Reading Mary Wroth

Reading Mary Wroth

REPRESENTING ALTERNATIVES
IN EARLY MODERN ENGLAND

Edited by Naomi J. Miller and Gary Waller

[signature: Gary Waller]

The University of Tennessee Press

KNOXVILLE

Frontispiece: Portrait of Lady Mary Wroth.
(Courtesy of the Viscount de L'Isle, V.C., K.G.,
Penshurst Place, Tonbridge, Kent)

The paper in this book meets the minimum requirements
of the American National Standard for Permanence of Paper
for Printed Library Materials.
∞
The binding materials have been chosen
for strength and durablility.

Library of Congress Cataloging in Publication Data

Reading Mary Wroth :
representing alternatives in early modern England
    edited by Naomi J. Miller and Gary Waller. — 1st ed.
        p.   cm.
    Includes bibliographical references and index.
    ISBN 0–87049–709–X (cloth: alk. paper)
    ISBN 0–87049–710–3 (pbk. : alk. paper)
    1. Wroth, Mary, Lady, ca. 1586–ca. 1640.   2. Women and
literature—England—History—17th century.
    3. Authors, English—Early modern, 1500-1700—Biography.
    I. Miller, Naomi J., 1960-   .   II. Waller, Gary F. (Gary Fredric),
1945–
PR2399.W7Z84   1991
828'.309—dc20   91–390   CIP

To our sons, Isaiah and Philip,
whose growth, from conception to birth,
first steps to first words,
has kept pace with the evolution
of this project.

Contents

Illustrations

Acknowledgments

The publication of these essays has been a pleasurable collaboration between the two co-editors, who have been helped by a variety of scholars, colleagues, and students, as well as friends and families. It originated, appropriately for something of a challenge to the canon of Renaissance literature, in a counter-discourse to a Spenser Society luncheon, and it led to many pleasant contacts with old friends and new. In particular, the editors wish to thank the enthusiastic editors at the University of Tennessee Press, especially Carol Wallace Orr and Lee Campbell Sioles, and the readers whose helpful comments and criticisms improved the volume enormously.

Specifically, Naomi Miller wishes to thank her fellow participants in the New England Seminar on Women in the Renaissance and the Reformation, at the Harvard University Center for Literary and Cultural Studies, for their thoughtful comments and suggestions about her ongoing work on Wroth: particularly Elaine Beilin, Pamela Benson, Mary Thomas Crane, Elizabeth Hageman, Ann Rosalind Jones, Barbara Lewalski, Carolyn Ruth Swift, and Susanne Woods. She appreciates also the remarks, in other contexts, of Emily Bartels, Heather Dubrow, Margaret Hannay, Carol Ann Johnston, and Josephine Roberts, and of her present colleagues Meg Lota Brown and Peter Medine. Special thanks go to her fellow editor for his energy and expertise. Finally, she wishes to thank her husband, Hugh, and her children, Fiona and Isaiah, for their loving support and patience during her work on this volume.

Gary Waller wishes to thank his fellow editor for her enthusiasm and scrupulousness, his colleagues Kathleen McCormick and Kris Straub for their comments on his paper, and for helpful and stimulating remarks: Jonathan Dollimore, Susan Rudy Dorscht, Janis Holm, Mary Ellen Lamb, Janel Mueller, Maureen Quilligan, Josephine Roberts, Gerald Rubio, Anne Shaver, and Susanne Woods. He has special thanks for

the students of his early modern literature and culture seminars, especially Kate Bellay, Craig Dionne, Doug Fedenick, Brett Molotsky, Stacia
Nagel, Michele Osherow, and John Timmins, not least for their willingness to read more of Wroth (and William Herbert) than might be
expected of the most conscientious. He hopes the Jacobean banquet at
semester's end was something of a compensation. He also wishes to
record his gratitude to the John Simon Guggenheim Foundation and
the Newberry Library for fellowships that allowed him to carry out
his research.

Abbreviations

Brennan   *Lady Mary Wroth's Love's Victory.* Ed. Michael G. Brennan. London: The Roxburghe Club, 1988.
CSP   *Calendar of State Papers*
HMC   *Historical Manuscripts Commission*
Roberts   *The Poems of Lady Mary Wroth.* Ed. Josephine A. Roberts. Baton Rouge: Louisiana State University Press, 1983.
Waller   *Pamphilia to Amphilanthus.* Ed. Gary Waller. Salzburg: Universität Salzburg, 1977.

Unless otherwise indicated, quotations from *Urania* are cited by page number from *The Countesse of Mountgomeries Urania* (London 1621) and by book and folio number from *The Secound Part of the Countess of Montgomerys Urania* (Newberry Library Case MS fY 1565. W 95).

Reading Mary Wroth

Introduction: Reading as Re-Vision

Naomi J. Miller and Gary Waller

The career of Mary Wroth, born Mary Sidney (c. 1587–1653), exemplifies the complex limitations and possibilities which faced a woman determined to achieve some significant degree of agency within a seemingly irresistible patriarchal family and social formation. Her life provides fascinating material for the history of gender assignment and gender politics, while her writings are important contributions to both the literature of early modern England and the rapidly developing story of women's writing in English. Wroth was perhaps the most accomplished woman writer in English before Aphra Behn (who may have been her granddaughter)[1]: she wrote the first Petrarchan sequence in English by a woman, *Pamphilia to Amphilanthus*; one of the first plays by a woman, *Love's Victory* (only recently published for the first time); and a long and intriguing prose romance, *The Countesse of Mountgomeries Urania* (first part published in 1621, with a two-volume critical edition of the complete work currently underway). In the past decade these writings, most particularly *Urania* and *Pamphilia to Amphilanthus*, have attracted increasing critical attention. The very range of genres represented by Wroth's works provides an unusual opportunity to examine not simply one surviving text by a woman of her time but a group of texts whose very diversity constitutes a challenge to the previous marginalization of women by many teachers and critics of Renaissance literature.

When Adrienne Rich asserted, in 1971, that "re-vision—the act of looking back, of seeing with fresh eyes, of entering an old text from a new critical direction—is for women more than a chapter in cultural history: it is an act of survival," she was discussing the awakening consciousness of twentieth-century women writers.[2] Two decades later, an established tradition of feminist scholarship—particularly well represented in recent collections of essays edited by Margaret Hannay, Mary Beth Rose, Margaret Ferguson, Maureen Quilligan and Nancy Vickers, and Anne Haselkorn and Betty Travitsky—has documented the existence of women writers in periods such as the Renaissance, when their silence, if not absence, had previously been taken for granted.[3] At the same time, a number of feminist critics have started to focus on more than the obvious oppression and victimization suffered by many early women writers (and noted by Rich in her essay), identifying their "acts of survival," the enabling strategies and legacies that can be identified in their works. While the facts of female subordination and the effects of gender hierarchy must not be underestimated, the significance of women as subjects generating writing and other actions must henceforth shape the analysis of any chapter in cultural history.

In the past decade or so, the early modern period in particular has been the site of multiple re-visions of cultural history and literary theory which have made possible the bringing together of the present collection of essays on Mary Wroth. Since the 1970s, the rediscovery of previously neglected writings of women from the early modern period has produced a major rewriting of the canon—and, perhaps even more usefully, helped call into question the ideological underpinnings of canonicity altogether. Henceforth, literary histories of early modern England will not be able to ignore the writings of Mary Sidney, Elizabeth I, Aemilia Lanyer, Elizabeth Cary, Mary Wroth, Anne Clifford, or the many other women, both well and lesser known, of the period. At the same time, the exciting and frequently contradictory impact of various feminisms, poststructuralisms, new historicisms, and other approaches to the production of texts has dramatically revised the ways we read. While the essays on Mary Wroth collected here do not articulate a shared theoretical position, inevitably they are written and should be read against the background of the theoretical rethinking that has made both literary studies, and early modern studies in particular, such exciting fields.

Yet even when we consider the gratifying examples of closer critical attention to women writers like Wroth, it becomes necessary to recognize that the enormous advances in critical awareness which have recently swept the field of early modern studies must not be allowed to generate a false sense of complacency. For all the recent attention to women writers, not one of the five major collections of critical essays concerned with early modern women which appeared in the second half of the 1980s included an essay on Mary Wroth.[4] Perhaps of even more concern, for teachers of the Renaissance, is the fact that the *Norton Anthology of Literature by Women: The Tradition in English*, edited by Sandra M. Gilbert and Susan Gubar, does not even mention Wroth, in spite of the notable variety and length of the works to her name.[5] In order to rewrite the canon, it is important to be able to read women writers as presences, not just absences, to read texts, not just contexts.

Likewise on the theoretical front, notwithstanding the appearance of some important collections of feminist essays on the early modern period, many recent collections of critical essays have tended to remain focused both upon traditional male-authored works and upon masculine preoccupations with political power in both literary and cultural texts of the period. As Carol Thomas Neely has observed, the effect of many of the new theoretical approaches has been paradoxically to further oppress women, repress sexuality, and subordinate gender issues.[6] Stephen Greenblatt's collection, *Representing the English Renaissance*, for instance, reinscribes "the" Renaissance in wholly male terms through its failure to consider any female-authored texts, while John Drakakis's collection, *Alternative Shakespeares*, follows a primarily "cult-historicist" line of interpretation (to use Neely's term), dismissing other, less "radical" approaches as not sufficiently "alternative."[7] Contributors to the present volume, by contrast, offer truly alternative interpretations to one another, drawing from feminist and psychoanalytic as well as various new historicist perspectives, and demonstrating, in particular, an awareness of alternative feminisms instead of attempting to inscribe a single feminist position.

The essays suggest how Mary Wroth, herself, engaged in representing alternatives to patriarchal Renaissance positions in her approach to gender and genre, to constructions of subjectivity and sexual difference. In her time, the primary roles of women in writing were still as figures in a discourse produced by men. Where women were able to write (and, especially, to publish), both external oppositions and internal tensions mark their prefaces and dedications — on the one hand, apologies for intervening in an activity forbidden to or at least deemed unsuitable for women; on the other hand, satisfaction that women were asserting themselves in an activity purported to be more natural to men. Wroth is one of the first woman writers in English who clearly saw herself as having the vocation of a writer, and in whose work a habitually submerged female discourse starts to emerge when self-conscious resistance to patriarchy finds written expression.

Since Mary Wroth's life is examined, from very different viewpoints, in the opening essays by Margaret Hannay and Gary Waller, here it is necessary only to provide the briefest biographical outline. She was born probably in 1587, the first child of Robert Sidney, later Viscount de L'Isle and Earl of Leicester. Thus she was born into a family prominent in politics and letters. Its most distinguished member, Philip Sidney, was celebrated (and mythologized) by successive generations as the ideal Renaissance courtier, a mystification of his contradictory and fascinating career, and other members of the family were almost as intriguing. Philip's father, Henry, was one of Queen Elizabeth's most dedicated public servants, not least for the thankless task of upholding the queen's parsimonious and often brutal Irish policy; his mother, Mary, likewise dedicated herself to the public duties of an aspiring court family, damaging her health while nursing the queen through an attack of smallpox. Philip's younger brother Robert, Mary Wroth's father, was an ambitious but anxious politician and (perhaps partly as a consequence) a fine poet whose writings record the strains of being a courtier in the increasingly paranoid court of the aging Elizabeth. Philip's sister, Mary, Countess of Pembroke, the mother of William Herbert, third Earl of Pembroke, was a much celebrated patroness and literary figure. As Margaret Hannay and Jeff Masten note in their essays, the title page of Wroth's *Urania* calls attention simultaneously to her literary and familial connections in naming her "Daughter to the right Noble Robert Earle of Leicester. And Neece to the ever famous, and renowned Sir Phillips Sidney knight. And to the most exelent Lady Mary Countesse of Pembroke late deceased."

Mary Wroth's childhood was spent at the family home, Penshurst Place, in Kent, with frequent visits to the Low Countries, where her father had charge of the English troops, and London, where the Sidneys usually stayed at the Earl of Pembroke's London residence, Baynards Castle. In the late years of Elizabeth's reign she came to court, and in

1605 married Sir Robert Wroth, a prosperous Essex landowner. After her marriage, which does not seem to have been particularly happy, she maintained unusually close connections with her family, in particular her father, with whom she shared an interest in poetry.

While Mary Wroth was acquainted with a number of literary figures, including Ben Jonson, who praised her poems, one of the most important relationships of her life—literary as well as personal—was with her first cousin, William Herbert, Earl of Pembroke (1580–1630), by whom she had two illegitimate children, William and Catherine, born after she was widowed in 1614. Some of her poetry can almost certainly be dated to before 1614, but the manuscript evidence suggests that she continued to work on it in these fruitful years of her early widowhood. The first part of her more major work, *Urania*, was also almost certainly written in these years following the death of her husband and published, with *Pamphilia to Amphilanthus*, in 1621—with some ensuing controversy. Her pastoral play, *Love's Victory*, was probably written in the early 1620s, at the same time as she was writing the second part of *Urania*. Indeed, it is arguable that the decade following 1614 was her most fulfilling as a writer and a woman: although she was under continual financial pressures, she was relatively independent, able to rely on both her Sidney and Pembroke connections; she was a lover, a mother, and a writer.

After the mid-1620s, records of Wroth's whereabouts and activities are sparse, but sufficient to give a general picture of her life. She outlived her cousin by some twenty or more years. Their children were supported by both the Sidneys and Pembrokes. She herself lived quietly, only occasionally surfacing in court or legal records. It is intriguing to speculate about these final thirty years of her life: Mary Wroth had in many ways radically challenged the cultural assignments laid down for a person of her class and gender—and it is likely that retirement was the safest and most fulfilling choice she could make. There are many fascinating, unanswered (and perhaps unanswerable) questions about her life from the 1620s on. What was she doing all those years? Was she with her children? Had the passion for her cousin burnt itself out? Did she choose, or was she in some sense forced, to live quietly, with her memories? Did she continue to write?

Most importantly, perhaps we can see Mary Wroth less as a forgotten, marginalized figure and more as one whose historical time had not so much passed as not yet come. In 1601, about the time that the young Mary Sidney came to court, another court lady, Mary Fitton, dressed up in men's clothes and visited William Herbert in his chambers. Such behavior was hardly to be condoned by Renaissance society, and the consequences the soon pregnant Mistress Fitton suffered were catastrophic by comparison to the temporary disruptions to his lordship's career and pleasures. In the same decade, Penelope Rich—years before in some sense the "Stella" of Philip Sidney's *Astrophil and Stella*— was hounded to penury and death by King James and his judiciary authorities not only for pursuing the man she loved but for marrying him: "outstanding in beauty, gifted in every quality of mind and body except for chastity," pronounced a (male) contemporary, she "contracted an unfortunate union . . . violated the sacred and proper law of matrimony and caused havoc in a most noble family." She died "neither wife, widow, or made."[8] Wroth's retirement (if such it was) might usefully be seen in this context. In her life as well as in her writings, she had asserted challenges to the dominant gender ideologies of her patriarchal culture, and the consequences of these challenges could not be escaped. Yet in her life choices, including (though not limited to) her writing, she served to expand the possibilities of a woman's choices and sense of agency.

Wroth's literary reputation in her own time was predictably confined to her family and literary circle. Any wider reputation for *Urania*, in particular, was hampered by a marginalization enforced by the court, some of whose members were threatened by the apparently subversive rhetoric of the work. The objections of some of King James's male courtiers to the book's apparently satirical references to their private lives forced her to withdraw *Urania* from sale in 1621, only six months after its publication.[9] Her primary attacker, Lord Denny, addressed Wroth as a "Hermophradite in show, in deed a monster," and advised her to "leave idle books alone / For wiser and worthyer women have writte none."[10] At least in part as a result of the court furor, only twenty-eight copies of the published *Urania* and only one copy of her unpublished continuation of the romance survive today, while the first complete edition of her romance is still in process. This publication history accords with Betty Travitsky's observation that a major deterrent to literary publication by Renaissance Englishwomen was "the negative attitude taken by the male arbiters of the time regarding works by women on subjects outside the spheres of religion and domesticity, which were considered the province of women."[11] Wroth in fact was attacked in part for her effrontery in presuming to write secular fiction and poetry, in contrast to her aunt's translations of religious poetry.

Although recent studies of women writers of the period have started to redress the previous marginalization of their works, as mentioned earlier, in Wroth's case the work of recovery has only just begun. Up through the first half of the twentieth century, Wroth earned brief and usually dismissive mention in studies of the English novel by J.J. Jusserand and Ernest A. Baker, and in surveys of women writers by Frederic Rowton and Bridget MacCarthy.[12] The late 1970s saw a burgeoning of interest in Wroth. The first modern edition of *Pamphilia to Amphilanthus*, edited by Gary Waller, appeared in 1977, and was followed by Josephine Roberts's edition of the complete poems in 1983. Wroth's poems subsequently received critical attention in articles by Roberts and Elaine Beilin, a longer study by May Nelson Paulissen, and, most recently, essays by Naomi Miller and Maureen Quilligan.[13]

Wroth's play, *Love's Victory*, was published for the first time only in 1988, and the manuscript versions of that play have been discussed in essays by Roberts, Carolyn Ruth Swift, and Margaret McLaren.[14] Before the past decade, Wroth's prose romance, *Urania*, received scant critical attention, save as a historical curiosity or pale imitation of the *Arcadia*. Even fairly recent scholarship has tended to undervalue the literary worth of Wroth's romance, defining her achievement primarily in terms of her uncle's generic influence.[15] Most recently, however, articles by Swift, Miller, Quilligan, and Roberts have tackled questions of female identity and authority both in Wroth's text and in the culture of her period, while Roberts is working on the first published edition of the complete *Urania*.[16]

The work of established scholars has been complemented by a number of unpublished doctoral dissertations, beginning with Charlotte Kohler's study of "The Elizabethan Woman of Letters" (1936), continuing with Margaret [Witten-Hannah] McLaren's pioneering study of *Urania* (1978), and extending into the 1980s and beyond with the dissertations of Naomi Miller (1987), Gwynne Kennedy (1989), Wendy Wall

(1989), and Kim Hall (1990).[17] The presence of significant dissertation-level studies of Wroth may be an indication that future critical directions in the study of early modern women should be charted not only according to the authoritative pronouncements of established scholars, particularly those concerned with reproducing "the[ir] Renaissance[s]," but also with reference to the newly identified concerns and subjects engaging the next generation of scholars-to-be. The diversity of the contributors to the present volume, from doctoral students to senior scholars, represents a range of the alternative perspectives possible not only on Wroth and her works, but also on gender issues in the early modern period.

The essays in this collection, then, provide an opportunity for an evaluation, and even a "re-vision," in Adrienne Rich's sense of the term, both of Wroth's achievements as a woman writer of the seventeenth century and of the culture in and of which she wrote. They are grouped in four sections. The first section focuses on the simultaneously constricting and empowering nature of Wroth's relation to her family bonds. Margaret Hannay suggests how Wroth found a voice as a writer through the example of her godmother and aunt, Mary Sidney Herbert, Countess of Pembroke, while Gary Waller addresses, from a cultural/psycho-analytic perspective, Wroth's relationship with her cousin, William Herbert, Earl of Pembroke, focusing on the question of the construction of gendered subjectivity.

The essays in the second section explore Wroth's poems, play, and prose romance in relation to the significant literary and cultural contexts which shaped their production. In each essay, the consideration of genre plays an important role in allowing for the examination of ideological constraints as well as aesthetic questions.[18] Jeff Masten analyzes the bibliographical evidence of the manuscript of *Pamphilia to Amphilanthus*, arguing that the poems, like the manuscript in which they are inscribed, encode a withdrawal from circulation, a refusal to speak in the public voice of traditional Petrarchan discourse. Barbara Lewalski examines Wroth's play, *Love's Victory*, in relation to the tradition of pastoral tragicomedy, finding that Wroth molds generic conventions in order to emphasize female agency. Josephine Roberts situates the marriage controversy in *Urania* with reference to a range of Renaissance marital contracts, scrutinizing the implications of Wroth's fictional engagement with an ongoing ideological controversy.

The third section of essays compares Wroth's work as a woman writer to related texts by two very different Renaissance writers, opening the question of how the writings of the period can be re-envisioned in gendered terms. Ann Rosalind Jones reads Mary Wroth and Veronica Franco together in order to suggest how, through verbal appropriation of elite spectacle, the Italian and the English poet rewrite their unstable social positions in order to represent themselves as public figures capable of new forms of feminine resistance and critique. Naomi Miller compares Wroth's construction of women's voices in *Urania* to the discourse of Shakespeare's female protagonists, focusing on how questions of gender can empower or subvert verbal constructions of identity, and arguing that Wroth foregrounds the gender-specific nature of speech in order to feminize the discourse of romance.

The essays in the final section examine definitions of female subjectivity, scrutinizing the relation between reading, writing, and gender in Wroth's inscription of her own discourse of sexual difference. Nona Fienberg suggests how, in rejecting the conventional reification of the beloved, Wroth sought alternative materials out of which to invent female poetic subjectivity, articulating the pleasures of the self in order to transform herself from object to subject. Heather Weidemann addresses dramatic rather than poetic subjectivity, contending that *Urania* introduces a new figure to the world of English letters — the theatrical woman — and relating some of the prevailing constructions of theatricality and female identity in the Renaissance to Wroth's vision of femininity as theater. Finally, Mary Ellen Lamb describes how Wroth authorized herself as a writer by subverting the cultural construct of the woman reader, challenging Renaissance ideologies of gender in order to invest women's reading with the independent subjectivity necessary to produce writing.

In "Constructing the Subject: Feminist Practice and the New Renaissance Discourses," Carol Neely calls for new ways to surround, contextualize and "over-read" men's canonical texts with women's "uncanonical" ones.[19] In order to "over-read" men's texts, it is necessary first to read and re-read women's hitherto uncanonical ones. The present collection of essays hopes to stimulate greater attention to Mary Wroth from all perspectives, so that, to paraphrase Rich, Renaissance criticism generally can benefit from the challenge of reading as re-vision.

NOTES

1. Sharon Valiant, "Sidney's Sister, Pembroke's Mother . . . and Aphra Behn's Great-Grandmother?", paper, American Society for Eighteenth Century Studies Conference in New Orleans (1989), argues for Wroth's daughter Catherine Lovell as Behn's mother.

2. Adrienne Rich, "When We Dead Awaken: Writing as Re-Vision," *On Lies, Secrets, and Silence: Selected Prose, 1966–78* (New York: W.W. Norton, 1979), p. 35.

3. See particularly Margaret Patterson Hannay, ed., *Silent But for the Word: Tudor Women as Patrons, Translators, and Writers of Religious Works* (Kent, Ohio: The Kent State University Press, 1985); Mary Beth Rose, ed., *Women in the Middle Ages and the Renaissance: Literary and Historical Perspectives* (Syracuse: Syracuse University Press, 1986); Margaret W. Ferguson, Maureen Quilligan, and Nancy J. Vickers, eds., *Rewriting the Renaissance: The Discourses of Sexual Difference in Early Modern Europe* (Chicago: University of Chicago Press, 1986); and Anne M. Haselkorn and Betty S. Travitsky, eds., *The Renaissance Englishwoman in Print: Counterbalancing the Canon* (Amherst: University of Massachusetts Press, 1990). See also Carole Levin and Jeanie Watson, eds., *Ambiguous Realities: Women in the Middle Ages and the Renaissance* (Detroit: Wayne State University Press, 1987); and Sheila Fisher and Janet E. Halley, eds., *Seeking the Woman in Late Medieval and Renaissance Writings: Essays in Feminist Contextual Criticism* (Knoxville: University of Tennessee Press, 1989).

4. See Hannay, Rose, Ferguson, Quilligan and Vickers, Levin and Watson, Fisher and Halley; only the most recent collection, edited by Haselkorn and Travitsky (1990), contains essays on Wroth.

5. Sandra M. Gilbert and Susan Gubar, eds., *The Norton Anthology of Literature by Women: The Tradition in English* (New York: W.W. Norton, 1985).

6. Carol Thomas Neely, "Constructing the Subject: Feminist Practice and the New Renaissance Discourses," *English Literary Renaissance* 18 (1988), 5–18.

7. Stephen Greenblatt, ed., *Representing the English Renaissance* (Berkeley: University of California Press, 1988), and John Drakakis, ed., *Alternative Shakespeares* (London: Methuen, 1985).

8. Richard Johnston, *Historia Rerum Britanniarum* (Amsterdam, 1655), p. 443; William A. Ringler, ed., *The Poetry of Sir Philip Sidney* (Oxford: Clarendon, 1962), p. 559.

9. For further discussion of the historical context, see John J. O'Connor, "James Hay and *The Countess of Montgomerie's Urania*," *Notes & Queries*, n.s. 2 (1955), 150–52; Josephine A. Roberts, "An Unpublished Literary Quarrel Concerning the Suppression of Mary Wroth's *Urania* (1621)," *Notes & Queries*, n.s. 24 (1977),

532–35; Paul Salzman, "Contemporary References in Mary Wroth's *Urania*," *Review of English Studies* 29 (1978), 178–81. See also Roberts, *Poems*, pp. 31–36.

10. For reproductions of Denny's verses, Wroth's rebuttal, and the accompanying correspondence, see Roberts, *Poems*, pp. 32–35, 233–45.

11. Betty Travitsky, ed., *The Paradise of Women: Writings by Englishwomen of the Renaissance* (Westport, Conn.: Greenwood Press, 1981), p. 114.

12. J.J. Jusserand, *The English Novel in the Time of Shakespeare* (1908; rpt. New York: AMS Press, 1965); Ernest A. Baker, *The History of the English Novel* (New York: Barnes and Noble, 1936); Frederick Rowton, ed., *The Female Poets of Great Britain* (London: Longman, 1848); Bridget MacCarthy, *Women Writers: Their Contribution to the English Novel, 1621–1744*, 2 vols. (Cork: Cork University Press, 1944).

13. Roberts, "Lady Mary Wroth's Sonnets: A Labyrinth of the Mind," *Journal of Women's Studies in Literature* 1 (1979), 319–29; Elaine V. Beilin, esp. "'The Onely Perfect Vertue': Constancy in Mary Wroth's *Pamphilia to Amphilanthus*," *Spenser Studies* 2 (1981), 229–45; May Nelson Paulissen, *The Love Sonnets of Lady Mary Wroth: A Critical Introduction* (Salzburg: Universität Salzburg, 1982); Naomi Miller, "Rewriting Lyric Fictions: The Role of the Lady in Lady Mary Wroth's *Pamphilia to Amphilanthus*," in *Renaissance Englishwoman in Print*, ed. Haselkorn and Travitsky, pp. 295–310; Maureen Quilligan, "The Constant Subject: Instability and Female Authority in Wroth's *Urania* Poems," in *Soliciting Interpretation: Literary Theory and Seventeenth-Century Poetry*, ed. Elizabeth D. Harvey and Katherine Eisaman Mauss (Chicago: University of Chicago Press, 1990), pp. 307–35.

14. Roberts, "The Huntington Manuscript of Lady Mary Wroth's Play, *Loves Victorie*," *Huntington Library Quarterly* 46 (1983), 156–74; Carolyn Ruth Swift, "Feminine Self-Definition in Lady Mary Wroth's *Loves Victorie*," *English Literary Renaissance* 19 (1989), 171–88; Margaret McLaren, "An Unknown Continent: Lady Mary Wroth's Forgotten Pastoral Drama, 'Loves Victorie,'" in *Renaissance Englishwoman in Print*, ed. Haselkorn and Travitsky, pp. 276-94.

15. See Graham Parry, "Lady Mary Wroth's *Urania*," *Proceedings of the Leeds Philosophical and Literary Society, Literary and Historical Section* 16, pt. 4 (1975), 55; Travitsky, *Paradise* (1981), pp. 135–36; and Suzanne W. Hull, *Chaste, Silent and Obedient: English Books for Women, 1475–1640* (San Marino: Huntington Library, 1982), p. 80.

16. Swift, "Feminine Identity in Lady Mary Wroth's Romance *Urania*," *English Literary Renaissance* 14 (1984), 328–46; Miller, "'Not much to be marked': Narrative of the Woman's Part in Lady Mary Wroth's *Urania*," *Studies in English Literature* 29 (1989), 121–37; Quilligan, "Lady Mary Wroth: Female Authority and the Family Romance," in *Unfolded Tales: Essays on Renaissance Romance*, ed. George M. Logan and Gordon Teskey (Ithaca, N.Y.: Cornell University Press, 1989), pp. 257–80; Roberts, "Radigund Revisited: Perspectives on Women Rulers in Lady Mary Wroth's *Urania*," in *Renaissance Englishwoman in Print*, ed. Haselkorn and Travitsky, pp. 187–207. Roberts is working on a two-volume critical edition of the complete *Urania* for the Renaissance English Text Society.

17. Charlotte Kohler, "The Elizabethan Woman of Letters: The Extent of Her Lit-

erary Activities," Ph.D. diss., University of Virginia, 1936; Margaret [Witten-Hannah] McLaren, "Lady Mary Wroth's *Urania*: The Work and the Tradition," Ph.D. diss., University of Auckland, 1978; Miller, "Strange Labyrinth: Pattern as Process in Sir Philip Sidney's *Arcadia* and Lady Mary Wroth's *Urania*," Ph.D. diss., Harvard University, 1987; Gwynne Kennedy, "Feminine Subjectivity in the English Renaissance: The Writings of Elizabeth Cary, Lady Falkland, and Lady Wroth," Ph.D. diss., University of Pennsylvania, 1989; Wendy Wall, "The Shapes of Desire: Politics, Publication, and Renaissance Texts," Ph.D. diss., University of Pennsylvania, 1989; Kim Hall, "Acknowledging Things of Darkness: Race, Gender, and Power in Early Modern England," Ph.D. diss., University of Pennsylvania, 1990.

18. See Janet Todd, *Feminist Literary History* (New York: Routledge, 1988), pp. 99–102, on the value of genre study to feminist criticism.

19. Neely, "Constructing the Subject," 16, 17.

PART ONE

Family Bonds

"Your vertuous and learned Aunt":
The Countess of Pembroke
as a Mentor to Mary Wroth

Margaret P. Hannay

I

The Renaissance woman writer was far more likely to experience the anxiety of absence than the anxiety of influence.[1] Whereas the Humanist tradition might give male poets a "joyful" self-confidence, female writers struggled to find authorization for their work in a culture which demanded silence and obedience of them, not eloquent self-assertion. As Tilde Sankovitch has noted, in France Madeline and Catherine des Roches sought a poetic "genealogy of their own making, suited to the needs of their gender"; in their mother/daughter relationship "of giving and receiving biological life" they found a parallel for "a reciprocal life-giving creative exchange." They articulate their "authority of origin" by displacing Apollo, the father of poetry, with "what they construe as a mother-of-poetry configuration" in the mother/daughter unit of Ceres and Proserpina.[2] Similarly, as Anne Prescott suggests, Marguerite de Navarre apparently found a role model in her mother, Louise de Savoie.[3]

In England the Countess of Pembroke became a pivotal figure in the formation of a female tradition of writing. She herself was far better placed than most Renaissance Englishwomen, for her mother's childhood friends formed a constellation of learned women—Queen Elizabeth, Lady Jane Grey, and the five Cooke sisters.[4] We often underestimate the importance of these articulate women for later women

writers. Although their work was typically restricted to the feminine
genres of translation, dedication, epitaph, and personal letters, they did
write and they did occasionally publish their works. Even if they published anonymously, in deference to strictures against women writers,
their authorship would have been an open secret in the English court.
Following their example, the Countess of Pembroke also wrote primarily translations, dedications, epitaphs, and personal letters; yet she
so far expanded the possibilities of those genres that her writings became a model for original work by later women writers, such as her
beloved niece Mary, Lady Wroth. When Wroth began to write, she
saw herself not merely as a woman, but as a *Sidney* woman with a clear
sense of poetic authority in her lineage. That sense of origin, of legitimacy as a writer, is far more important to Wroth's achievement than
are specific parallels between the works of these two women. Before
a writer chooses her genres or her topics, she must first decide to write.
The works of the Countess of Pembroke proved to Mary Wroth that
the label "woman writer" was not an oxymoron.

By astute use of the permitted feminine genres, the countess had
developed a literary career. Translation was thought to be the work
most appropriate for women, but as Sankovitch reminds us, translation
can be "a road into positive intertextuality."[5] Closely allied with Protestant leaders on the Continent, the Countess of Pembroke was also con-
versant with contemporary Continental literature. If we look at what
she did achieve, instead of at the limits placed on her work by her gender, we discover that through her translations she brought sophisticated
literary genres to England. For example, her translation of Petrarch's
"Trionfo della Morte" was the first English translation to maintain
Petrarch's original *terza rima*, making it of considerable interest for its
technical achievements, but it may be even more important for opening
up the Petrarchan canon in English. Male poets, who looked only at
the early part of Petrarch's sonnet sequence, present a passive Laura who
speaks only through silence; the countess, in her translation of the
"Triumph of Death," presents Laura as a vibrant, eloquent woman.[6] Her
translation of Robert Garnier's *Marc Antoine* introduced a vogue for the
avant garde French historical tragedy, with its emphasis on character
rather than action. Most importantly, her *Psalmes*, inspired primarily
by the French psalter of Clément Marot and Théodore de Bèze and

other European models, were skillful, original poems, valuable in their own right and important also for their influence on seventeenth-century devotional poets such as George Herbert and John Donne.

Through her translations the countess not only imported sophisticated literary genres but also commented on politics and social justice. Her interest in politics was well known. For example, Robert Sidney typically reported the court news to her in his letters, and Samuel Daniel says that, after he had dedicated sonnets to her, she encouraged him to try more serious genres: "[She] call'd vp my spirits from out their low repose, / To sing of state, and tragicke notes to frame," as he says in his *Cleopatra*.[7] The countess herself finds a way to "sing of state" in the *Discourse*, in *Antonius*, and in the *Psalmes*. Her translation of Philippe de Mornay's *Discours de la Vie et de la Mort* was one of a series of translations undertaken by Philip Sidney and his Continental friend to support Mornay and the Huguenot cause. The *Discourse* also allows the countess to comment on the abuses of the English court, using the ventriloquism of translation. Her *Antonius* helped to naturalize Continental historical tragedy in England, using Roman history to comment on English politics in a way that anticipated Shakespeare.[8] And she used her *Psalmes* for political commentary in the spirit of the Geneva Protestants who were so closely allied with her family.[9]

Her four extant original poems likewise make a strong religious and political statement. Her elegies, "The Dolefull Lay of Clorinda" and "To the Angell Spirit of the most excellent, Sir Philip Sidney," both mourn the death of her brother and celebrate Sir Philip as a Protestant martyr, slain while fighting for Dutch independence against Catholic Spain in a campaign his family believed was doomed by inadequate support from the queen.[10] Her two poems for Queen Elizabeth, "Even now that Care" and "Astrea," also have a political sub-text. "Even now that Care," conjoined with "To the Angell Spirit" in the dedication of her *Psalmes*, instructs the queen to be active in the Protestant cause, at home and on the Continent. Her encomium, "Astrea," is fully self-conscious of its own genre, debating the truth of conventional praises of the queen.

With the possible exception of "Astrea," all of these works were technically within the approved feminine genres. Like Queen Elizabeth, who cleverly adapted the strictures of chastity into a public relations triumph (the cult of the Virgin Queen), the Countess of Pembroke used her public role as "Sydneys sister Pembrokes mother"[11] to push back the boundaries for women, even while appearing to remain within them. If she speaks from the margins of literature, she nevertheless speaks clearly. So when Mary Sidney, later Mary Wroth, was named for her aunt and godmother, she was thereby given a literary mentor such as no Englishwoman had had before her.

The relationship been these two brilliant women has been obscured by stereotypes: the Countess of Pembroke as a somewhat dour religious figure, Mary Wroth as a romance writer whose fiction grew out of her own unhappy love affair. In fact, both women were witty, articulate, cognizant of Continental literature, active in politics, and proud of their heritage as Sidneys. As the Countess of Pembroke called herself "Sister of Sir Philip Sidney,"[12] so Wroth is identified by family references in the title of *The Countesse of Mountgomeries Urania. Written by the right honorable the Lady Mary Wroath. Daughter to the right Noble Robert Earle of Leicester. And Neece to the ever famous, and renowned Sir Phillips Sidney knight. And to the most exelent Lady Mary Countesse of Pembroke late deceased.*[13] Wroth also followed her aunt's lead in using an "S fermé" (ß) in her letters; both women thereby emphasized their identity as Sidneys although their signatures were, respectively, "Mary wrothe" and "M. Pembroke."[14] Like the countess, Wroth also retained the Sidney pheon for her own seal after her marriage, instead of adopting her husband's device.

As a writer, Mary Wroth was widely judged as a Sidney. Ben Jonson, in his highest tribute to her, declares that even her appearance would make the observer "Know you to be a Sidney, though unnamed." That name itself, Jonson declares, is the true "imprese of the great."[15] Jonson's poem is the most famous tribute to her as a Sidney, but Joshua Sylvester likewise praised her in *Lachrimae Lachrimarum*, his elegy for her brother Sir William Sidney, declaring "None, but a *Sidney's* Muse/ Worthy to sing a *Sidney's* Worthyness," thereby praising her as a Sidney poet and also making the familiar Wroth/Worth pun. She is "AL-Worth Sidnëides."[16]

Like Jonson and Sylvester, Sir Edward Denny evaluates her as a Sidney, but he finds her lacking. In their quarrel over topical allusions in her 1621 *Urania*, Denny charges that she had not lived up to her heri-

Title page from *Urania*, published in 1621.

(Courtesy of the Newberry Library, Chicago)

tage. Taking her lineage with the same seriousness as he would that of a man, he admonishes her to "repent you of so many ill spent yeares of so vaine a booke" and "redeeme the tym" by writing "as large a volume of heavenly layes and holy love as you have of lascivious tales and amorous toyes." She had departed from her role as a Sidney, he is saying, but she may yet "followe the rare, and pious example of your vertuous and learned Aunt, who translated so many godly books and especially the holly psalmes of David."[17] His warning is ironic, for in all but caution she was following the example of her learned aunt. The Countess of Pembroke had used translation as a strategy of indirection, enabling her to circumvent the ridicule directed at original works by women and to make political statements safely. Ever conscious of envy and slander at court, she had set her political statement in Roman times, a strategy followed by Samuel Daniel, William Shakespeare, and other dramatists. Wroth, more confident in her role as a writer, openly transgressed the boundaries for women by creating original works and the boundaries for political satire by writing a transparent pastoral romance, wherein court references were displaced neither by historical reference nor by translation. Perhaps she had not originally intended to publish the *Urania*, since it also contains family references.[18] Wroth did write the *Urania* as a Sidney and included complimentary references to her "vertuous and learned Aunt," with whom she had spent many happy times.

II

Mary Sidney Wroth may well have been born at Baynards Castle, the London home of the Earls of Pembroke, like several of her brothers and sisters, for in 1587, probably shortly before her birth, Robert Sidney wrote to "my most deerly beloued wif Lady Sydney at Bainards Castle."[19] Throughout her childhood, young Mary was often cared for by the Countess of Pembroke. During the invasion of the Spanish Armada in 1588, for example, "Little Mall," as her father called her, was taken by her mother to Wilton, where they were under the protection of the countess along with Thomas Sidney (Robert and Mary Sidney's adolescent brother), and the countess's own three surviving children: eight-year-old William, five-year-old Anne, and three-year-old Philip. Their response to the anticipated invasion can be traced through the letters of Robert Sidney to his wife, Barbara Gamage. Robert Sidney writes to his "deerly beloued wif" from Baynards Castle to Wilton on 26 April 1588, as the Spanish Armada was gathering in Lisbon. He sends her a "fan of fethers" and concludes, "farewell sweete wench and make much of little mall."[20] His next letter is addressed to Lady Sidney at Ivychurch (the favorite resort of the Countess of Pembroke, next to Clarendon Park and overlooking the Avon River near Salisbury) where he plans to join her. In a postscript he directs her to "kiss my Lady of Pembrokes hands and doe your best to excuse my not writing. And make much of Tom: Sydney."[21] On May 29th he is still apologizing for not arriving, but promising her that he will be with her in Ivy-church on Saturday.[22] By the end of July, Lady Sidney and the countess had moved with their children back to Wilton, where Robert Sidney once again apologizes for delay in coming to her and says "you must excuse mee if you heare not oft from mee for our matters bee so busied as I can not write so often as I would." He attempts to reassure her, "you shall euer bee most deer unto mee, and whyle I liue I will haue the same care of you as of mine owne life."[23] On 5 August, Sidney writes to her from "camp" at Tilbury, where Queen Elizabeth made her famous speech, but he saved the political news for "my Ladye of Pembrokes letter."[24] On the following day, the attack appeared immi-nent: he tells his wife "leaue not to pray for mee."[25] Because the Sidney women were becoming frightened by rumors that the Spanish would attack southern England, they began making plans to flee with their young children to "Wales," probably to Ludlow Castle, far from the dangerous coastal ports of Milford Haven and Cardiff. Robert Sidney tries to reassure them: "For ought I can see my Lady of Pembroke neede not stir for any feare of the ennimie, for I thinck hee will doe us no greate harme this year."[26] He promises a frightened Barbara that he will care for her no matter what happens: "if the ennimie come not I will send for you, and if he doe I will send you mony to prouide for your going into Wales." Even if the Spanish do attack they "will not bee heer so soone but that I shall haue leasure to take order for you."[27] The women and children were quite safe at Wilton on the first of young Mary's many visits.

Because most of the women's personal correspondence has been lost, we have only a few direct references to young Mall's relationship with her aunt and godmother. The countess's affection for her young god-daughter is shown in her one extant letter to Barbara Sidney, in which she sends her love to her "pretey Daughter" Mary, who was not quite four years old.[28] From the occasional references in letters and account books, we can deduce that young Mary was frequently in the company of her learned aunt, particularly during her mother's many pregnancies. In July 1594, for example, Robert Sidney asked his wife "to commend me to my sister" who was with her at Penshurst, and negotiated for lodgings in London for Lady Sidney and the children at Baynards Castle.[29] In November 1595 Lady Sidney was staying at Baynards Castle with the countess and her children. On the 12th Robert Sidney's agent Rowland Whyte reported, "This day yt appeares that Mrs. Mary hath the Mesels, but, God be thancked she is nothing sicke withall."[30] Her mother, then nine months pregnant, would "not by any persuasion be moued to keape from her, and with much ado brought to lie from her. The child her self humbly beseaching my Lady to haue a care of her own health, as she loued her." Her brother William bravely visited her "for he saies his turn wilbe next." Predictably, Lady Sidney did come down with the measles just before her delivery. Young Robert Sidney was born full of the measles, but he suckled and cried and showed good strength. (He lived to be the beloved Rosindy described in the *Urania*.) The Countess of Pembroke was there for his christening on New Year's Day.[31] It is usually difficult to be certain whether any of the Herberts were with the Sidneys at Baynards Castle, or whether they had stayed in Wiltshire, but in these letters Whyte specifically mentions the Earl and Countess of Pembroke and "my Lord Herbert." They all usually went up to London at least for the Accession Day festivities and for New Year's Day, and there were frequent additional journeys on court business.

The Countess of Pembroke may also have been present for the birth and christening of Mary's sister Barbara in December 1599. Mall, who was then about twelve years old, went with her brother William and her younger sister Katherine "to meet the Ladies at there coches and brought them vp to my Lady, which they did of an excellent Behauior and Grace," as Rowland Whyte reported.[32] The godparents were the Earl of Worcester, the Lady Nottingham, and the Lady Buckhurst. Nineteen-year-old William, Lord Herbert, the Countess of Pembroke's son, would have been godfather, but he was "sicke of an ague at Ramsbury," the Pembroke estate in northern Wiltshire. His mother may have stayed with him there. In the winter of 1600–1601 Mary's family was again at Baynards Castle, according to the account books, which list "milke for [little] Mrs. Barbara Sydney."[33]

In addition to inviting Robert and Barbara Sidney and the children to visit her at the various Pembroke estates, the countess also visited them at her own childhood home, Penshurst Place. The most extensive visit for which we have documentation is July through September of 1604, when the widowed countess helped to prepare for young Mary's wedding to Sir Robert Wroth. William Herbert, who had recently inherited his father's title of Earl of Pembroke, contributed a third of her dowry, one thousand pounds. At the beginning of September Robert Sidney tells his wife, "I hope you haue made much of my sister: I ame sorry truly that I haue not bin there since her coming theither." He is pleased by his sister's letter, since she "hath desired mee to giue you thanks for the entertainment shee receaues which shee shews to take very kindly."[34] In this, as in his earliest letters, he says "Commend me to Mall and the rest of my children and bless them from me." Young Mary Sidney was married to Sir Robert Wroth on 27 September 1604; two days later, the countess hurried to London on pressing business, but she returned to Penshurst in October to visit with Mary Wroth and her new husband.[35]

Robert Sidney continued his earlier pattern, established during the Armada scare, of sending personal news to his wife and reserving political news for his sister: "Such litle news as there is I have written to my sister and desired her to show you," he says, "For I as I thinck she wil bee with you this night or tomorrow."[36] These family letters establish that young Mary was frequently with her aunt while the Countess of Pembroke was supervising the publication of Sir Philip Sidney's works and publishing her own translations. Not surprisingly, when Wroth began to write she modeled her work on that of her famous uncle, both in her pastoral romance, *The Countesse of Mountgomeries Urania*, and in her poems, *Pamphilia to Amphilanthus*. Wroth apparently saw *The Countess of Pembrokes Arcadia* as a work that legitimized a fe-

male voice, because of the involvement of the Countess of Pembroke
in its production. Whether or not the countess had contributed ideas
for the plot and characters, Sidney's familiar letter of dedication suggests that she did have some part in its creation (it was written "onley
for you, only to you").[37] Furthermore, as Hugh Sanford tells the reader
in the 1593 edition, her editorial supervision means that "it is now by
more than one interest *The Countess of Pembrokes Arcadia*; done, as it
was, for her, as it is, by her."[38] Since Wroth's *Urania* is named for a
character in the *Arcadia*, she may have thought of her work as — in some
sense — continuing Sir Philip's unfinished romance, even as her aunt
was completing the *Psalmes*.

The two women must have talked frequently about their literary
work. Wroth's 1621 *Urania* tantalizes us with what appears to be a depiction of their continuing relationship. Anne Prescott suggests that by
presenting members of her family under the thinnest of disguises in
a narrative framework, Wroth may be imitating the *Heptameron* of
Marguerite de Navarre, wherein the storytellers represent Marguerite
herself as Parlamente, her husband, Henri de Navarre, as Hircan, her
mother, Louise de Savoie (or her friend Louise de Daillon), as Oisille,
and so on.[39] As has long been recognized, in the *Urania* Pamphilia is
one of several self-designations for Wroth, Amphilanthus bears a remarkable resemblance to William Herbert, Earl of Pembroke, and there
are many other family references, such as Rosindy, who represents
Wroth's brother Robert. Only recently we have noted that the Countess
of Pembroke is figured in *Urania* as the widowed Queen of Naples,
mother of Amphilanthus and "the brauest of Ladies of her time." If
this reference is, as it appears to be, equally biographical, then Mary
Wroth and the Countess of Pembroke maintained their literary and personal relationship even after Wroth's marriage. Indeed, the Queen of
Naples, who was "rare in Poetry" (415–16), helps to authorize the writings of Pamphilia even as the Countess of Pembroke helped to authorize
the writings of Wroth.

Pamphilia met her aunt "with ioy and respect, knowing her so worthy,
as she was onely fit to bee mother to such a sonne, who alone deserued
so matchlesse a mother" (316). As was decorous, Pamphilia approached
"with a low reuerence, which loue made her yeeld her," but the Queen
embraced her. Their time together was spent in witty and profitable

talk, for "no time was lost betweene them, for each minute was fild with store of wit, which passed betweene them, as grounds are with shadowes where people walke: and the longer they discoursed still grew as much more excellent, as they, to nightward seeme longer" (316). Their discourse is on politics, love, and poetry.

When the two queens discuss politics, they imitate the Countess of Pembroke and Mary Wroth. The Queen asks Pamphilia for news "of the warres in *Albania*," which appears to be a reference to the Netherlands. Mary Wroth had traveled to Flushing with her mother in her youth and continued to maintain her interest in affairs there, even recommending particular soldiers in the garrison for promotion and extra pay. Other women turned to her for news of Continental affairs. For example, Anne Clifford records in her diary that at the funeral of Queen Anne in 1619 she talked with the Countess of Pembroke and Lady Wroth, "who brought news from beyond the sea."[40] For members of the Protestant alliance, such news would probably concern the Netherlands and the Palatine. In the *Urania* the news given is, naturally enough in a romance, about another unhappy love affair producing a national crisis, neatly solved by Amphilanthus. For the happy resolution "all must thanke Amphilanthus," Pamphilia says. "And hee your loue (said the Queene) who thus commendeth him" (318). This passage is intriguing for it may imply that the Countess of Pembroke sanctioned Wroth's love for her son William, perhaps on the grounds that her marriage had been a political and economic convenience planned by others for their own ends, or perhaps because of *de praesenti* marriage vows which predated young Mary's marriage to Robert Wroth, as Josephine Roberts suggests in her essay in this volume.[41] Pamphilia "blushed to heare her iudgement so free with her. [The Queen of Naples] kissed her, and willd her not to feare, though she discouered her" (318). The situation is deliberately obfuscated, however, for a few pages later the Queen of Naples does not seem to know whom Pamphilia loves. The two women walk, "still taulking of loue, the braue Queene longing to heare the young Queene confesse, shee willing enough if to any shee would haue spoken it, but hee, and shee must only bee rich in that knowledge" (320). Wroth may have perceived the Countess of Pembroke as a restraining influence, for as soon as they leave the Queen of Naples, Pamphilia and her friends sail away on a sea of passion and are imprisoned by enchantment. They had been careful not to let the Queen of Naples know that they were leaving "least their iourney might be hindred; thus they plotted to deceiue themselues, and ranne from safety to apparent danger" (320).

Equally intriguing are the literary activities shared by these two queens. Pamphilia presents a lengthy poem to the Queen of Naples, supposedly written by another character (318–19). The Queen of Naples is herself "as perfect in Poetry, and all other Princely vertues as any woman that euer liu'd, to bee esteemed excellent in any one, [but] shee was stor'd with all, and so the more admirable" (320). She walks "in the sweet woods" with her ladies," where "they passed the time together, telling stories of themselues, and others, mixed many times with pretty fine fictions, both being excellently witty, and the Queene of Naples rare in Poetry" (415). *Urania* then presents a sample of "Verses framed by the most incomparable Queene, or Lady of her time, a Nightingale most sweetly singing, vpon which she grounded her subiect."

> O That I might now as senselesse bee
> Of my felt paines, as is that pleasant Tree,
> Of the sweet musique, thou deare Byrd dost make,
> Who I imagine doth my woes partake.
> Yet contrary we doe our passions mooue,
> Since in sweet notes thou dost thy sorrowes prooue.
> I but in sighs, and teares, can shew I grieue,
> And those best spent, if worth doe them beleeue.
> Yet they sweet pleasures make me euer finde
> That happinesse to me, as Loue is blinde,
> And these thy wrongs in sweetnesse to attire,
> Throwes downe my hopes to make my woes aspire.
> Besides, of me th'aduantage thou hast got,
> Thy griefe thou vtter'st, mine I vtter not.
> Yet thus as last we may agree in one,
> I mourne for what still is, thou, what is gone (415).

After she has sung, Perissus gives her great praise, saying "that he neuer had heard any like them, and in so saying, he did right to them, and her who knew when she did well, and would be vnwilling to lose the due vnto her selfe, which he gaue her, swearing he neuer heard any thing finelier worded, nor wittilier written on the sudden" (416). Since we know that a poem in *Urania* attributed to Amphilanthus is included in various seventeenth-century miscellanies as the work of William

Herbert, Earl of Pembroke, we may well ask if this lyric, attributed to the Queen of Naples, is one of the lost works of Mary Sidney.[42] The characterization of the poet as one "who knew when she did well, and would be vnwilling to lose the due vnto her selfe" certainly fits what we know of the Countess of Pembroke, who added a proud postscript on a business letter, "It is the Sister of Sir Philip Sidney who yow ar to right and who will worthely deserue the same."[43] Since her late twenties, the countess had received extravagant praise for her poetry and would continue to expect that praise, despite the traditional self-deprecation in her dedicatory poems.

After the Queen of Naples has presented her own poem, a sketchy narrative provides excuse for other poems. The probability that these stories do give us a glimpse of the literary amusements of the countess and Mary Wroth is increased by both external and internal evidence.

External evidence includes the testimony of other witnesses to the countess's habit of encouraging storytelling and poetry. The literary activities of the Queen of Naples, as she walks "in the sweet woods" with her ladies, where they "passed the time together, telling stories" (415–16), sound much like the descriptions of Pembrokiana and her friends in Abraham Fraunce's *Ivychurch* poems, written for the Countess of Pembroke. For example, in *The Third Part of the Countesse of Pembrokes Iuychurche. Entituled, Amintas Dale*, Pembrokiana honors her brother's death by storytelling in the woods at Ivychurch:

> Matchless Lady regent, for further grace to *Amyntas*
> Late transformed to a flowre; wills euery man to remember
> Some one God transformd, or that transformed an other:
> And enioynes each nymph to recount some tale of a Goddesse
> That was changd herself, or wrought some change in an other.[44]

Each story is interpreted by the learned Elphinus as the company sits under the trees. As Mary Ellen Lamb suggests, the Countess of Pembroke may have commemorated her brother in this way.[45] The Pembroke's physician Thomas Moffett plays with similar classical tales in *The Silkwormes and their Flies*, comically adapting them to his discussion of silk making for "Mira" [an anagram for Mari], her daughter "Panclea" [Anne], and "the Gentlewomen attending upon Mira and her daughter."[46]

Internal evidence that the literary activities in the *Urania* reflect those of the countess and Mary Wroth is found in the conflation of fiction and autobiography on two levels, that of the characters and that of the author. The characters display a sophisticated self-awareness of the nature of their fiction. The Queen of Naples and the ladies "passed the time together, telling stories of themselues, and others, mixed many times with pretty fine fictions," we are told. That is, they deliberately present autobiography and biography in a fictional form. Furthermore, Pamphilia tells a tale, "faigning it to be written in a French story," in one of Wroth's most transparent biographical references, the story of Robert Sidney's courtship of Barbara Gamage. "A braue young Lord . . . second sonne to a famous Nobleman . . . was by means of a brother in Law of his, married to a great Heyre in little Brittany, of rich possessions. This Lady was wooed and sought by many, one she affected and so much loued, as she was contented to thinke him worthy to be her husband, and so for worth, he was." Her father would not permit her to marry, but after his death, when she was neglected by her "first seruant . . . she chang'd her minde, and gaue her selfe to valiant and louely *Bersindor*" (424). This tale reflects the life of Barbara Gamage, "a great Heyre in little Brittany" (Wales), who had been betrothed to Herbert Croft but married Robert Sidney, "the "second sonne to a famous Nobleman" (Sir Henry Sidney). The match was arranged "by means of a brother in Law of his" (Henry Herbert, Earl of Pembroke.) They had "many faire and sweet children" who were well bred. The eldest daughter was Lindamira (Lady Mary), rather immodestly described as a "Lady of great spirit, excellent qualities, and beautifull enough to make many in loue with her" (424).

Such autobiographical references are scattered throughout the *Urania*. For example, another lady begins her account of her sorrows in love with the parentage of her beloved, in an equally transparent description of William Herbert: "My father [Robert Sidney] had a sister [Mary Sidney] married to one of the noblest and greatest Princes of this Countrie [Henry Herbert, Earl of Pembroke], as rich in possessions as any, yet possessed he not so much treasures, as hee did vertues, being richer in them, then any other of this land, true noblenesse and noble hospitalitie abounding in him" (243). The reference to the immensely wealthy Earl of Pembroke is obvious, particularly since the Pembrokes were renowned for their hospitality, dispensed on a feudal scale. Like Pembroke, this Prince had three children, "two Sonnes and one Daughter" who were his heirs. His eldest son was "called Laurimello,[47] who had been much in my fathers house, his father putting that trust in his brother in Law, as to leaue his dearest part of comfort with him: besides, my Fathers estate lay nearer to the Citie of *Buda*, which was a convueniecy, by reason of the Courts lying there, for his seeing, and frequenting that: by reason whereof, after his fathers death he brought his sister likewise thither, betweene whom and my selfe, there grew an entire friendship" (243). Penshurst was far closer to London than was Wilton, Ivychurch, or the other Pembroke estates in Wiltshire. We know that William Herbert often stayed at Penshurst; in fact, Barbara Sidney, when scolded by her husband for her extravagant housekeeping, explained that they only served luxurious fare when it was necessary to treat William, Lord Herbert, according to his rank. It is quite probable that after his father's death, young Pembroke brought his sister Anne to Penshurst frequently, for Anne and Mary had spent many months together during childhood, were at court together early in the reign of James I, and acted together in Jonson's *Masque of Blacknesse*. In *Urania*, the speaker wants to marry her beloved Laurimello, but "he not once imagining my end, married another Lady, rich, and therefor worthy" (245), perhaps a reference to Pembroke's marriage to Mary Talbot, daughter of the Earl of Shrewsbury. Under severe pressure from her family, the lady finally accepted the original suitor and had two years of unhappiness: "I liu'd an ill, and froward life with him, for some two yeares, while ignorance held me, and willfulnes liued in him" but they became "good friends, and like kinde mates" for three years (245–46). Having "beene bred in Court," she did not appear sufficiently modest, but her husband eventually came to realize that "more innocency lyes vunder a fayre Canope, then in a close chest." The company meets her husband and learns that she loves her cousin chastely but openly — and her husband does not mind. Eventually, the lady's husband is overthrown in a joust by Amphilanthus and accidently killed, "leauing his delicate wife, as perfect and excellent a widdow" (247).

The 1621 *Urania* ends with the joyful reunion of Pamphilia and Amphilanthus. Amphilanthus is called to Germany, "but intreates Pamphilia to goe as far as Italy with him, to visit the matchles Queene his mother," who apparently approves of their joyful love. Preparing for the journey, "all now merry, contented, nothing amisse; grief forsaken, sadnes cast off, Pamphilia is the Queene of all content; Amphilanthus ioying worthily in her" (558). Significantly, the Queen of Naples still understands their love in the second half of the *Urania,* even after their marriages to others. Her "deerest mother-Aunte" is a most welcome visitor to Pamphilia on the morning after her wedding, "for she was onely the true secretary of her thoughts" (II:fol.23r). Later, Amphilanthus walks between the Queen of Naples and Pamphilia, "who though loath to bee parted, yett soe deerely loued the partision, as they thought they joined both in him" (II:fol.24v), suggesting that the widowed Wroth either had, or wished to have, the Countess of Pembroke's approval of her love for William Herbert.[48]

As Wroth followed her uncle's example in writing a pastoral romance, so in her closet drama, written for performance within the household, she followed the genre of her aunt's *Antonius.* Using the story of Antony and Cleopatra, the countess had explored the conflict between personal and political duties, particularly for her female protagonist; Wroth focused more on personal than on public affairs in her play, *Loves Victorie.* In a fascinating adaptation of family members for fictional purposes, she has Sir Philip Sidney appear as Philisses (a reference to his own self-designation in the *Arcadia,* Philisides), who is in love with Musella, who could be interpreted both as the Muse and as Stella (Penelope Devereux, Lady Rich), although in this cheerful adaptation of the Romeo and Juliet plot, Philisses and Musella are eventually freed to marry.[49] The Countess of Pembroke also figures in *Loves Victorie,* wherein Simena (Mary Sidney) loves Lissius (Sir Mathew Lister, a court physician known for his learning and for his good looks), who scorns love.[50] Predictably, Lissius is eventually vanquished by love, but wins Simena "with too little paine" for Venus to be satisfied.[51] Venus and Cupid therefore separate the lovers by rumors that Lissius is secretly wooing another woman. After Musella finally brings about their reconciliation, Simena and Lissius abjure jealousy and become "the couple Cupid best doth love."[52] We will probably never know how much of this is truth and how much fiction, for the appearance of Sir Philip Sidney as one of the living lovers and the complete reworking of his relationship with Penelope Devereux make the balance between fiction and truth far more complicated than the usual *roman à clef.* Nonetheless,

Wroth was comfortable portraying her widowed aunt, "vertuous and learned" though she may have been, as a lover—at least in the Platonic sense. The countess, who had translated and sponsored closet drama herself, may well have taken part in a reading of *Loues Victorie*.

Surely Denny was wrong to suppose that the Countess of Pembroke should be invoked to frighten Mary Wroth back into appropriately feminine genres. Mary Sidney, Countess of Pembroke, the most important literary woman of her generation in England, was a mentor to Mary Sidney, Lady Wroth, the most important woman writer of the next generation. In her literary work, as well as in her social position, Mary Wroth was "Neece . . . to the most excelent Lady Mary Countesse of Pembrooke."

NOTES

1. "Introduction," *Silent but for the Word: Tudor Women as Patrons, Translators, and Writers of Religious Works*, ed. Margaret Hannay (Kent, Ohio: The Kent State University Press, 1985), p. 1.

2. Tilde Sankovitch, "Inventing Authority of Origin: The Difficult Enterprise," in *Women in the Middle Ages and the Renaissance: Literary and Historical Perspectives*, ed. Mary Beth Rose (Syracuse: Syracuse University Press, 1986), 229–33.

3. Conversation with Anne Prescott, 9 May 1990, Kalamazoo, Michigan. See also Prescott, "The Pearl of the Valois and Elizabeth I: Marguerite de Navarre's *Miroir* and Tudor England," in *Silent but for the Word*, ed. Hannay, pp. 61–76.

4. See "The Cooke Sisters: Attitudes toward Learned Women in the Renaissance," in *Silent but for the Word*, pp. 107–25.

5. Sankovitch, p. 234.

6. On the Countess of Pembroke's poetic legacy, see Nona Fienberg's essay in this collection.

7. Samuel Daniel, *Delia and Rosamond Augmented. Cleopatra* (London: Simon Waterson, 1594), sig. H5.

8. See Margaret Hannay, *Philip's Phoenix: Mary Sidney, Countess of Pembroke* (New York: Oxford University Press, 1990), pp. 119–29.

9. On the political nature of her *Psalmes* and on the Dudley/Sidney/Herbert Protestant alliance of her family with the Huguenots, see *Philip's Phoenix*, particularly the prologue and chapters 3 and 4.

10. *Philip's Phoenix*, ch. 4. Beth Wynn Fisken has recently demonstrated that "To the Angell Spirit" is "quietly subversive" on a personal level as well, for the countess camouflages "the assertiveness of her style with the self-abnegation of her subject matter," in "'To the Angell spirit . . .': Mary Sidney's Entry into the 'World of Words,'" in *The Renaissance Englishwoman in Print: Counterbalancing*

the Canon (Amherst: University of Massachusetts Press, 1990) ed. Anne M. Haselkorn and Betty S. Travitsky, pp. 265–66.

11. William Browne, "On the Countesse Dowager of Pembroke," British Library Lansdowne MS. 777, f. 43v.

12. Countess of Pembroke to Sir Julius Caesar, 8 July 1603, British Library Additional MS 12,503, f. 151.

13. London: John Marriott and John Grismand, 1621.

14. See, for example, the Countess of Pembroke's letter to the Earl and Countess of Shrewsbury, where she signs her name "Pembroke" with the S fermé around her signature (Talbot Papers, Lambeth Palace MS 3203, f. 259). She had signed her name "M. Pembroke" until her daughter-in-law, Mary Talbot Herbert, adopted that signature. Thereafter the countess was simply "Pembroke" with the identifying design to distinguish her title from her son's. Lady Wroth uses the device after the salutation in her letter to George Villiers, Duke of Buckingham (Bodleian MS Add. D III, ff. 173r-v; reproduced in Roberts, p. 77); on folios 5 and 10 of the Huntington manuscript of *Loves Victorie* (HM 600); and on the binding of the Penshurst manuscript of *Loves Victory* (described in Brennan, p. 16).

15. *Ben Jonson: The Complete Poems*, ed. George Parfitt (New Haven, Conn.: Yale University Press, 1982), p. 165.

16. Joshua Sylvester, *Lachrimae Lachrimarum* (London: H. Lownes, 1613), sig. H2. Roberts, p. 19, notes that "AL-WORTH" is an anagram for "La. Wroth."

17. Sir Edward Denny to Lady Mary Wroth, 27 February 1622, Cecil Papers 130/118-119, printed in Roberts, pp. 238–39.

18. See Lady Mary Wroth to the Duke of Buckingham, 15 December 1621, Bodleian Library MS Add. D. III, ff. 173r-v. Printed in Roberts, p. 236.

19. Robert Sidney to Barbara Sidney, "This Tuesday 1587," De L'Isle MS U1475 C81/1, the first in the series of 323 letters from Robert Sidney to his wife that she preserved. De L'Isle MSS quoted with the permission of the Viscount De L'Isle, V.C., K.G., from his estate at Penshurst Place.

20. Robert Sidney to Barbara Sidney, 26 April 1588, C81/2. This may have been young Mary's first extended visit with her cousin William, who, like Bellamira's beloved in the *Urania*, found a cause of love in their "breeding together, which though in our infancies, yet the more naturally bred loue, and increased it, adding to loue, as the smalest sticks doe with number to the fiers of triumph" (329). They would indeed have been bred together, for among the Sidneys and Herberts, as was customary in aristocratic families, there were frequent exchanges of children. For example, "Bess," Sir Philip Sidney's ten-year-old daughter Elizabeth, was sent from Penshurst to Wilton in September 1594. Robert Sidney enclosed a letter from his sister by which "you may see how much my Lord longs for Bess; there is a coach and a gentlewoman come vp for her; let her be sent hither as soon as you may." Robert Sidney to Barbara Sidney, September 1594, C81/46.

21. Robert Sidney to Barbara Sidney, 24 May 1588, C81/3.

22. Robert Sidney to Barbara Sidney, 29 May 1588, C81/4. On 31 May he has again been delayed but is still trying to reach her, C81/5.

23. Robert Sidney to Barbara Sidney, 27 July 1588, C81/6.

24. Robert Sidney to Barbara Sidney, 5 August 1588, C81/7.

25. Robert Sidney to Barbara Sidney, 6 August 1588, C81/8.

26. Robert Sidney to Barbara Sidney, 5 August 1588, C81/7.

27. Robert Sidney to Barbara Sidney, 6 August 1588, C81/8.

28. Mary Sidney, Countess of Pembroke, to Barbara Sidney, 9 September 1590, British Library, bound in Additional MS 15,232.

29. Robert Sidney to Barbara Sidney, 11 July 1594, C81/42; not listed in HMC De L'Isle.

30. Rowland Whyte to Robert Sidney, 12 November 1595, C12/23.

31. Rowland Whyte to Robert Sidney, 8 December 1595, C12/40.

32. Rowland Whyte to Robert Sidney, 22 December 1599, C12/198.

33. Baynards Castle diet book, October 1600–March 1601, De L'Isle MS U1475 A27/4.

34. Robert Sidney to Barbara Sidney, 2 September 1604, C81/110.

35. Dowager Countess of Pembroke to the Earl and Countess of Shrewsbury, 29 September 1604, Lambeth Palace MS 3203, f. 259. Just a few days after the wedding, Wroth had gone up to London, leaving Mary Wroth at Penshurst. "My son Wroth," Robert Sidney reported, has "found somewhat that doth discontent him" although he would not say what. "It were very soon for any unkindness to begin," Sidney observes. Robert Sidney to Barbara Sidney, 10 October 1604, C81 / 117.

36. Robert Sidney to Barbara Sidney, 2 October 1604, C81/113.

37. *The Countesse of Pembrokes Arcadia* (London: William Ponsonby, 1590), sig. A3. The dedication was apparently written for the *Old Arcadia* but was included in the first publication of the *New Arcadia*.

38. *The Countesse of Pembrokes Arcadia* (London: William Ponsonby, 1593), sig. A4.

39. Conversation with Anne Prescott, 9 May 1990, Kalamazoo, Michigan. Like Wroth's names "Rosindy" and "Lindamira," several of Marguerite's names are anagrams, such as "Oisille" for "Louise" and "Hircan" for "Hanric" or "Henri."

40. *The Diary of the Lady Anne Clifford*, ed. Vita Sackville-West (New York: Doran, 1923), p. 77.

41. See Josephine Roberts's essay in this volume, "'The Knott Never to Bee Untide': The Controversy Regarding Marriage in Mary Wroth's *Urania*."

42. The poem "Had I lou'd but at that rate," included in *Urania*, is attributed to Pembroke in British Library MS Harley 6917, ff. 33v–34. See Roberts, p. 217.

43. Mary Sidney, Countess of Pembroke, to Sir Julius Caesar, 8 July 1603, Additional MS 12,503, ff. 151–52.

44. Abraham Fraunce, *The Third part of the Countesse of Pembrokes Iuychurch. Entituled, Amintas Dale. Wherein are the most conceited tales of the Pagan Gods in English Hexameters together with their auncient descriptions and Philosophicall explications* (London: Thomas Woodcocke, 1592), p. 1.

45. Mary Ellen Lamb, "The Countess of Pembroke's Patronage," Ph.D. diss., Columbia University, 1976, p. 135.

46. Thomas Moffett, *The Silkwormes and their Flies* (1599), ed. Victor Houliston (Binghamton, N.Y.: Medieval and Renaissance Texts and Studies, 1989), p. 40.

47. Laurimello is a reference to Petrarch's Laura, thereby emphasizing the chaste love of the fictional cousins. Wroth herself, however, apparently bore William Herbert a son and a daughter.

48. I am indebted to Professor Helen Hackett for noticing this reference in the

Newberry Manuscript. Helen Hackett to Margaret Hannay, 31 May, 1990. See "'Yet tell me some such fiction': Lady Mary Wroth's *Urania* and the 'Femininity' of Romance," in *Interventions: Women, Texts and Histories, 1575-1760*, ed. Diane Purkiss and Clare Brant (London: Routledge, forthcoming).

49. The ending of the play, now available in Brennan's edition, is discussed by Carolyn Swift, "Feminine Self-Definition in Lady Mary Wroth's *Loves Victorie* (c. 1621)" *English Literary Renaissance* 19 (1989), 171–88.

50. The identification was made by Josephine A. Roberts, "The Huntington Manuscript of Lady Mary Wroth's *Loves Victorie*," *Huntington Library Quarterly* 48 (1983), 156–74. There may be a connection between this story and that of the Marygold widow in the *Urania*, who reacts jealously to her lover (268). For gossip about the Countess of Pembroke and Sir Mathew Lister, see John Aubrey, *Brief Lives*, ed. Oliver Lawson Dick (London: Secker and Warburg, 1949), p. 139; and John Chamberlain to Sir Dudley Carleton, *Letters of John Chamberlain*, ed. Norman Egbert McClure (Philadelphia: American Philosophical Society, 1939. Reprint, Westport, Conn.: Greenwood Press, 1979), vol. 2, pp. 69 and 400.

51. Brennan, p. 133.

52. Brennan, p. 163. The same wording is used in the Huntington Library MS HM 600, f. 18v.

Mary Wroth and the Sidney Family Romance:
Gender Construction in Early Modern England

Gary Waller

If anyone is inclined to turn away in horror from this depravity of the childish heart or feels tempted, indeed, to dispute the possibility of such things, he should observe that these works of fiction, which seem so full of hostility, are none of them really so badly intended, and that they still preserve, under a slight disguise, the child's original affection for his parents.

Freud, "Family Romances"

I

In 1908, in his *Der Mythus von der Gerburt des Helden* (Myth of the Birth of the Hero), Otto Rank printed Freud's "Der Familienroman der Neurotiker" (the neurotic's family romance). Remarking that "the liberation of an individual, as he grows up, from parental authority is one of the most necessary though one of the most painful" events of life, Freud describes the symptoms of "the family romance." These all involve the desire to change one's family circumstances—to have richer or more powerful parents, or not to share one's parents' love with siblings. Other symptoms include a boy's hostility coupled with an intense desire to bring his mother—the subject, says Freud, "of the most intense sexual curiosity"—into "situations of secret infidelity" with him. Related phantasies may include incestuous feelings for siblings, desires to return to fancied (or perhaps real) conditions in early childhood when the child was unindividuated from the mother, and the child's "most intense and momentous" general wish, "to be big like his parents." In children, such symptoms emerge as wish fulfillments with, Freud says, aims that are simultaneously erotic and ambitious, not only to emulate (or seduce) the parents but to be free of their control. In adults, the family romance is symptomized by desires to recapture a lost state of autonomy, which may be projected, negatively or positively, upon a variety of love-objects—lovers, siblings, parents, or children—who thereby become incorporated into the neurotic patterns laid down early in the adult's own family history. For many post-Freudians, of course, most notably Deleuze and Guattari, the incestuous family romance as outlined by Freud is not a primary desire, but a particular form that desire assumes because of the repression to which it is necessarily subject by society. The unrealizability of infantile desires forces us back into the family as the site where we struggle, inevitably imperfectly, to realize some substitute for them.[1] We can also use the term "family romance" to refer to the psychological soap operas of erotic attraction between siblings or cousins, the erotic entanglements, say, of Oates's *Childwold* or Nabokov's *Lolita*, or the *cris de coeur* of the adolescent lovelorn, as witness this extract from "Ask Beth" in the *Boston Globe* for March 25, 1988:

> Dear Beth: My cousin is extremely precious to me, but killing me. She says she loves me. We have had intimate contact several times, but she also has sex with many boyfriends. She lives so far away I only see her a couple of times a month . . . every time I see her, I fall in love all over again.—Far Gone in Heartache
> *Your cousin is a "sexpot," and your attraction is strongly sexual. . . . Intimate relations with first cousins aren't very healthy anyway. You'd be much better off developing real friendships closer to home with girls you can have dates with. When you've made a loving relationship, your awkward passion for your cousin will fade.*

My subject is, indeed, a pair of first cousins, not just their "awkward passion," but how they were constituted within a particular cultural conjunction as gendered and familial subjects. Mary Wroth and William Herbert were cousins, lovers, writers, and parents: their separate and conjoined histories make up a fascinating variant of the "family romance" and the contradictory social, familial, and gendered discursive practices by which they were constructed.

The Freudian models of family and gender have been criticized for underplaying social forces beyond the individual psyche. As Mark Poster notes, "while the family generates a psychological pattern of internalized age and sex hierarchies, it also participates in larger social institutions." Such factors as the quaternity of cultural materialist criticism, *gender, race, class,* and *agency,* allow us to see how individuals are constituted as familial and gendered subjects. In this case, though class is clearly deeply implicated, and race (given the Sidneys' involvement in Ireland and Wales) by no means irrelevant, the most important of these categories are gender and the attendant question of agency.[2]

Contrary to essentialist assumptions—whether they be liberal humanist, biogrammatic, or certain readings of Freud—gender is a category of social construction: it is, in complex and overdetermined ways, assigned to human subjects within the material practices of different societies, not least the family. The categories "man" and "woman" are always sites of contestation. The fundamental asymmetry of the two in the early modern period produced an almost exclusive "feminine" milieu—domestic activities, passivity in the marriage market, childbearing, the priority of sexual over public activity—which for the majority of women at the time seemed to constitute prototypical feminine experiences. It is also true that of the various models that try to explain how people, whether as individuals or in groups, interact—by force, dominance, persuasion, bargaining, or nurturing—the dominant one in the early modern period was quite openly that of authority. Viable subject positions beyond those sanctioned by the dominant ideology are therefore rare, and inevitably marginalized or compromised. Having (or "being"? or "being afforded"? rarely would it be "possessing") the body of a woman, and as the daughter of an aspiring family, Mary Wroth inherited a sexual destiny that was to a large extent not her own. It was her father who played the dominant role in her early life— entering her life infrequently in person yet supervising her education, deciding upon her marriage, arranging her dowry (ironically with the help of Pembroke), and giving her access to an area of relative agency when, through her writing, she came to emulate him, her aunt Mary, and her uncle Philip. His letters are full of affection for her as a child and, even after her marriage, he seems more concerned for her than his other children. Yet however benevolent he was, his daughter's marriage was simply one step in what on the surface was a smooth transition from girlhood and dependence on her paternal family to marriage and an equally dependent place in her husband's family. In the assigned practices of her class and gender within the family lay her destiny. Considering the unconscious as a desiring machine, in Deleuze and Guat-

tari's term — a flow of desires produced by the interactions of the social
and the biological and then cathected onto the world — the family is
a primary locus of control and recuperation, the place where desires
are tested, transformed, or distorted under the incessant pressure of the
social formation that in part engenders them. Parents, husbands or
wives, siblings, cousins, children, and lovers therefore are all both a major source of desire and the means of its denial.[3]

Yet, as Gramsci repeatedly argued, hegemony is never total, and the
family is also the material and metaphorical structure in which the
young girl strives for differentiation and independence by looking for
alternatives to her parents. In Wroth's case, the struggle seems to have
been, initially at least, one over which she had little control. Dominated by men, or more accurately, by her internalization of the socially
constructed power of men — first her father, then (to a limited extent,
at least) her husband and, probably over the course of twenty years,
her cousin-lover — Wroth's life shows a consistent struggle to come to
terms with her idealization of the figure of the distant father. This im-
aginary contruct is reinforced if, as in this case, he is rarely at home
with the family. A familiar version of the family romance involves casting him in the role of the glamorous or permissive hero who rescues
the daughter from the humdrum and oppressive; another version casts
the father in the role of the censor and inhibitor who drives her back
to culturally predetermined roles. These two father-figures, in historically specific forms — the idealized "day father" and the threatening
"night father" who brings "all the dangers of cruelty and seduction
in his train and mobilizes anxious nightmares" — lie behind the male
figures in Wroth's writings, just as she seems to have projected them
upon the major male figures in her life, her "real" father, her husband,
and her cousin.[4]

What, if any, alternatives could Wroth turn to? Within the tightly
controlled early modern family, were there distinctive chances of autonomy and self-assertion? Were there areas of woman's agency that
as Nancy Hartsock puts it, can "be characterized as feminine or female?"[5]
What, for instance, was the force of such matters as the importance
of women's primary identification with the family, the changing nature
and value of women's work, the separation from most "public" events,
the impact of the female life cycle, risky and frequent childbirth, aging,

the lack of adequate contraception or medical knowledge, or the development of special networks and alliances? If we tackle the Freudian argument head on, another crucial area is the silenced power of women's own sexuality. In short, in (as it were) the cultural unconscious, to what areas of autonomy did a woman have access—at least on the level of fantasy? What collective fantasies can we cite for evidence of emergent aspirations or practices? What for instance, did it mean to a woman to be interpellated into the collective fantasy of domination, individual heroism, and ostentation centered upon the warrior-prince, the courtier, the patriarch? Required to be decorative, inspiring, constant, and domesticated, women occupied essential parts in that elaborate and destructive structure—in the case of aristocratic women, if not as homebodies, let us say, at least as "great house" bodies. In the *Urania*, whereas the men are in continual movement—pursuing adventure in an expansive, half real, half fantastic, landscape—the women are either expected to wait at home, however restless or trapped they appear, or else are continually at risk for their boldness and, as Ann Shaver argues, their outspokenness. Judging from Wroth's writings, a recurring fantasy for women in the period is that they might emulate the autonomy and mobility of the courtly-chivalric heroes. My speculation is supported by Simon Shepherd's work on the figure of the Amazon and by recent studies of women's likely reactions in the theaters to both women characters and fellow spectators.[6] In fiction, however, such a fantasy could only temporarily focus women's dreams of autonomy—the end of *As You Like It* rewards men for their tolerance by restoring the patriarchal control of both father and husband over Rosalind, appropriately dressed as a virgin bride, her frank desires now tamed to their uses. It is well that we learn of Orlando's prowess in killing the lioness and overthrowing the Duke's wrestler; otherwise we might wonder about his ability to control the raging passions of his eager wife.

What do Wroth's writings tell us of the areas which women have historically carved out for themselves in defiance or independence of male domination and the cult of heroic violence—whether wrestling, lion-killing, or some other? The first that emerges from Wroth's life as well as her writings is a distinctive sense of community among women that has been termed "womanspace"—groups, allegiances, and friendships that provide women with strength and a measure of independence by excluding or circumventing men. In the Countess of Pembroke's case, as Hannay shows in her recent biography, such an area was provided by the "little court" at Wilton.[7] In Mary Wroth's case, this function was served by her friendships with other members of the extended Sidney-Herbert families, notably with her father and Pembroke's sister-in-law, Lucy, Countess of Montgomery, to whom the *Urania* was dedicated. Both the *Urania* and *Love's Victory* stress the importance of networks of women friends, which provided opportunities for private spaces where the more brutal aspects of hegemonic male power might be escaped.

Another space, associated with the regulation of women's distinctive sexual capacities, is childbearing. Do women's bodies and specifically motherhood provide, as Julia Kristeva argues, a pre-cultural given that plays a determinative, trans-historical role in women's lives? This is, understandably, a difficult argument to make at the present time, especially in some feminist circles: as Kristeva notes, at a time when "feminism demands a new representation of femininity," such an argument may seem to identify motherhood with an "idealized misconception" and so "circumvents the real experience that fantasy overshadows."[8] We need to historicize and particularize here, distinguishing perhaps between the patriarchal institution of motherhood and the experience of childbearing. In Wroth's case, is it possible to view her childbearing — not so much her one legitimate child as her two illegitimate children — at least in part as a defiance of the patriarchal system in which her marriage had imprisoned her? On the evidence not only of her life, but also of the *Urania*, especially the unpublished continuation, bearing her two illegitimate children may have suggested not so much Wroth's acceptance of her role in dynastic politics as the assertion of her sexuality against a repressive world. Certainly, much of what we can see of Wroth's sexuality was assigned to her — in particular, the submission to familial aggrandizement betokened by her marriage. For a woman of her rank, sexuality in marriage was part of the family obligation: she was to marry and supply her husband and his estate with a male heir. Her drives to achieve bodily satisfaction were not permitted in themselves to be the means to autonomous intimacy or pleasure. Of course, we do not know, except indirectly, how sexuality operated in Mary Wroth's marriage or her other relationships. But we can perhaps tell something from two recurring patterns in her writing: one of male dominance and female masochism—what the *Urania* terms the "molestation" women suffer (409); the other, the repeated stories of women daring to make sexual choices. In her life, her affair with Pembroke had sufficient stability or at least recurrence to produce two children; it is possible that she was attempting to carve out an unusual degree of specifically sexual agency. Paradoxically, perhaps, by contracting a relationship with a close to forbidden degree of consanguinity, she could both defy convention and enfold herself back into the family romance. Each of these "adventures"—to borrow a recurring word in her romance—constitutes a distinctive breach with her conventional gender assignments in early seventeenth-century society.

Wroth's sexual defiance—ironically afforded by the family, within the family romance—is, then, one area in which she strove to assert herself. The other is her activity as a writer. Wroth is one of the first women writers in English in whose work a habitually submerged female discourse starts to emerge. Hegemony is never total cultural dominance, the obliteration of all alternatives, and it is the everyday contestations of sexual and familial life that eventually produce what, to adapt Raymond Williams's phrase, we can call the "long" revolution in the history of gender assignment.

II

First, then, to the place of Mary Wroth's sexuality in the Sidney Family Romance. Her marriage, however advantageous to the two families, seems not to have been either an immediate or long-term success. Ben Jonson told Drummond of Hawthornden that "my Lady Wroth is unworthily married to a jealous husband." Only two weeks after the wedding, there are two letters from Robert Sidney to his wife, referring to "words of grief" which she had put "in the end" of a letter written while the newly married couple were with her at Penshurst. Sidney refers to "that which you tolde me somewhat of the morning when I came away. If it be so," he writes, "I must confess it a great misfortune to us all, and yet I see no reason why we may not have hope of ammendment of it. But for the time it is very necessary that it be very secret kept and that by no circumstance it be discovered." The day after, Robert again replied to his wife's concerned remarks, this time explicitly mentioning Robert Wroth's "discontent:"

> I finde by him that there was somewhat that doth discontent him: but the particulars I could not get out from him: onely that hee protests that hee cannot take any exceptions to his wife, nor her carriage towards him. It were very soon for any unkindness to begin; and therefore whatsoever the matters bee, I pray you let all things be caused in the best manner til wee all doe meet. For mine ennimies would be very glad for such an occasion to make themselves merry at me.

McLaren speculates that the letters refer to the "possible non-consummation" of the marriage; it could equally be the discovery that his wife's affections were placed elsewhere: it certainly sounds as if there are sexual overtones to the incident. Pembroke's marriage, contracted about the same time, was clearly uncongenial to him, but while the evidence for some family anxiety about both the cousins' marriages is clear enough, we have no certain knowledge that there was a connection.[9] There is also, however, the start of the lengthy estrangement between Pembroke and his mother—a phenomenon upon which Margaret Hannay strangely barely comments in her recent biography of the countess—but which was to last some ten years.

Regardless of any exotic diversions or rumors that might have constituted "discontentment," the Wroth marriage brought together incompatible interests and temperaments. As one of Queen Anne's group of ladies, Mary continued her life at court, taking part in masques and entertainments, while her husband spent most of his time in local affairs—pursuing tenancies, consolidating his forest holdings, and hunting. Mary Wroth spent much of her time in London at Baynards Castle, Pembroke's London house. The Sidney family correspondence shows a constant movement between Loughton and Durance (the Wroths' main residences in Essex), Pembroke's London residence, Baynards Castle, and Penshurst: for instance, Mary is at Penshurst on August 1610; Robert Sidney is anxious to see his daughter there a month or so later; early in October, Mary is back at Loughton; her husband visits her at Durance a week later and again the following month; Mary and the Countess of Montgomery visit Baynards a few months later, and they are again together at Penshurst in August 1611.[10] The men involved—her father, her cousin—frequently overlap; her husband is occasionally mentioned but is rarely present away from his estates; Pembroke's wife is barely mentioned except as an embarrassment.

As Hannay has argued in the previous chapter, there is a strong sense that although she married into the Wroth family, Mary remained, though "unnamed," a Sidney. And as a Sidney, she inherited something of the family's reputation for patronage, and a number of poets addressed her—some by her married name but usually making reference to her parentage. On the other hand, her husband had other interests. As William Gamage, himself probably a distant relation of Wroth's mother, noted: "Thy Durance keeps in durance none, I heare / 'Lesse be to pertake of thy bounteous cheere." Gamage footnotes "thy" with an explanation that Wroth was "a famous housekeeper," an opinion echoed by Ben Jonson. *The Forrest*, in which "To Penshurst" and "To Sir Robert Wroth" occupy the first places (after the mock-dedicatory "Why I Write Not of Love") is a kind of manifesto praising the Sidneian ideology of "housekeeping." Philip Sidney is invoked as both a commitment to the past ("To Penshurst") and a prophecy of the future ("To Elizabeth Countess of Rutland"); the volume contains a poem associated with Pembroke and possibly Wroth ("That Women Are But Mens Shaddowes") and with one of Lady Wroth's brothers ("To Sir William Sydney, On His Birthday"). Of the fifteen poems in the collection, five—and among those four of the most significant—are associated with the Sidney/Herbert family.[11]

Jonson's poem to Sir Robert Wroth has usually been read as a celebration of the reciprocity and generosity which are supposedly upheld in "To Penshurst." According to this reading, Jonson sees the Wroth estates as images of rural contentment and natural innocence. But if we set the poem in the context of Wroth's marriage, his wife's activities, and the ideals of manhood which the poem purports to uphold, a very different reading emerges. The poem opens, in fact, with an immediate back-handed compliment. Wroth inherited his father's distrust of the court and preference for hunting and country life. Jonson, the urbane haunter of coffee-houses and taverns, exclaims: "How blest art thou, canst love the country, Wroth / Whether by choice, of fate, or both," going on to praise Wroth's lifestyle: while his estates are "neere the citie, and the court," he is fortunately untainted by this proximity, since unlike ambitious courtiers, glittering court ladies, or dissipated masquers, he does not resort to the pleasures of the city. In particular, Jonson eulogizes: "Nor, throng'st (when masquing is) to have a sight / Of the short braverie of the night." As a frugal housekeeper, Wroth is invited to contemplate disapprovingly "the jewells, stuffes, the paines, the wit / There wasted, some not paid for yet!"

When we consider not only to whom Jonson was writing but who was hovering in the background of the poem, we must be struck by the risks he was taking. As he looked over his shoulder, he saw, first, Wroth's wife, one of those for whom "the short braverie of the night" was a central part of life. The other he would have seen was Wroth's wife's cousin, whose intimacy with her was probably at the very least rumor, and who was still owed for her dowry, so who in a sense had pointedly given the Wroths some "jewells" and "stuffes," that were "not paid for yet." Is Jonson indulging in sarcasm? Or in irony? As the poem goes on, when we consider the multiple audiences, it is as if Jonson is trying to satisfy all of them. For Wroth, it was probably a compliment not only to have a poem addressed to him by a poet of Jonson's reputation (especially among his wife's relations), but also to be praised precisely for what he, not she, wanted to do—for staying "at home," in "thy securer rest." But his wife and her cousin, for their part, might well laugh up their sleeves when Wroth is described as dwelling "mongst loughing heards, and solide hoofes." Jonson is praising Wroth for exactly the characteristics his wife scorns. While she is masquing at court, he is at home with the cattle and the local squires. Jonson celebrates Wroth's rural life not as a moral exemplum but as that of an unsophisticated country gentleman. Unlike the Sidneys at Penshurst, for whom country hospitality is part of a moral responsibility, for Wroth it is an opportunity for a "rout of rural folke" to "come thronging in." What Jonson quite explicitly calls "their rudenesse" is something that Wroth (as it were by nature) overlooks while his "noblest spouse" is sufficiently condescending to afford "them welcome grace." Jonson's conclusion praises Wroth by explicitly emasculating him:

> And such since thou canst make thine owne content,
>   Strive, *Wroth*, to live long innocent.
> Let others watch in guiltie armes, and stand
>   The furie of a rash command,

Goe enter breaches, meet the cannons rage,
That they may sleepe with scarres in age.

Behind this praise is a rejection of the masculine pursuits of politics, arms, law, business, "money, warre, or death." The poem concludes:

Let thousands more goe flatter vice, and winne,
By being organes to great sinne,
Get place, and honor, and be glad to keepe
The secrets, that shall breake their sleepe.

The kind of man Jonson is praising Wroth for not emulating—indeed, rejecting—is undoubtedly best exemplified in his immediate circle by Pembroke himself.

Even more ironic are the metaphors of gender that dislocate the poem's apparent harmonious vision. As in "To Penshurst," housekeeping is depicted as a return to an undifferentiated relationship with the mother, a primitive unity where food, satisfaction and acceptance are all instantly available. As Raymond Williams pointed out, in "To Penshurst," nobody actually works to produce the feasts; the fish offer themselves to be caught; all nature and its plenty are part of a universal flow.[12] It is a gently comic pre-oedipal fantasy of how nature and human beings were once united and provided for. In such a pattern the court represents an oedipal break; it is, by contrast to the idealized country, a raw, crude masculine world. Staying at home, therefore, Wroth is demasculinized and sneered at. His wife is clearly most fulfilled when part of the court's perpetual movement, part of the masculine world dominated by the king and her cousin; he stays at home, since "when man's state is well, / Tis better, if he there can dwell." "Such," Jonson says to Wroth with, it seems, magnificent bravado, "be thou." The poem is full of such mystifications. Wroth is praised for avoiding the litigious pursuit of land at court. And yet we know that is precisely what he was perpetually involved in, and that it was his wife who wrote, successfully, to the queen for interventions to be made on his behalf so he might rebuild Loughton. Someone—and it was more often his wife and her family, including her increasingly influential cousin—had to "sweat, and wrangle at the barre." Likewise, it is precisely because his wife, cousin-in-law, and father-in-law "goe flatter vice, and winne / by being organs to great sinne," that he could enjoy the prestige of having the king come to hunt on his lands. Masculine power, most powerfully represented in the king, makes possible both the life of virtuous retirement and the world of the glittering court. The material details of labor, financial investment, and exploitation—which in fact produce the harvest, enclose the forest, and pay the huntsmen—are, as in "To Penshurst," carefully ignored. As David Norwood notes, "someone living so close to Theobald's was bound to feel the need to keep up with the massive scale of conspicuous consumption indulged in by Cecil and the King." Cecil was referred to as "Robin the encloser of Hatfield wood," and Wroth himself was described by Chamberlain as "a great commander or rather by the Kings favor an intruder in Waltham forest." J.C.A. Rathmell points out that "To Penshurst" can usefully be read as, in part, an expression of Jonson's anxiety that Robert Sidney might forget his moral duty and try to emulate the "costly piles." With "To Sir Robert Wroth," Jonson is skating, with typical verve and bravado, on very thin ice indeed. As Lord Chamberlain, Pembroke had a major influence on the revels, in which Jonson and Inigo Jones received employment, and annually gave Jonson £20 for books and—if Jonson's dedications to *Catiline* and the *Epigrams* are evidence—supported and admired him.[13]

Whether the wit of "To Sir Robert Wroth" afforded its primary addressee satisfaction, and his wife (and her cousin) some very different kind of amusement, we cannot be sure. But we do know that the unease Mary's father expressed over his daughter's marriage may find support in the fact that the Wroths did not have a child until 1614. Except where prevented by impotence or infertility, being a woman in the upper classes inevitably meant rapid childbearing as part of the duty of forwarding the ambitions of the husband's family. Yet Mary Wroth's legitimate child, which was presumably fathered by her husband, was born only a month before he died. Her two illegitimate children were born in her period of widowhood—the first probably soon after she became a widow, the second within the next few years.

In 1614, a month after the birth of her son James, Lady Wroth was widowed. Her husband's will was made the day before James was christened—with Pembroke as one of his sponsors, standing in for the king—and twelve days before his death at Loughton on March 14, 1614, probably of gangrene. He left behind him, as Chamberlain noted, "a young widow with £1,200 fortune, a son a month old, and his estate £23,000 in debt." Wroth left her a legacy of £1000, adding in his will that "I hartelie desire my sayed deere and loving wife that she will accept hereof as a testimony of my entire love and affection towards her, albeyet her sincere love, loyaltie, virtuous conversation, and behavioure towards me, have deserved a farre better recompense, yf the satisfying of my debts and supporting my house would have permitted the same."[14]

So, in 1614, Mary Wroth was twenty-seven, a widow with a month-old son and a heavily indebted estate. It does not sound a promising situation and yet arguably the next decade of her life was to prove the most eventful and, probably, the most satisfying. She was a widow, a lover, a mother, and a writer. All the roles were, in their different ways, places in which she carved out distinctive loci of agency for herself. First, despite her indebtedness, widowhood forced her to develop a degree of involvement in public affairs and autonomy that she clearly had in part to suppress as a married woman. We can trace some of her movements — in this period journeying abroad was always more representative of the autonomy of the male — in the first decade after her husband's death. She engaged in other conventionally male activities — especially in ongoing legal disputes over her land and to preserve her financial independence.

Her sexual independence can also be adequately, if not lavishly, documented. It is likely that many records of both the Sidney and Herbert families have been destroyed — in the former case, possibly deliberately; in the latter, in the Wilton House fire of 1647–48 — but there are sufficient to indicate that the most significant relationship of her life was with her cousin. The evidence for Mary Wroth's involvement with Pembroke is a tantalizing mixture of public documentation and circumstantial surmise. There are the facts of the family birth records. Pembroke died without a will, the usual place to mention children, even illegitimate ones (Sir Walter Raleigh provided for his natural daughter in his will), but in two of the family manuscripts in the Cardiff Public Library, there are mentions of "William his base son" by "the Lady Mary Wroth Da[ughter] of Rob[er]t Sidney E[arl] of Leicester" and Katherine, his daughter, who, one manuscript indicates, married a Mr. Lovel. A highly effective cover-up by the Sidneys meant that nothing surfaced in biographical accounts of Lady Wroth — apart from puzzlement about the occasional "mistaken" mention of a second son—until M.A. Beese discussed the Cardiff documents in her 1935 Oxford thesis edition of Pembroke's papers. With the Wilton papers destroyed, and the Sidney papers probably carefully combed to purge most references to the event, the relationship was successfully concealed.

Adultery? In the Jacobean court, a fig, as Iago puts it. More significant are, first, that Wroth could, with the connivance of her family, assert her sexual independence in maintaining her affair with Pembroke; second, that the relationship had sufficient stability to produce two children; and third, that Wroth's lover should be her first cousin. In a society, as Shorter notes, "which maximizes male domination over females at every level," coercion was the rule, and coupled with a widespread suspicion, even fear, of women's sexual appetites, it meant that women who demanded sexual choice or independence often suffered dire social consequences. Sexually independent women were regarded with great hostility in the period, but the surveillance under which they lived varied by class. Church courts existed in large part to bring offenders against moral law into conformity, but women of Wroth's class were usually exempt from the courts' surveillance. In the aristocracy, scandals erupted periodically and there were a number of celebrated independent noble women who were courageous enough to claim a degree of sexual autonomy. But it was still only the lucky and powerful woman who, engineering some degree of social or economic control by means of her family's or husband's positions, could afford to indulge her sexual choices. A widow might be doubly vulnerable. There might well be resentment towards women who remarried, but it would have been no less suspicious to remain single. As Chaytor comments, "a too hasty remarriage could have been regarded as a dishonor to the dead husband but a lifetime of sexual freedom while enjoying his property might have been considered the greater insult."[15]

Hannay speaks of Wroth's "unfortunate" relationship with Pembroke," and asserts, in quaintly Victorian phraseology, that Wroth's "sexual indiscretions undoubtedly humiliated her parents and her godmother";[16] however, not only were the "indiscretions" presumably committed by both Wroth and Pembroke, but almost all the evidence we have on reactions of family members is positive. Lord Herbert of Cherbury wrote a charming poem on the birth of one of the children, and more especially, the Herbert and Sidney families gave both children support and advancement. Lamb has shown, too, the extent to which Wroth was preoccupied with and indeed proud of the illegitimate children who appear in the second part of the *Urania*.[17] There are other signs that Mary Wroth thought of herself as acquiring a degree of sexual independence in her return to being a single woman. From letters, her own and others, it is clear that she spent frequent amounts of time in her cousin's household at Baynards Castle, probably writing much of the *Urania* there. From the fact that there were two children, there must have been a continuing or at least recurring relationship with Pembroke. There may have been other relationships. Some letters she wrote to Sir Dudley Carleton, then ambassador at the Hague, carried by her father, make rather cryptic reference to a possible visit to Carleton and to his visiting with her at Loughton, and regret at her lack of happiness: "I must not expect any happiness I soe much desire never yett having received any cause to flatter my self with hope. . . ." In the second letter, she writes to thank Carleton for some unstated "favor and delicate present . . . being soe rare and wellcome a juell to me as by the estimation my injoyment is the greatest that may bee imagined for such a creature. . . ."[18] Was she courting the garrulous, witty, married Carleton? Or was he acting as a friend and confidante, perhaps with regard to her relationship with Pembroke? That she wrote the first letter from Pembroke's house and that the bearer was her father seems to favor the latter reading.

We can, however, only speculate about much of the cousins' relationship throughout their lives. As Hannay indicated in the previous essay, the Sidneys had frequently stayed at Baynards Castle during Mary's childhood, and the closeness of the young William Herbert to his uncle is another fascinating aspect of the Sidney Family Romance that I shall take up in another place. One set of records in which they are brought together is especially tantalizing. In early September 1608, Robert Wroth was at Loughton, very ill, but his wife remained at Baynards Castle until September 19 when she seems to have left with Pembroke, Robert Sidney immediately writing to his wife that Mary had been at Baynards Castle "till now, but this afternoon doth go to Loughton." On September 20, Sidney further reports to his wife that Pembroke had been visiting Mary. His words are tantalizingly cryptic: "My Lord

Pembroke told me yesternight that he had left my daughter that morning." By early October, she had returned to Baynards Castle where she met again with her father, who accompanied her back to Loughton. By then, Wroth was making his will and Sidney expresses some surprise about the generosity of its provisions for her, which included the forgiving of part of the dowry remaining, to use Jonson's phrase, "not paid for yet." He then notes that his daughter was leaving Loughton, probably going back to Baynards Castle.[19]

One of the most intriguing aspects about the relationship is that Mary Wroth and William Herbert were first cousins. In the England of the day, first cousin marriage was not forbidden. The marriage of "cousin germans" was "always *lawfull*, and sometimes . . . *Expedient*," as an expert later in the century expressed it. [20] Both married for family aggrandizement—Pembroke to acquire money and lands, marrying a woman of apparently little physical attractiveness or social grace, who eventually went insane or, more accurately, for the financial benefit of her husband's family, was declared so. Wroth, as we have seen, was married in a typical transaction between a powerful family with a daughter and a prosperous but socially inferior son: namely, for riches. In her chapter, Josephine Roberts speculates on an implicit or *de praesenti* marriage between them, but there does not seem to be a question of that. However tempting it is (the family romance in the vulgar sense, in this case), we have little evidence for a fantasy of two tragic figures, cousins yearning to marry across forbidden bonds. In fact, a more interesting pattern of connections emerges if we see the relationship in the context of the family romance in the more specifically psychoanalytical sense. William Herbert was brought up in a family notable for its intense Protestant idealism and courtly ceremony. The intellectual contradictions of the countess and her circle at Wilton are, I have argued elsewhere, notoriously extreme—in their lives and in their writings they try to hold together militant Protestantism and courtliness, Calvin, as it were, with Castiglione.[21] But such contradictions are not only observable as thematic tensions within literary texts. They have distinctive personal, familial, and wider ideological dimensions. As a successful courtier and, as Clarendon put it, "immoderately given to women,"[22] William Herbert was focused and fixed on conquest: on power, place, riches, prestige—and on women. Inevitably, the object woman, as

Freud described the pattern of the family romance, is initially encoded as a woman within the family: first a boy's mother, and then his sister—or, in this case, his cousin. To complicate it further, Mary Wroth was in a sense Pembroke's sister, since when his own father died, William transferred much of his battle against his father for independence to Mary's father. A sister is frequently the focus of an adolescent boy's voyeuristic sexual experiences—and both William and Mary grew up in an atmosphere permeated by the voyeuristic gaze of the court, epitomized in that most scopophiliac of poetic forms, the sonnet, which both wrote to and about each other. In the classic Freudian pattern, the son is beaten back by the father from the mother, so transfers his desire from the mother to some other woman, and thereafter the incestuous desires for the mother are projected upon her replacement—in this case, a cousin who is not, legally, a forbidden blood relative, but one who stands in for the forbidden sister and mother.

This kind of speculation is not a re-essentializing of the classic Freudian pattern. The details of the family romance are articulated in the material practices of a specific social formation. Likewise, we avoid the suspicious and even sentimental transcendentism of Kristeva's valorization of childbearing, yet see motherhood as part of Wroth's desire for self-assertion against the conventions and expectations of her gender assignment. We have no idea, it needs to be emphasized, whether her pregnancies were the result of stray encounters with a close and intimate relation to whom she felt obligated as well as attracted, and we can only speculate about a continuing romantic attachment. Some of the mixture of celebratory fantasy and embitterment projected into clearly autobiographical aspects of the *Urania* could reflect the latter, though they could equally reflect Susan Brownmiller's observation that rape underlies all traditional power relations, that in Shorter's words "the women we encounter in the lists of unwed mothers" in the early modern period "are almost all women who were forced to go along" with the dominant male.[23]

But from Wroth's viewpoint, motherhood may have enfolded her back into the family with a higher degree of independence than when she left it. The experience of motherhood as a Sidney rather than as a Wroth enabled her to recover a state of fusion with the family, the nurturing matrix or mother-function. As the mother of illegitimate children, the advantage she had in being part of a powerful family was the possibility of secrecy. Like adultery, illegitimacy was under increasing surveillance by church courts. A statute of 1576 empowered local justices to order parents of bastards to maintain them and to punish both mother and father, including (by an act of 1610) a requirement that mothers be confined in houses of correction, at the expense of the father. But such legislation did not touch a family like the Sidneys. As part of a residual indifference to aristocratic bastards, it was not uncommon for them to be brought up with legitimate brothers and sisters. As Pinchbeck and Hewitt comment, "in the households of the great, throughout the sixteenth century and for many years after, acceptance of a man's illegitimate children persisted" among the aristocracy by contrast with a hardening of social attitudes towards middle and lower class occurrences. The "inescapable fact" is that "the state was only concerned with illegitimacy among the poor." Wroth's children were well protected by the Sidneys and Herberts. William was helped by the Fourth Earl of Pembroke to a "brave living in Ireland"; Catherine married a "Mr Lovel neare Oxford," possibly a tutor in the household of Wroth's brother, Robert Sidney, second Earl of Leicester, in the 1640s. As Sharon Valiant has ingeniously speculated, Catherine's daughter (and, so, Wroth's granddaughter) may well have been the woman later known as Aphra Behn.[24] If motherhood may have given Mary Wroth more fulfillment than the structures of dynastic marriage had afforded her, and may be read as an affirmation of her own erotic worth, it also took her back into the Sidney family structure, even though on very different terms from those on which she left it. The windings and rewindings of the romance of the family are rarely simple or without irony.

The other major space which she attempted to carve out for herself and for which she is best known is her writing. Again, the family connections are complex and fascinating. Poetry was her greatest continuing tie to her father, and one that also links her with other members of the Sidney family. It is obvious that she studied her uncle's and father's poetry well; but it is perhaps significant that she was less affected by her aunt's pious poetry. Although, as Hannay argues in the previous essay, there is a generous fictional portrait of the countess in the *Urania*, Denny's sarcastic suggestion that Wroth follow the countess's pious example may, indeed, reflect something of Mary Wroth's indiffer-

ence for her cousin's mother. But clearly, writing served as both self-
assertion and displacement for both women. As I have argued elsewhere, the "strange passion" felt by the Countess of Pembroke for her
brother Philip both controls and empowers her writing.[25] In Wroth's
writing, likewise, we can see signs of her struggles within contradictory patterns laid down in the family. We have usually simply assumed
that Wroth's father and her aunt "encouraged" her to write: the only
evidence we have, however, is *that* she wrote. What psychological, and
ideological dynamics were involved? Was it emulation? rivalry? the conscious or unconscious rejection of the mother in favor of the power
of the father? The intriguing contradictions in this corner of the family
romance require more than pieties about Wroth's aunt's (or father's)
"influence" or "encouragement." Her writing might, for instance, be
described as neurotic displacement, a vulnerability to depression and
helpless passivity before the father figure, but, nonetheless, the very act
of writing—the assertion of the significance of fantasy, the detailed plan-
ning, revision, circulation and publication (as well, as Jeff Masten's essay
suggests, her choice to refuse to circulate or publish) demonstrates a
degree of agency that confounds the gender stereotypes to which she
was otherwise assigned.

Not only did Wroth grow up in a household in which her father,
uncle, and aunt would have been held up as literary models, but it is
intriguing to speculate on the connections with Pembroke's poetry. Do
we have here a writing couple, what Cixous has termed "the historically heterosexual, famous, totally necessary to each other, oh too human, writing couple"? As with other areas of Wroth's life, her writing
career was certainly heavily dependent upon men—a phenomenon,
Cixous argues, that is a "seeming historical necessity for the heterosexual woman who wants to create, to write—and be read—to couple
herself, in fact or fantasy . . . with a man who also writes or wrote."[26]
I do not simply mean that references to her love for her cousin constitute the primary meaning of the poems. While there are unquestion-
ably references to Pembroke in *Pamphilia to Amphilanthus* (as there are
in the *Urania*) Wroth's struggles have a far wider cultural significance.
That many of the poems are a projection of Wroth's wish fulfillment
fantasies about her relationship with Pembroke seems undeniable. The
two lovers of the *Urania* are also transparent. They are first cousins

whose love must be kept secret (31). In Pamphilia's poems there are recurring puns on the name "will," too many to be coincidental. One
in particular makes the biographical reference extremely clear when it
concludes: "Yet love I will till I butt ashes prove." As Roberts notes,
this is "one of the very few places in which the identification of Amphilanthus is made explicit."[27]

The poems present a fantasy of autonomy by a woman struggling
in what they repeatedly term a "labyrinth." I suggested earlier that
Wroth's writing is an act of self-assertion, but she is unavoidably caught
up in discursive positions that she can occupy only at the cost of self-
violation. In psychoanalytic terms, to turn to writing is to turn from
the mother to the father, to choose assertion, activity, possession of the
phallus over passivity, castration, and masochism. Yet the choice is
never easy, especially in a society where women's writing was so marginalized, and its difficulty is registered in the tensions and contradictions of Wroth's poems. Her frequent references to "molestation" are
recurring signs of this tension. Behind the term are both physical realities and multiply encoded cultural myths. Sexual assault and masochism
may well have been part of Wroth's own experience of love but, as
well, she is evoking part of a historically specific cultural unconscious,
the fears built into being a woman in a particular masculinist society.
It may be too that a woman expressing any degree of sexual autonomy
or demand falls victim to one of patriarchy's recurring myths about
sexual molestation, which warns women that if they stray from their
assigned place they may suffer rape. Molestation is thus what Anna
Clark terms an "extension of the social construction of male sexuality
as active, dominant and aggressive."[28]

Filtered through her rewriting of the Petrarchan sequence, these concerns emerge in Wroth's poems as a discontented passivity, a restless
masochism. The conventional Petrarchan emphasis on love as an invasion encourages a passivity in a woman, but Wroth gives that assigned role a distinctively masochistic edge. As part of what is presented sometimes as enforced passivity, sometimes as chosen withdrawal,
the feeling that love "indeed was best, when I did least it move"(36),
is the awareness that she is being both watched by others for signs of
her love and in a sense given an identity by their gazes. At times Pamphilia is "molested" by her role as an object of the desiring gaze, at

others she tries to escape the gaze of lover and others, in loneliness, isolation, or sleep. Such reactions can be read, perhaps, as struggles to avoid the constructing of sexual relations by patterns of domination and submission. Given both the literary tradition in which she was working and the residual power of her gender role, she was engaged in heroic but nearly hopeless contradictions. The dominant language of the erotic in Petrarchanism is that sexual excitement is founded on hostility, domination, and absence, not in indulgence or *jouissance*—most certainly not for the woman. The traditional Petrarchan situation against which *Pamphilia to Amphilanthus* is written is part of a historical pattern of "normal" sexuality as defined by Western society, in which, as Stoller puts it, "an essential purpose is for one to be superior to, harmful to, triumphant over another."[29] The seeming neutrality of "one" in Stoller's remark covers the preponderant historical identification of the gaze and its wider cultural associations with the male. Beneath the language of sexual dependence, idealized admiration, even of sexual reciprocity that Petrarchanism lays claim to, there is a one-sided emphasis on domination and submission, underlaid by the destructive dynamics of hostility, revenge, and destruction.

One of the poems in Wroth's opening sequence in *Pamphilia to Amphilanthus*, however, makes a remarkable critique of this tradition. Acknowledging the seemingly "natural" status of control of women by the male gaze, it attempts not to overthrow but to subvert and appropriate the dominant male subject position by making claim not only to the gaze, but to its pleasure:

> Take heed mine eyes, how you your lookes do cast
>   Least they beetray my harts most secrett thought;
>   Bee true unto your selves for nothings bought
>   More deere then doubt which brings a lovers fast.
>
> Catch you all waching eyes, ere they bee past,
>   Or take yours fixt wher your best love hath sought
>   The pride of your desires; lett them be taught
>   Theyr faults for shame, they could not truer last;
>
> Then looke, and looke with joye for conquest wunn
>   Of those that search'd your hurt in double kinde;
>   Soe you kept safe, lett them themselves looke blinde
>   Watch, gaze, and marke till they to madnes runn,

> While you, mine eyes injoye full sight of love
> Contented that such happinesses move. (P39)

The poem opens with a warning against indiscretion, but it is unusually paranoid, as if guarding not just against betrayal of a secret which has been entrusted to the speaker, but of the multiple "selves" in which she must live. Her tactics for survival, indeed, become not the passive slipping into a role of secret lover or even the modest one of acknowledging that one is an object of a forbidden desire, but the more aggressive one of "catching," or trapping and neutralizing "all waching eyes." Given that public identity consists in being assigned a multiplicity of roles, that very multiplicity and its contradictory assigned positions, can become her basis for action. The possibility of agency arises from contradiction. Agency within a female subject position is based on her returning the gaze, on reminding herself to "looke with joye for conquest wunn," and acknowledging that it is her own active desire, accepting her construction by the contradictory gazes and returning them, that affords some possibility of power. Stoller remarks—irritatingly essentializing but nonetheless usefully pointing to a seemingly fixed aspect of Western patriarchy—on the little boy's assumed "right to sexual looking and a little girl's training that she is not to permit that looking."[30] Wroth's Pamphilia marks a breach in such a pattern. She is not merely fixed by the gaze but turns it to an active and defiant exhibitionism. She has started to reappropriate herself as a subject.

In this respect, too, the *Urania* constituted for its author at least in part an enacted daydream in which she imagined, in the residual, masculinist, terms of chivalric romance, what her life as her cousin's "truest wife" might "really" be like, as she puts it in the Newberry manuscript (II:fol.26). As in her own life, fantasizing and storymaking, the writing of poetry, the withdrawal of a character to write or sing her inner thoughts, and the sharing of gossip, tale or anecdote, all play central roles in the fiction. But the multiple adventures of the *Urania* are not a purely personal romance. If they constitute Pamphilia's—and to an extent her creator's—"adventures," like all daydreams, they are articulated within the narrative forms and ideological contradictions produced by their culture. Their projections of unachieved, even unachievable, agency compulsively repeat yearnings for autonomy and transcendence

that are at once private and intimate and at the same time banal and
collective. Whatever our degree of embarrassment, we would all recognize our own fantasies and daydreams as the products in part of the
common narrative structures and commonplace motifs of our own
culture — struggles for achievement, control, conquest, fame, achievement through struggle — that are placed within and provided with
language by patterns of culturally produced discourses that name and
layer our unconscious.

Of special interest to the family romance that is acted out in the
Urania is the archaic genre, the chivalric romance of male heroism, that
provides the main metaphorical vehicle for its female author's fantasies.
The ideology of violence and subjugation that is articulated in chivalry
has had extraordinarily and destructively intimate connections with the
Western male psyche. This ideology is so culturally dominant that it
has seemed to be outside gender. What difference, then, does it make
that a woman is writing in what had hitherto been an overwhelmingly
masculinist genre? Elaine Beilin has argued that Wroth makes of romance "a potentially 'feminine' genre," but we need to probe more
deeply into the psycho-cultural complexities of such a potential transformation than to simply note that women characters predominate, or that
the "spirituality" or "virtue" of women is affirmed. Similarly, to argue
that Pamphilia is the "first extended fictional portrait in English of a
woman by a woman" may not only involve an unhelpful essentialism
but may also take for granted the masculinist values of the romance
world of chivalry: domination and violence.[31] What — if anything, we
need to ask — counterbalances that dominance of the masculinist chivalric world which must have been epitomized for Mary Wroth by her
cousin? The residually feudal warrior code of the Renaissance was centered upon a core of violence and insecurity that was figured in the
linkage of "honor" and desire. Passionate celebrations of ritual violence — seen in tourneys, jousts, and the stories of heroic romance as
well as in religious and nationalistic wars — were compounded with a
traditional view of the male warrior as an innocent, idealistic (and
humanistically educated) youth for whom tournaments and war were
rituals of maturity, spiritual as well as physical rites of passage. This
ideology covered over a tragically self-destructive complex of masculine
immaturity that resembles what Klaus Theweleit, using Margaret Mah-

ler's work on "psychological birth" in his studies of fascist militarism, has analyzed as the condition of the "not-yet-fully-born" that dominates the family romance of fascism. Such people seek violence and destruction—however transferred into socially approved rituals and duties— as the means of achieving a lost unification with the maternal, and tend to develop a "social" rather than an "individual" ego that is "painfully drilled into and fused onto the individual." Theweleit argues provocatively that this inability to achieve adequate individuation which Mahler isolated in children is widespread in what he terms "soldier males" throughout Western history.[32]

Seen in such a light, the battles, jousts, and journeys in Wroth's *Urania* cannot simply be described as traditional "literary" conventions. These are emblems of the desires and anxieties that lie at the core of a whole culture's myths of violence and domination within both the family and the wider structures of the culture. In the figure of Pamphilia, Wroth projects a fantasy formed from the materials that reinforced her own assignments within the early modern class and gender systems. Like a modern adolescent dreaming of movie stardom even while sensing the corruption and superficiality of Hollywood, the queen is a fanciful self-construction. Her adventures, together with those of the interconnected families of the interlaced narratives, comprise an elaborate family romance in which the various participants experience passions, challenges, and achievements on a grandiose scale, all the while that Pamphilia is predominantly a victim, unhappy, unrewarded, "molested." Wroth thereby creates an elaborate image of the confusions and contradictions that attended a woman's struggle for a subject-position in the early modern period. Even in Wroth's fantasy, the structures and assumptions that constructed a woman's life emerge as "naturall," unavoidable rather than culturally assigned. A revealing remark records that Pamphilia "raild at the uncareful people who permitted her to have her fond desires without limiting her power," as if only the limitation imposed by male dominance could make her happy. The firmer the limitation, the less discontent for a woman, so runs the implication, even for a queen in a world of make-believe. Other women in the romance may have, temporarily and sometimes with disastrous consequences, their own "adventures," but Pamphilia is constant to her ideal of helpless love. "Tis pittie," Amphilanthus's sister, Urania, tells

her, "that ever that fruitlesse thing Constancy was taught you as a vertue" (351). For Pamphilia, women "bred in Loves Schoole knew" their
"paine," and Pamphilia, largely cast in the role of masochistic victim,
accepts "misfortunes" that "farr surpas'd any happiness she had ever
seene" (223).

There are, however, some (literally) small spaces in which we can
detect a striving for some way out of the destructive and pessimistic
impasse that is Pamphilia's usual position in the *Urania*. One space
opens up in her desire for privacy. When she is alone (so far as attendants, suitors, and walled gardens will allow) she, like Wroth herself,
is able to populate her mind—as Wroth herself was—with thoughts
that, while constructed out of others' words, nonetheless suggest an
area of potential agency. This stress on solitude might be taken for the
fantasy of a woman who was rarely able to be alone, continually aware
of her subjection to and dependence on family support, yet who is striking out to find a private space, if only to bewail her lot. But the focus
of her solitary thoughts is revealing. Like Wroth's own, Pamphilia's
fantasy life centers on desire and writing, sexuality and language. In
the *Urania*, we can read a multiple projection of both conscious autobiography, wish-fulfillment fantasy and deeper demands of the culturally
produced unconscious upon a fantasy landscape. *Urania* obsessively
displaces personality, familial, gender, and broader social contradictions
into a series of compulsively repeated narratives. Wroth's romance shows
how women function as a terrain for the male fantasies within the incestuous family structure, but it also shows how a woman's fantasies,
productions of her place in the complexities of the incestuous/patri-
archal family romance, can nonetheless trigger a search for ways to
dramatize not just its author's own voice but an increasingly insistent
collective voice.

After the *Urania*, of course, within Wroth's own life, that voice is
largely silent. So far as we know, there were no plans to publish the
second part of the romance. Wroth's literary voice was silenced by the
disapproval of the court just as she was marginalized by her lifestyle
and the choices made for her by her status as widow, mistress, and
mother. Within this particular family romance, the mother/sister figure
is called to demonstrate that she too is consumed by suffering and self-
denial because she is unable, finally, to fall into the embrace of the

son/brother. Mary Wroth must have fulfilled many of the fantasies of her cousin/brother, but at the cost, except for perhaps six or seven years after being widowed, of her own voice and her own autonomy.

And yet, in those six or seven years, perhaps, we can see, when we place her within the broader cultural patterns emerging from early modern England, the pre-emergent signs of something that, in later centuries, has become far less marginal. In a discussion of the discourse of deviance in Shakespeare, Jonathan Dollimore makes an important distinction that is relevant here. He argues that there are "two com-plementary modes of materialist criticism." Although both are con-cerned to "recover the text's history," they do so differently. The first, which locates history within the text, does so by constructing the con-ditions of the text's production, which "even if not addressed directly by the text can nevertheless still be said to be within it." The other, which places the text within history, addresses history itself directly, making explicit what may have had no voice at the time, the develop-ment of which, Dollimore argues, is necessarily "another and later story."[33] It is this latter mode of historical analysis that exactly catches the value for us of Wroth's struggles. Historical criticism's traditional task has been to make the silence of a text speak: to bring the political, religious, and material practices of a culture that, as it is conventionally put, "influenced" that text to bear upon our reading of it. In reading for absences, by contrast, we do not so much read them *into* the text (implying a crude appropriation) as read it in terms of the historical patterns into which the text flows, to which it points and, whether in large or small ways, to which it contributes. We all live within sys-tems of representations that both enable and limit our articulations as living (and writing or reading) subjects; the absences of a particular historical conjunction can often be articulated only by later readers who see them precisely as absences, as signs perhaps of a pre-emergent break with the epistemic limits of a particular society, class, gender, or family, and who link that "absence" with a (by now) more visible preoccupa-tion within their own society. With Wroth, issues of gender point clearly to such a major set of absences. I have presented her as a woman "written" by men—in particular by her father and her cousin, with the two sometimes not easily distinguished. She occupied the classic posi-tion of woman as mediatrix for men's desires within the family romance:

her mind and body—as daughter, sister, cousin, wife, and mother—were the sites of struggle for men and their language, for their particular family romances. In occupying the place in which they struggled, she managed nonetheless—in, as I have suggested, her sexual and maternal independence as well as in her writing—to carve out, however temporarily, an area of agency, a place in which some of her stories could be told. In doing so, both her life and work point forward to other and later struggles and stories.

Slowly emergent cultural changes often first become visible within the practices of marginal groups, and in the contradictions, achievements, and failures of Wroth's battles with her assigned gender roles, we may sense the hints of triumphs of later centuries. The contemporary exploration of the New World was a work of masculinist domination, of conquering, destroying, pillaging, populating. It contrasts with what might have been another opening up, something closer at hand, the frontiers of bodily freedom and ego formation through sexual expansion, which (perhaps because historically centered in the female) was so much more gradual, and had to wait many centuries. In Wroth's articulations of her family romance—which was at once her own and yet produced by cultural determinants beyond the family structures in which she lived—we can see both the struggles and triumphs of later cultural history.

NOTES

1. Sigmund Freud, "Family Romances," *The Standard Edition of the Works of Sigmund Freud*, ed. and trans. James Strachey, vol. 9 (London: Hogarth Press, 1952), pp. 237–41. See also *The Complete Letters of Sigmund Freud to Wilhelm Fliess 1887–1904*, trans. and ed. Jeffrey Moussaieff Masson (Cambridge: Harvard University Press, 1985), pp. 317–18; Helene Deutsch, *The Psychology of Women* (London: Research Books, 1946), p. 6. For a discussion of Deleuze and Guattari's re-reading of Freud, see Klaus Theweleit, *Male Fantasies, Volume 1: Women, Floods, Bodies, History*, trans. Stephen Conway (Minneapolis: University of Minnesota Press, 1988), p. 327.

2. Mark Poster, *A Critical Theory of the Family* (New York: Pluto Press, 1978), p. 160.

3. Gilles Deleuze and Felix Guattari, *Anti-Oedipus: Capitalism and Schizophrenia*, trans. Robert Hurley, Mark Seem, and Helen R. Lane (Minneapolis: University

of Minnesota Press, 1983), ch 1. In this and some subsequent paragraphs, although the focus is somewhat different, I draw on "Mother/Son, Father/Daughter, Brother/Sister, Cousins: The Sidney Family Romance," *Modern Philology*, 88 (1991), and wish in particular to acknowledge the careful scrutiny and helpful suggestions of Janel Mueller, the editor of *Modern Philology*.

4. Deutsch, *The Psychology of Women*, p. 195.
5. Nancy M. Hartsock, *Money, Sex, and Power: Toward a Feminist Historical Materialism* (London: Longman, 1983), p. 2.
6. Ann Shaver, "Outspoken Women in Book I of Lady Mary Wroth's *Urania*," *Sidney Newsletter* 10, no. 1 (1990), 89; Simon Shepherd, *Amazons and Warrior Women: Varieties of Feminism in Seventeenth-Century Drama* (Brighton: Harvester, 1981); Jean Howard, "Crossdressing, the Theatre, and Gender Struggle in Early Modern England," *Shakespeare Quarterly* 40 (1989), 418–40.
7. Hannay, *Philip's Phoenix: Mary Sidney* (London: Oxford University Press, 1989); Alison M. Jaggar, *Feminist Politics and Human Nature* (Totowa, N.J.: Rowman and Allan Held, 1983).
8. Julia Kristeva, "Stabat Mater," in *Tales of Love*, trans. Leon S. Roudiez (New York: Columbia University Press, 1987), p. 234. For a recent restatement of Kristeva's views, see the interview with her with Josyane Savigneau, in *Le Monde*, March 9, 1990, trans. in *Manchester Guardian Weekly* 142, no. 19, May 13, 1990, p. 16.
9. Ben Jonson, *Discoveries*, ed. G.B. Harrison (Edinburgh: Edinburgh University Press, 1966), p. 15; HMC, De L'Isle and Dudley, III, pp. 139, 140, 127–28, 134; Margaret McLaren, "Lady Mary Wroth's *Urania*: The Work and the Tradition," Ph.D. diss. (University of Auckland, 1978), p. 34.
10. HMC, De L'Isle, IV, pp. 44, 63.
11. Ben Jonson, *The Complete Poems*, ed. George Parfitt (New Haven, Conn.: Yale University Press, 1982), pp. 81–84.
12. Raymond Williams, *The Country and the City* (London: Paladin, 1973), p. 17.
13. David Norwood, *Poetry and Politics in the English Renaissance* (London: Routledge, 1984), pp. 190, 192. J.C.A. Rathmell, "Jonson, Lord Lisle, and Penshurst," *Elizabethan Literary Renaissance* 1 (1972), 250–60.
14. Roberts, 23.
15. Edward Shorter, "On Writing the History of Rape," *Signs* 3 (1977–78), 475; Miranda Chaytor, "Household and Kinship: Ryton in the late 16th and 17th centuries," *History Workshop Journal* 10 (1980), 44. For the church courts, see Martin Ingram, *Church Courts, Sex and Marriage in England, 1570–1640* (Cambridge: Cambridge University Press, 1987).
16. Hannay, *Philip's Phoenix*, p. 210; and see Hannay's essay, this volume.
17. *The Poems of Edward, Lord Herbert of Cherbury*, ed. G.C. Moore Smith (Oxford: Clarendon, 1923), p. 42; Mary Ellen Lamb, *Gender and Authorship in the Sidney Circle* (Madison: Wisconsin University Press, 1990), pp. 145–47; Roberts discusses the family's support for the two children and prints Herbert of Cherbury's poem, pp. 25–26.
18. CSP Dom. James I 1619–1623, pp. 37, 40.
19. HMC, De L'Isle and Dudley, III, pp. 127, 233, 343–44, 347–48; IV, p. 63.

20. *The Marriage of Cousin Germans, Vindicated from the Censures of unlawfullnesse, and Inexpediency* (London, 1673), p. 5.

21. See G.F. Waller, *Mary Sidney, Countess of Pembroke (1561–1621): A Critical Study of her Writings and Literary Milieu* (Salzburg: Institut für Anglistik und Amerikanistik, 1979), p. 61; "'This Matching of Contraries': the influence of Calvin and Bruno on the Sidney Circle," *Neophilologus* 56 (1972), 331–43.

22. Edward Hyde, Earl of Clarendon, *The History of the Rebellion and Civil Wars in England* (Oxford: Clarendon, 1849), vol. 1 89.

23. Susan Brownmiller, *Against Their Will: Men, Women and Rape* (New York: Simon and Schuster, 1975); Shorter, "History of Rape," 476.

24. Ivy Pinchbeck and Margaret Hewitt, *Children in English Society*, vol. 1, *From Tudor Times to the Eighteenth Century* (London: Routledge and, Kegan Paul, 1969), p. 203. For the connections with Behn, I am indebted to Sharon Valiant, of New York City, for sharing her researches and a copy of her unpublished paper, "Sidney's Sister, Pembroke's Mother . . . and Aphra Behn's Great-Grandmother?", delivered at the American Society for Eighteenth-Century Studies conference in New Orleans, 1989.

25. Waller, *Mary Sidney*, pp. 99–100.

26. Quoted in Alice Jardine, "Death Sentence: Writing Couples and Ideology," in *The Female Body in Western Culture*, ed. Susan Rubin Suleiman (Cambridge, Mass.: Harvard University Press, 1986), pp. 85–86.

27. Roberts, p. 115.

28. Anna Clark, *Women's Silence Men's Violence: Sexual Assault in England 1770–1845* (London: Routledge, 1987), p. 6.

29. Robert J. Stoller, *Perversion: The Erotic Form of Hatred* (London: Mansfield Library, 1975), p. 90.

30. Stoller, p. 90. For some of the remarks on Wroth's poem, I am grateful to a conversation with Stacia Nagel.

31. Elaine Beilin, *Redeeming Eve: Women Writers in the Renaissance* (Princeton: Princeton University Press, 1987), pp. 212, 208, 215.

32. Klaus Theweleit, *Male Fantasies*, vol. II, trans. Jessica Carter (Minneapolis: University of Minnesota 1987), pp. xx, 213, 222, 316–19.

33. Jonathan Dollimore, "Transgression and Surveillance in *Measure for Measure*," *Political Shakespeare* (Manchester: Manchester University Press, 1985), pp. 85–86.

PART TWO

Con/Texts

"Shall I turne blabb?":
Circulation, Gender, and Subjectivity
in Mary Wroth's Sonnets

Jeff Masten

I

W hat immediately strikes the modern reader of Mary Wroth's sonnet sequence *Pamphilia to Amphilanthus* is its sustained lack of reference. Trained to mine the Riches of the biographically thick Sidneian sequence, to register Stellas, Astrophils, Shakespearean Wills, and Spenser's three Elizabeths, we find within Wroth's sonnets little reference to their writer, no mention of the beloved by name (except in the title), few allusions to contemporary events (in the old-historical sense), and little attempt to engage outside interlocutors. Indeed, these sonnets center exclusively on, and are the intense poetic efflux of, a persona who claims she is in love. As such, they seem to speak an almost inscrutable private language.

What little we know about the sequence as material object—the "external evidence"—replicates the privative experience of reading it. The sequence exists only in an undated holograph manuscript (Folger v.a. 104) and in the published *Urania*, where it occupies a separate section at the end; we do not know which version of the sequence is earlier. Josephine A. Roberts argues that, since the watermark of the Folger copy resembles those of two other manuscripts dated 1587 and 1602, the manuscript version of the sequence precedes its publication in 1621. This evidence, however, provides only a very tentative *terminus a quo* (since such a procedure attempts to date the paper not the sonnets), and could likewise support the argument that Wroth began writing the sonnets no earlier than the year of her birth, probably 1587; Gary

Waller more tentatively dates them after Robert Wroth's death.[1] Furthermore, we know virtually nothing about the Folger manuscript's contemporary history, function, or readership, and the poems have not been discovered in published miscellanies or in manuscript commonplace books extant before 1621. Roberts cites Sylvester's *Lachrimae Lachrimarum* (1613) as evidence of circulation "long before . . . 1621," but the lines merely imply that Wroth was writing (something) by 1613 and mention no specific texts. Strangely, Roberts also cites Jonson's *Underwood* 28 as evidence of early circulation, though the poem was not published until 1640 and no prior date for it has been established, as Waller notes.[2] Jonson could just as well be "exscribing" the sonnets after publication.

In an article surveying the movement of Renaissance poetry "From Manuscript to Print," J.W. Saunders shows that such activities as the interpolation into manuscripts of commentary and verse in other hands, the transcription into one manuscript of another's poems, the circulation of manuscripts at four and five removes from the original writer, and the circulation of multiple copies (as many as twenty to thirty) were the common practice when Wroth was writing. Saunders sketches a picture of mobile, permeable texts which constantly gesture toward aspects of their own writing and widespread circulation in an open, collaborative, setting. The manuscript of *Pamphilia to Amphilanthus* is notably at odds with this larger cultural practice. It contains no interpolations by, additions from, or transcriptions of others, and, in contrast to Margaret Ezell's description of the circulating writings of other women during the period, it has no title page, preface, dedication, or date and does not seem to be addressed to a family audience, friend, or patron.[3] There are no references to the sequence before 1621 and no multiple versions to indicate that the poems circulated before their publication.

In fact, the manuscript known as *Pamphilia to Amphilanthus* may not be a circulating sonnet sequence at all — or at least not in the way we have understood it to be. In her edition of Wroth's poems, Roberts asserts that the manuscript represents an early version of *Pamphilia to Amphilanthus* and assumes that Wroth circulated her sonnets among her friends. Roberts equates the Folger manuscript with the sequence *Pamphilia to Amphilanthus* — a possible interpretation of the evidence, if only because the first group of poems (and in the absence of a title page, apparently the whole manuscript) is designated by that title. But such a construal underplays the presence of other poems (some of which appear in *Urania*) and other important evidence. We might as easily read the manuscript as several distinct sequences of poems copied into a single manuscript, including *Pamphilia to Amphilanthus* (the first fifty-five poems) and the distinctly organized "crowne of Sonetts." This explains the manuscript's unusual numbering (which begins again with "1" at several points), the placement of blank pages between sets of poems, and the distinctive arrangement of these different sets on the page—as well as the regular alternation of sonnets and songs in the first set of poems in contrast to the rest of the groupings. In other words, rather than a circulating version of *Pamphilia to Amphilanthus* with a few *Urania* poems tacked on at the end, the manuscript may represent Wroth's own collection of several of her (more or less discrete) sonnet sequences, along with some other non-sequential poems. Both Roberts (whose structural analysis and continuous numbering impose unity and continuity upon the manuscript) and Elaine V. Beilin (whose novelistic narrative posits a totalizing structure) obscure discrete groupings within the manuscript. McLaren's and Paulissen's divisions of the manuscript into two and four parts respectively are, I think, conservative estimates. That the manuscript contains alterations in Wroth's hand and lacks dedication and title-page suggests it was a fair copy for her own use, not a presentation copy.[4]

In the following discussion, I suggest that interpreting this bibliographical evidence is part of, not simply prior to, the reading process, for the poems themselves—like the anomalous manuscript in which they are inscribed—encode a withdrawal from circulation. The sonnets stage a movement which is relentlessly private, withdrawing into an interiorized space; they foreground a refusal to speak in the public, exhibitionist voice of traditional Petrarchan discourse; in the context of the published portion of *Urania* they articulate a woman's resolute constancy, self-sovereignty, and unwillingness to circulate among men; they gesture toward a subject under self-control. In their insistent privacy and refusal to circulate, the poems reproduce the actual situation of their writing. And, as we shall see, privacy and circulation are tied closely to gender in this first sonnet sequence by an Englishwoman.

At the beginning of the seventeenth century, Francis Barker observes, "the public and the private as strong, mutually defining, mutually exclusive categories, each describing separate terrains and distinct contents, practices, and discourses, are not yet extant."[5] As twentieth-century readers of Wroth's texts, we must remind ourselves that concepts we may take as the organizing categories of existence are constructed in history, that the terms "public" and "private" are emergent in the discursive world we interrogate here. Wroth's texts, we shall see, are both documents and instruments of that construction; they do not merely reflect the emergence of a public/private distinction "in the culture," but also work to create that distinction.

Arthur F. Marotti has asserted that the sonnet sequence was a public, courtly genre, circulating widely, expressing "social, political, and economic suits in the language of love,"[6] and from the outset *Pamphilia to Amphilanthus* seems to contest the place of a female speaker within that "public" tradition of Petrarchan verse. In the initial sonnet Pamphilia watches as, in a dream vision, Venus inserts a Petrarchan burning heart into her breast, authorizing her position as a Petrarchan speaker: "one hart flaming more then all the rest / The goddess held, and putt itt to my breast, / Deare sonne, now shutt sayd she . . ." (1/P1). The poem's final lines, with their ricochet of glosses for the speaking subject, emphasize that this sequence will contest woman's place in the Petrarchan lover's discourse: "I, waking hop'd as dreames itt would depart / Yett since: O mee: a lover I have binn."

But at the same time that these images place the fictional Pamphilia firmly within the Petrarchan tradition, the sonnet also represents a withdrawal from public signification. Like so many of these poems, it deploys images of night, blackness, darkness, and sleep to register privacy and privation. The heart transplant is, as Roberts notes, a recurrent image in the English tradition of Petrarchanism, but the insertion it signifies, the movement inward at this inaugural moment, recurs throughout the sequence as a withdrawal into an interiorized corporeal space: "now shutt sayd she. . . ."[7] In sonnet 22/P25, for example, Pamphilia memorably compares herself to "the Indians, scorched with the sunne . . . they doe as theyr God adore." The Indians are outwardly marked by their worship of the sun, but Pamphilia asks to "weare the marke of Cupids might / *In hart* as they *in skin* of Phoebus light. . . ." The next sonnet makes this privatization more explicit still:

> When others hunt, my thoughts I have in chase;
> If hauke, my minde att wished end doth fly,
> Discourse, I with my spiritt tauke, and cry
> While others, musique choose as greatest grace.

Here the speaker appropriates public (and one might argue, male) "pastimes" and brings them into a private space, "free from eyes" (1, 5). And what seems perhaps a merely metaphorical conversion of public activity into private introspection is enacted in the couplet (indeed, in the entire sonnet and the sequence at large), as the speaker explicitly "discourses" with her "spiritt."[8]

Sonnet 36/P41 stages a comparison of the public lover and Pamphilia's private love, not by appropriating the public but by repudiating it. The inserted heart of the first sonnet again registers the authenticity of this inward pain: "How well poore hart thou wittnes canst I love. . . ." But Pamphilia emphasizes her difference from the Petrarchan tradition of displayed corporeality: "Yett is itt sayd that sure love can nott bee / Wher soe small *showe of passion* is descrid." Wroth's dismissal of the typical Petrarchan speaker's outwardly demonstrative body accords with Barker's argument that the construction of the public/private distinction "in its modern form" occurs simultaneously with the "disappearance of the body from public view."[9] The sonnet concludes with a strong repudiation of love theatrically displayed, positing instead a self-enclosed authenticity of expression: "For know more passion in my hart doth move / Then in a million that make show of love."

Here Pamphilia writes in Petrarchan discourse to write against it, and the other sonnets are implicated in this strategy. Returning to those poems, we can read the figures against which she establishes herself (the Indians, the hunters and hawkers) as representations of the male speakers of the popular English Petrarchan tradition — the million that make elaborate textual show of love — as practiced most significantly by Wroth's uncle in *Astrophil and Stella*. The worship of the master/mistress as a sun and Wroth's citations of hunting, music, and discourse recall dozens of other sonnets from the tradition.

Furthermore, Shakespeare's "As an unperfect actor on the stage"

(Sonnet 23) and Spenser's "Of this world's Theatre in which we stay" (*Amoretti* 54) exploit the lover's theatrical "shows." In her sonnets, then, Wroth transforms seemingly ungendered signs into markers of her gender-difference from the tradition in/against which she writes; moreover, in each case she displaces public, male exhibition with a discourse seeking to register a private authenticity of feeling. To put Hamlet's memorable phrase in a gendered context, Pamphilia explicitly refuses the "actions that a man might play" (*Hamlet*, I.ii.84).

Read in this context, the speaker of sonnet 38/P44 becomes one "bannish'd" from enjoying "pastimes" the earlier poems gendered as male:

> What pleasure can a bannish'd creature have
>   In all the pastimes that invented arr
>   By witt or learning, absence making warr
>   Against all peace that may a biding crave;
> Can wee delight butt in a wellcome grave. . . .

The "creature" of the first line and the "wee" of the second quatrain read as signifiers for the banished and speechless female Other of the male-authored Petrarchan sequences (see *OED* definition 3b for gendered examples of "creature"). Furthermore, the syntactically difficult lines 3–4 seem to connect "absence" not with an absent lover but with the speaker herself, banished as she is from Petrarchan language as it is usually spoken. The next sonnet, one of the few which focus explicitly on writing, again takes up Pamphilia's position in relation to Petrarchan discourse: "Nor can I as those pleasant witts injoy / My owne fram'd words, which I account the dross / Of purer thoughts, or recken them as moss . . ." (39/P45). Reflecting on her own elaborately fram'd sonnets, Pamphilia argues that her texts are the expression of inward emotion and distinguishes herself from the "witt sick" "witts," whom she views as (merely) playfully discursive. Admitting that her words are but pale reflections of an inward authenticity, she nonetheless argues that her poetry, unlike theirs, grounds itself in an emotional reality. Confronting them directly, she adds: "Alas, think I, your plenty shewes your want, / For wher most feeling is, words are more scant. . . ." The sonnet thus sets up a number of oppositions important to the sequence at large: plenty versus want, empty Petrarchan discourse versus full emotion, show versus authenticity.

Addressing the "witts" again, the next sonnet acts as a gloss on its predecessors, stressing in particular the inauthentic theatricality of stock Petrarchanism:

> Itt is nott love which you poore fooles do deeme
> > That doth *appeare* by fond, and *outward showes*
> > Of kissing, toying, or by swearings glose. . . .
> 'T'is nott a *showe* of sighes, or teares can prove
> > Who loves indeed . . . ;
> Butt *in the soule* true love in safety lies. . . . (40/P46)

Pamphilia's anti-theatricality is strikingly similar to Hamlet's statement in a different context that he has "that within, which passeth show; / These, but the trappings, and the suites of woe" (I.ii.85–86). As in Barker's reading of that play, Pamphilia here makes a decisive claim "for qualitative distinction from the corporeal order of the spectacle"; however, to do so in her case is to foreground a gender difference — to repudiate the rhetorical trappings and metaphorical suites of male Petrarchan discourse.[10]

Interestingly, given Wroth's uncle's sequence, sonnet 41/P47 comments on the "blessed starrs which doe heavns glory show" and resonates with a later sonnet (6/P100) that subtly writes against Sidney's star-struck sequence. Asking in that poem "that noe day would ever more appeere," the speaker concludes:

> Lett mee bee darke, since bard of my chiefe light . . .
> To mee itt seems as ancient fictions make
> > The starrs all fashions, and all shapes partake
> > While in my thoughts true forme of love shall live.

Pamphilia speaks at one level in a Platonic vocabulary, comparing the mere "shapes" of love to her own "true forme," and at another level about "ancient" astrology, with its constellations of animal and human shapes. But the mere mention of star-study by a member of the Sidney family brings with it resonances of *Astrophil and Stella*, which might have seemed by Wroth's time an "ancient fiction."[11] And the Petrarchist discourse which makes its Stellas and Astrophils into "all fashions and all shapes" is here set against the interior private space — "thes haples rooms," playing on the Italian *stanza* — site of articulation for the authentic version of love, spoken by an individual who claims the tradi-

tionally non-discursive space of a "darke" lady. As before, the "shapes"
and "fashions" are associated with the inauthenticity of "stage play like
disguised pleasures."

The earlier set of sonnets culminates with a defense of interior authenticity and the most strident anti-theatricality of the sequence:

> If ever love had force in humaine brest?
>> If ever hee could move in pensive hart?
>> Or if that hee such powre could butt impart
>> To breed those flames whose heart brings joys unrest.
> Then looke on mee; I ame to thes adrest,
>> I, ame the soule that feeles the greatest smart;
>> I, ame that hartles trunk of harts depart
>> And I, that one, by love, and griefe oprest;
> Non ever felt the truth of loves great miss
>> Of eyes, till I deprived was of bliss;
>> For had hee seene, hee must have pitty show'd;
> I should nott have bin made this stage of woe
>> Wher sad disasters have theyr open showe
>> O noe, more pitty hee had sure beestow'd. (42/P48)

As in sonnet 36/P41, where the speaker claims "more passion. . . / Then
in a million that make show of love," this poem insists on interior and
superlative feeling, "the soule that feeles the greatest smart." If interiority exists (and that existence is, in an important way to which
we will return, precisely what this sequence maps out), the speaker
claims with her repeated and emphatically punctuated "I, ame" that
she is its exemplary embodiment. The poem's opening conditional
clauses (made doubly conditional by the unusually situated question
marks) contest the very existence of emotion "in humaine brest," and
the insistence of the second quatrain ("Then looke on mee") indicates
the novelty of this discursive situation. Here the speaker does not repudiate spectacle as she had in earlier sonnets but instead laments that she
has herself been made to participate in public, theatrical signification,
"this stage of woe / Wher sad disasters have theyr open showe. . . ."
Finally, this sonnet associates the emergent private space with (de)pri-
vation and emptiness; in a way that resonates with the opening sonnet,
the speaker here is "that hartles trunk of harts depart." Absence as a
palpable presence pervades Wroth's verse, but as the syntactically vexed
"bannish'd creature" sonnet shows, referents for this absence are ambiguous or absent themselves. Does "absence" refer to the Amphilan-

thus present only in the title? to the speaker herself? to "the hartles trunk of harts depart"? Or does the speaker use the absent lover as a device for speaking of this newly postulated private discursive space? In other words, does Wroth appropriate the machinery of Petrarchanism, with its absent/distant lover, as a convenient discourse for figuring a private self?[12]

These are questions to which we will return; sonnet 45/P52, one of the few sonnets to engage an interlocutor, capitalizes on this ambiguity. "Good now bee still, and doe nott mee torment," the speaker exclaims, and demands that she be allowed to withdraw into the interiority valorized elsewhere in the sequence: "only lett mee quarrell with my brest." The initial quatrains read as the attempted escape from "Divell"-ish public discourse, with its "toungue torture" and "multituds of questions," into the private domain. Read in this context, the sestet is not so much a ruse to free the speaker from the interlocutor (a madness play-acted by sanity) as it is a gloss upon the lines which have preceded it, an attempt to explain a novel discursive position in terms the interlocutor can understand:

> Well then I see noe way butt this will fright
> > That Divell speach; Alas I ame possesst,
> > And mad folks senceles ar of wisdomes right,
> The hellish speritt absence doth arest
> > All my poore sences to his cruell might. . . .

Pamphilia appropriates the familiar discourse of demonic possession, but, importantly, she is "possesst" not by some definitive intruding demon (this is not the earlier "Divell") but rather by "the hellish speritt absence." And once again absence defers a referent.

The sonnets' insistent withdrawal — their repudiation of public Petrarchan discourse and its inauthentic "open shows," "shapes," and "fashions" — registers at a number of levels a refusal to circulate. Pamphilia refuses to construct herself or circulate as a Petrarchan sign, eschewing the signifying body of both the Petrarchan master and mistress (though she could fill either role, as writer or as woman): "Take heed mine eyes, how you your lookes doe cast / Least they beetray my harts most secrett thought . . ." (34/P39, 1–2). Furthermore, as Roberts's survey of "The Biographical Problem" suggests, the sequence makes few particular references outside itself which would serve to draw in a reading "public," and, with few exceptions, there is nothing here resembling the male Petrarchists' engagement of other public (courtly) personae — or of the master/mistress/other itself.[13] If, returning to Marotti's conclusions, we agree that Wroth's chosen genre was otherwise relentlessly public — circulating at large to express male "social, political, and economic suits in the language of love" — then *Pamphilia to Amphilanthus* is a woman's privatization of that genre toward other ends. The published books of Wroth's *Urania* place this privatizing poetics within the context of romance narrative.

III

Pamphilia, noted by Maureen Quilligan as the *Urania*'s privileged poet-figure,[14] is also "the most silent and discreetly retir'd of any Princesse" (50). In an extremely public narrative — detailing the wanderings of innumerable characters across a seemingly boundaryless Eurasian landscape — she is remarkably immobile, and her poetic process is closely linked with retirement. She writes sequestered in a "fine wood, delicately contriu'd into strange, and delightfull walkes" (74), to which she alone has a key. The first of her many poems in the text is signaled by a vow (like the speaker of the sonnets) "not to carry the tokens of her losse openly on her browes, but rather to weare them priuately in her heart" (76). Furthermore, in response to her suitor Leandrus's suggestion that she acquire the protection of a male lover, Pamphilia defends her garden "walkes" as a distinctly independent domain: "My spirit . . . as well guards me alone, as in company; and for my person, my greatnesse, and these walls are sufficient warrants and guardians for my safety . . . for strength I had rather haue these [walls], then ones power I could not loue" (178). Pamphilia effectively genders her garden, privileging the autonomy of this private female space over the protection of a male lover-guardian.[15]

A later break in the narrative makes emphatic the opposition of a public, male world and Pamphilia's withdrawal into a privatized locus of female poetic expression. The long-awaited conquest of Albania, in which almost every important male character participates, is abruptly interrupted by a mid-paragraph shift to Pamphilia "in her owne Coun-

try," "walk[ing] into a Parke she had adioyning to her Court . . ."
(264). Talking to herself, she hears her words repeated by an echo, which
she silences: "Soft said she, shall I turne blabb? no Echo, excuse me,
my loue and choyce . . . must not be named by any but my selfe. . . .
As none but we doe truely loue, so none but our owne hearts shall
know we loue" (264). Just as she remains embowered in her garden
(and that embowerment is juxtaposed to the male boundary-transgressions
of war), her thoughts remain enclosed; they must not circulate beyond
herself.[16] Moreover, Pamphilia exercises self-containment even in "public": "shee could bee in greatest assemblies as priuate with her owne
thoughts, as if in her Cabinet, and there haue as much discourse with
her imagination" (391). Such physical and verbal discretion clearly recalls aspects of the sonnet sequence.

Pamphilia's hallmark, as the text makes clear at every available point,
is her unflagging constancy to Amphilanthus. Constancy distinguishes
her from virtually every other character; it is, she explains, the basis
of her identity: "I can neuer [let in that worthlesse humour change]
till I can change my selfe, and haue new creation and another soule . . ."
(391). Pamphilia's constancy and her identity as a female subject might
thus seem to be based on Amphilanthus (that is, on a male being exterior to her self). But as both Quilligan and Miller have emphasized,
Pamphilia, by citing the constancy of her love for Amphilanthus rather
than the love itself, foregrounds autonomy.[17] Though her love is male-
directed, her constancy (the privileged virtue) is self-maintained. In an
important way to which we will return, then, Pamphilia's "constancy"
may represent the proto-virtue of a bourgeois subject only beginning
to emerge at this point in history, for it is a virtue constructed as interior to the self, self-authorized and unchanging. Rather than subject-
ing herself to a protecting male lover as Leandrus suggests, Pamphilia
constructs her own "walls" in a prototypical gesture of subjection to
the self.

Constancy is also a defense against circulating in the text as a mar-
riageable female. Though Pamphilia constant/ly stresses her devotion
to Amphilanthus, their marriage is always deferred, for no apparent
reason—at least on the level of plot. She doesn't marry Amphilanthus
through 558 pages of the published narrative, and, unlike other characters, she steadfastly refuses to marry any but her one true love. Pam-

philia thus avoids what Gayle Rubin has called the basis of the "sex/
gender system" in patriarchal cultures: "the traffic in women." Men,
Rubin argues, trade women as conduits of but not participants in patriarchal power. Women are thus subjected but are not subjects; that is,
they are allowed no self-control, and a woman can begin to occupy a
subject position only by blocking her trafficking.[18] By asserting her
withdrawal from the "traffic" that characterizes both the romance text
and the culture in which Wroth wrote, by refusing to allow herself
to be bestowed upon a husband by a father as a gift between men, Pamphilia establishes that she is "subject" to her self.

Wroth figures this self-control in the discourse of female political
sovereignty; Pamphilia tells her father that he "had once married her
before, which was to the Kingdome of Pamphilia, from which Husband
shee could not bee diuorced, nor ever would have other . . ." (218). For
her emergent female subject Wroth thus appropriates her culture's only
available model of a sovereign female self (subjected only to herself,
singularly able to control her own circulation within the traffic in
women), the virgin queen Elizabeth. Urania makes the connection
when she asks Pamphilia, "how can you command others, that cannot
master your selfe, or make laws, that cannot counsel, or soueraignise
ouer a poore thought?" (398). Whereas a married woman would be
governed by her husband, this queen withdraws into the political space
she rules independently of patriarchy. Married only to her country, her
name is appropriate for an emergent female subject: she "soueraignises"
over Pamphilia—her country and her self.

A refusal to circulate between men and the important ramifications
for the formulation of a female subject are foregrounded in *Urania*'s
treatment of poetic manuscripts. The narrative privileges manuscript
protection, while manuscript circulation is often problematic. Love
letters are forged and intercepted (231, 513–14), and circulating poems
lead to a love triangle in which a woman is shared sexually by two men
(384). Nereana circulates verses to a lover and goes mad when they fail
to have the desired effect (417–20). Steriamus gives Urania a book of
verses to explain his decision to love her; circulating verses rationalize
an act of inconstancy, a change of love-object (276). In Pelarina's narrative, a woman's loss of control over her manuscript is worse than the

loss of her virginity; her lover's reading of her poems motivates her conversion to virtuous constancy and a pilgrimage to Jerusalem (453–54).

Notably, Pamphilia's poetic practice is altogether different; her first verses in the text are "buried" almost as soon as she writes them (51–52). Later, when Antissia discovers Pamphilia's poem carved on a tree in her private garden, Pamphilia coyly argues that the poem does not refer to her own situation — that it has no publicly significant referentiality. Furthermore, at an important moment in book 3, Pamphilia refuses to recite her verses and instead tells the prose tale of Lindamira — "faign[ed] to be written in a French Story" and detailing the life of the anagrammatically related Ladimari Wroth. The story culminates in Lindamira's public dishonor: "her honour not touched, but cast downe, and laid open to all mens toungs and eares, to be used as they pleas'd" (425). Public/ation — the "laying open" and "use" of a woman's narrative — is figured in sexual terms, and this discursive violation occurs at the very point in *Urania* where the autobiographical Lindamira, the narrator of Lindamira's story, and the narrator of *Urania* (Lady Mary?) become indistinguishable in a narrative which describes all three: Lindamira "complain'd, which complaint, because I [Pamphilia] lik'd it, or rather found her estate so neere agree with mine, I put into Sonnets . . . ; for thus the Booke leaues her, the complaint is this diuided into seauen Sonnets" (425). Who is speaking in the final clause, and about which Booke? Lindamira's tale? the French Story? book 3 of *Urania*, which concludes with these poems?

This complex juncture of autobiography and fictions — centered on the public/ation of a woman's story — produces *Urania's* only interpolated sonnet sequence. Pamphilia's transcription of Lindamira's complaint displaces the "laying open" and making public of Pamphilia's own verses. However, unlike the explicit prose narration introducing it, the surrogate sequence is seemingly non-referential, a sustained inscription of emotion suggestive of *Pamphilia to Amphilanthus*. Once again sonnets are deployed as a withdrawal into a privatized discursive space — deployed against the making public, the circulation, of a woman's story.

IV

To assert that Pamphilia figures an "emergent female subject," is not, as that term suggests, to argue that a female subject rises fully constituted from these texts. Several Wroth critics have indeed discerned or assumed a full-fledged modern subjectivity in the sonnets. Roberts finds that "Wroth analyzes . . . universal psychological conflicts," while Beilin argues that Wroth "explores the psychology of woman's passion." Both read the sonnets as unproblematic transcriptions of a "state of mind" and make Wroth inappropriately our psychological, psychoanalyzable contemporary. Such arguments, like Carolyn Ruth Swift's attempt to locate a "feminine consciousness" in *Urania*, are perhaps both canonic and essentialist. To posit "universalist" psychological conflicts in the texts of a heretofore unacknowledged woman writer is to prepare her for entrance into a humanist great-books canon. To read for evidence of an essential female psychology is to read gender at the expense of history — rather than gender through/across history.[19] Instead — and here I am following and gendering Stephen Greenblatt's provocative formulation — I think we can read *Pamphilia to Amphilanthus* as a text which gestures toward and contests the very notion of female subjectivity — the eventual construction of which has made such psychological interpretations possible. Like so many Renaissance texts, Wroth's sonnets speak a language which seems simultaneously to invite and deny our reading Pamphilia as a humanist subject.[20]

In the context of a larger argument detailing the emergence of the subject of "bourgeois culture," Francis Barker argues that in the early seventeenth century subjection "does not properly involve subjectivity at all, but a condition in which place and articulation are defined . . . by incorporation in the body politic. . . ." As a part of the larger spectacle, the typical character in *Hamlet* (Barker's example) has meaning not through "an interiorized, self-recognition," but through its acting of certain roles within a publicly displayed hierarchy. In contrast, the atypical Hamlet can insist on his own exception from this rule, announcing he has "that/Within, which passeth show." But as Barker notes, Hamlet's "Within" is never articulated, is always deferred "as a central obscurity which cannot be dramatized." Because it is historically "premature," an interiorized subjectivity is imagined "outside the limits of the text-world in which it is as yet emergent only in a promissory form."²¹ *Pamphilia to Amphilanthus* shares important aspects of this formulation. Pamphilia voices a refusal to signify publicly and insists instead upon a private authenticity beyond/beneath the text. Likewise, she denounces the courtly theatricality that constructs meaning in the world around her. But (as in Barker's formulation) the subjectivity mapped "in" Pamphilia is not only private but privative; the text figures it in terms of emptiness, lack, loss, and absence. *Pamphilia to Amphilanthus* clears a space for a nascent subject without articulating what it is that fills that emergent private space. Pamphilia, though constant to herself, is "possesst" by "absence" (45/P52).

But Pamphilia differs from Hamlet in the crucial matter of gender, and, as Catherine Belsey has persuasively argued, the construction of the male subject in this period was accomplished against a female Other.²² The question then becomes: How did Wroth, writing in a culture which generally denied women a stable place from which to speak, negotiate the gendered positions of speech and silence to construct an emergent subject's voice? Part of the answer lies in Wroth's remarkable personal history. Descending from a line of prolific poets, as Hannay and Waller argue in their essays, she continued even after her marriage to be associated closely with the Sidney family name and its poetic heritage. Wroth's class position and illustrious family precursors served as an authorization to write and to be read; the *Urania* title page announces Wroth as "Daughter to the right Noble Robert Earle of Leicester. And Neece to the ever famous, and renowned Sr. Phillips Sidney knight. And to ye most exelent Lady Mary Countesse of Pembroke. . . ." Furthermore, as Miller and Quilligan have argued, Wroth created at least one of her texts as reaction to and rewriting of her uncle's; her romance begins by turning his inside out, making articulate in *The Countesse of Mountgomeries Urania* the voice of a woman prominently silent in *The Countess of Pembroke's Arcadia*.²³

Wroth works a similar transformation in *Pamphilia to Amphilanthus*. If "Petrarchism is one of the discourses in which a recognizably modern mode of subjectivity . . . is first articulated and actively cultivated,"²⁴ Wroth's sequence appropriates that discourse to map the position of a female subject. But, as the initial lines of the sequence make clear, she can attest to the emergence of this subjectivity only in terms of its lack:

"When nights black mantle could most darknes prove, / And sleepe deaths Image did my senceses hiere / From knowledg of my self. . . ." Finally, unlike the male subject constituted by the writing and circulation of verses within a courtly Petrarchan context, Wroth's female subjectivity is predicated on a refusal to circulate.

Speaking of the decades around 1600, Saunders has noted that "there must have been widespread traffic (and perhaps marketing, white and black) in poetic manuscripts, and a large number of people must have prized and collected them" (521). Given what we have seen in the *Urania*, it seems no mere coincidence that Saunders's observation applies equally to poetic manuscripts and to women in Wroth's culture. At this intersection of bibliography and gender, we can read *Pamphilia to Amphilanthus* — both the "external" and "internal" evidence — as a suggestion that Wroth's control over and containment of her poetic manuscripts figures control over herself as a potentially trafficable woman. Recognizing the risks involved for women who (like Elizabeth Cary's Mariam) "with publike voyce runne on,"[25] Wroth seemingly constitutes her distinctively private female subjectivity against the traffic in both women and words.

Pamphilia, we remember, is "the most silent and discreetly retir'd of any Princesse," and the word *discreet*, wonderfully resonant in this context, recurs in descriptions of her. In the early seventeenth century, spelling was only beginning to differentiate meanings we now separate into "discreet" and "discrete"; as the *OED*'s glosses suggest, both meanings apply to Pamphilia and to Wroth's writing:

> *discreet* Showing discernment or judgement in the guidance of one's own speech and action; . . . circumspect, cautious; often esp. that can be silent when speech would be inconvenient.
>
> *discrete* Separate, detached from others, individually distinct.

In an era before lexical standardization, a single word fuses the construction of a female subject — a woman "separate, detached from others, individually distinct" — with one who withdraws from public discourse into "circumspect," even "silent" speech.

To discuss *Urania* and *Pamphilia to Amphilanthus* in a context of "privacy" and non-circulating silence, however, elides one of the few definitive facts one can state about these texts: they were made public and did circulate in the elaborate folio *Urania* of 1621. Unfortunately, this is virtually the end of certainty when one speaks of the volume's publication. Strangely, *The Countesse of Mountgomeries Urania*, written by one prominent noblewoman and named for another, contains "no dedicatory epistles, poems, or prefatory material," as Roberts notes. The narrative ends with a provocative "And," and the sonnets appear in a separately paginated and signed section at the end. We do not know whether Wroth initiated, assisted, or otherwise participated in the volume's printing, and she is on record in a letter to the then Marquess of Buckingham as both opposing and supporting its publication.[26]

What, then, are we to make of the sonnets' appearance in this cryptically published, ambiguously public volume? The answer lies in the project I have outlined thus far. To insert oneself into Petrarchan discourse in order to register one's subject position and (simultaneously) to keep private the texts which construct that position is at best a mute gesture. Dis/course runs to and fro; by definition it circulates. More simply: if a woman writes in a forest (or garden) and no one reads her, has she written anything? Wroth, as a woman-writer, must resist publication as a form of male trafficking, yet that resistance can only register if it is made public. It is ironically appropriate, then, that Pamphilia marries not in the published *Urania* but in the unpublished continuation. Paradoxically, the published texts must announce their resistance to public/ation, in the multiple senses of the word; they stage their own privatization.

Wroth's letter to Buckingham carefully balances such concerns: "I have with all care caused the sale of [my booke] to bee forbidden, and the books left to bee shut up, for thos that are abroad, I will likewise doe my best to gett them in, if itt will please your Lordship to procure mee the kings warrant to that effect, without which non will deliver them to mee, besids that your Lordship wilbe pleased to lett mee have that which I sent you . . . what I ame able to doe for the getting in of books (which from the first were solde against my minde I never purposing to have had them published) I will with all care, and diligence parforme."[27] Within the confines of a single sentence Wroth says both that she never meant to publish the volumes and that she sent a presentation copy to one of the most public figures in the kingdom. Indeed, by requesting the king's warrant, Wroth injects the controversy into the very arena she elsewhere seems most eager to avoid. At the same time, she stages her anxieties about publication; to publish is to set meaning loose, to allow the possibility of "strang constructions" circulating "abroad."

To be sure, there is ample evidence of male aristocrats protesting their unwillingness to engage in publication and circulation, but the situation for women goes far beyond gestures of mere reluctance. Lord Denny's verses to Wroth following *Urania*'s appearance illustrate exactly what a woman risked in publishing her work. His gender-specific attack ("leave idle bookes alone / For wise and worthyer women have writte none") portrays Wroth in precisely the ways she repudiates in the sonnets; a "Hermophradite in show," she becomes in his view a sexual and theatrical "monster"—indiscreet (in both senses) and open to the view of "all men."[28] Denny's attack thus reproduces the perceived correspondences in the period between a woman's sexual transgressiveness, "her linguistic 'fulness' and her frequenting of public space."[29] In writing to Buckingham, Wroth stages anxieties of publication in comparable spatial metaphors; the offending books—like Pamphilia herself in the sonnets and romance—she promises to "shut up" and "gett in."

To argue that Wroth "stages" anything at all in so vehemently antitheatrical a text as *Pamphilia to Amphilanthus* may seem contradictory. And yet it is this very anti-theatricality and self-enclosure which Wroth must dramatize in her construction of the authentic, articulate subject. Returning to sonnet 42/P48, "If ever love had force in humaine brest?," we see that the poem makes an exhibition of its privacy, demanding that the reader "looke on mee"; however, the drama the reader witnesses is the demonstrative Petrarchan body interiorized: "in humaine brest," "in pensive hart," in "the soule." Like a soliloquy, this sonnet presents itself as interior discourse, all the while alluding to its public performance. The speaker likewise asserts in order to register submission, expressing what will come to be the condition of bourgeois subjectivity—a freeing of the self from exterior constraints which becomes, instead, a subjection in and to the self, the self in and under control: "I, ame the soule that feeles the greatest smart; / I, ame that hartles trunk of harts depart / And I, that one, by love, and griefe oprest. . . ." Finally, the speaker obscures her own agency in the anti-theatrical drama she stages: "I should nott have bin made this stage of woe / Wher sad disasters have theyr open showe."

Wroth's sonnets thus demonstrate several points crucial to our understanding of subjectivity, genders, and writing in the Renaissance. To withdraw from "the traffic in women" is to imagine the possibility of female subjectivity; likewise, to withdraw from the traffic in manuscripts — to exercise control over one's words — is to imagine the possibility of a voice of one's own, a speaking female subject. And yet, ironically, the subject's "mastery" over her words and her self can only be acknowledged by in some measure relinquishing absolute privacy and control. If the subject is constituted in and through discourse, she must speak to exist. "Soft said she, shall I turne blabb?" Publish or perish.[30]

NOTES

1. See Roberts's stemma in *The Poems of Lady Mary Wroth*, p. 65, and Waller's stemma in his edition of *Pamphilia to Amphilanthus*, pp. 22–23; for the question of dating, also see Waller, p. 8.

2. Roberts, *Poems*, pp. 62, 19; Waller, *Pamphilia to Amphilanthus*, p. 8.

3. See J.W. Saunders, "From Manuscript to Print: A Note on the circulation of poetic MSS in the sixteenth century," *Proceedings of the Leeds Philosophical and Literary Society* (1951), 507–28; Margaret J.M. Ezell, *The Patriarch's Wife: Literary Evidence and the History of the Family* (Chapel Hill: University of North Carolina Press, 1987), ch. 3.

4. Roberts, *Poems*, pp. 44–46; see Elaine V. Beilin, *Redeeming Eve: Women Writers of the English Renaissance* (Princeton: Princeton University Press, 1987), ch. 8; Margaret [Witten-Hannah] McLaren, "Lady Mary Wroth's *Urania*: The Work and the Tradition," Ph.D. diss., University of Auckland, 1978, p. 143; May N. Paulissen, "The Love Sonnets of Lady Mary Wroth: A Critical Introduction," Ph.D. diss., University of Houston, 1976, p. 191. That the 1621 *Urania* volume prints much of what appears in the ms. as if it were a single sequence cannot be construed as Wroth's intention. Because it is more accessible than the Folger ms., I follow (somewhat reluctantly) the other essays in this collection in quoting from Roberts's edition, giving both Wroth's and Roberts's numbering. All emphases are mine. Roberts's copy-text in most cases is the ms., though it is important to note that she rearranges the ms. sonnets in the order of the 1621 printed text. She asserts that the 1621 ordering of the sonnets is authorially intended, but that other aspects of the printed text are not. Waller prints the 1621 text in the 1621 order. Sonnet order is not crucial to my argument; I merely wish to point out that no printed edition reproduces the unusual and significant arrangement of the ms.

5. Francis Barker, *The Tremulous Private Body: Essays on Subjection* (London: Methuen, 1984), p. 34.

6. Arthur F. Marotti, "'Love is not Love': Elizabethan Sonnet Sequences and the Social Order," *English Literary History* 49 (1982), 399.

7. Roberts, *Poems*, p. 85. I am grateful to Ann Rosalind Jones for pointing out to me the more contextually consistent reading of this line: Venus orders Cupid to shoot Pamphilia's heart. I would note, however, that, as the *OED*'s entries for both "shoot" and "shut" suggest, the spelling "shutt" signified prolifically in the period; I am proposing here a more inclusive reading that does not preclude the possibility that the word aligns Pamphilia's entry into a lover's discourse ("shoot") with her corporeal enclosure ("shut").

8. See also Jones's and Fienberg's discussions of the poem in their essays in this volume.

9. Barker, *Tremulous Body*, p. 14.

10. Barker, *Tremulous Body*, p. 35. Given the resemblance to Hamlet's speech in the presence chamber, Wroth's appearance in Jonson's *Masque of Blackness*, and her later removal from court, a probable target of Pamphilia's denunciation is courtly display. For the courtly context of Petrarchan poetry, see Marotti, "Love," and Louis Adrian Montrose, "The Elizabethan Subject and the Spenserian Text," in *Literary Theory/Renaissance Texts*, ed. Patricia Parker and David Quint (Baltimore: Johns Hopkins University Press, 1986), pp. 303–40.

11. See Alan Hagar, "The Exemplary Mirage: Fabrication of Sir Philip Sidney's Biographical Image and the Sidney Reader," *English Literary History* 48 (1981), 1–16. See also Naomi J. Miller, "Rewriting Lyric Fictions: The Role of the Lady in Lady Mary Wroth's *Pamphilia to Amphilanthus*," in *The Renaissance Englishwoman in Print: Counterbalancing the Canon*, ed. Anne M. Haselkorn and Betty S. Travitsky (Amherst: University of Massachusetts Press, 1990), pp. 295–310.

12. See Quilligan, "The Constant Subject: Instability and Female Authority in Wroth's *Urania* Poems," in *Soliciting Interpretation: Literary Theory and Seventeeth-Century English Poetry*, ed. Elizabeth D. Harvey and Katharine Eisaman Maus (Chicago: University of Chicago Press, 1990), pp. 311–12; Montrose, "Elizabethan Subject," p. 325; and Jones's and Fienberg's essays in this volume.

13. Josephine A. Roberts, "The Biographical Problem of *Pamphilia to Amphilanthus*," *Tulsa Studies in Women's Literature* 1 (1982), 43–53. Sonnet 9/P71 seems to record four significant words from an addressee (Amphilanthus?): "I must bee gone."

14. Quilligan, "Constant Subject," p. 315.

15. Peter Stallybrass notes the association of enclosed gardens, the state, and the female monarch: see "Patriarchal Territories: The Body Enclosed," in *Rewriting the Renaissance: The Discourses of Sexual Difference in Early Modern Europe*, ed. Margaret W. Ferguson, Maureen Quilligan, and Nancy J. Vickers (Chicago: University of Chicago Press, 1986), p. 129. Margreta de Grazia has suggested to me the similarity of Urania's "contriu'd walkes," seventeenth-century gardens, and the "labourinth" enclosing the speaker of Wroth's "Crowne of Sonetts."

16. Women who do circulate (geographically and sexually) are compared to ill-kept gardens. Nereana, who goes on an international "Knightlike" quest for her beloved, is "a garden [which], neuer so delicate when well kept under, will without keeping grow ruinous" [279].

17. Quilligan, "Constant Subject," p. 322–23; see also Miller's essay, "Engendering Discourse," in this volume.
18. Gayle Rubin, "The Traffic in Women: Notes on the 'Political Economy' of Sex," in *Toward an Anthropology of Women*, ed. Rayna Reiter (New York: Monthly Review Press, 1975), pp. 157–210.
19. Roberts, "Biographical Problem," p. 51; Beilin, *Redeeming Eve*, pp. 233, 236; Carolyn Ruth Swift, "Feminine Identity in Lady Mary Wroth's Romance *Urania*," *English Literary Renaissance* 14 (1984), 328–46.
20. Stephen Greenblatt, "Psychoanalysis and Renaissance Culture," in Parker and Quint, *Literary Theory/Renaissance Texts*, 210–24.
21. Barker, *Tremulous Body*, pp. 31, 36.
22. Catherine Belsey, *The Subject of Tragedy: Identity and Difference in Renaissance drama* (London: Methuen, 1985).
23. Quilligan, "Constant Subject," p. 310; Naomi J. Miller, "'Not much to be marked': Narrative of the Woman's Part in Lady Mary Wroth's *Urania*," *Studies in English Literature* 29 (1989), 126–27.
24. Montrose, "Elizabethan Subject," p. 325.
25. Elizabeth Cary, *The Tragedie of Mariam, the faire Queene of Iewry*, ed. A.C. Dunstan (Oxford: Malone Society Reprints, 1914), sig. A3.
26. See Roberts, *Poems*, pp. 69–70.
27. Roberts, *Poems*, p. 236. There may be a public/private distinction within the realm of print itself. Donne writes: "I am brought to a necessity of printing my Poems, and addressing them to my L. Chamberlain. This I mean to do forthwith; not for much publique view, but at mine owne cost, a few Copies." See Arthur Marotti, "John Donne and the Rewards of Patronage," in *Patronage in the Renaissance*, ed. Guy Fitch Lytle and Stephen Orgel (Princeton: Princeton University Press, 1981), p. 232.
28. Roberts, *Poems*, pp. 32–33.
29. Stallybrass, "Patriarchal Territories," p. 127.
30. With clarifying criticism of this essay's early versions, Margreta de Grazia, Jay Grossman, and Wendy Wall have in important ways saved me from turning blabb, and I thank them.

Mary Wroth's *Love's Victory*
and Pastoral Tragicomedy

Barbara K. Lewalski

M ary Wroth's pastoral tragicomedy, *Love's Victory*, has recently been published for the first and only time;[1] it was unknown except to a small contemporary coterie, and is still virtually unread. Only one complete manuscript is extant, at Penshurst; the Huntington Library has a partial manuscript.[2] Both are holograph. The date of composition is uncertain: Wroth's editors, Josephine Roberts and Michael J. Brennan, suggest the 1620s on the strength of a few parallels to an early section of the unpublished second part of Wroth's *Urania*, extant only in one manuscript at the Newberry Library.[3] We know more about Wroth than about most women writers of the Elizabethan and Jacobean era, as discussed in the essays by Margaret Hannay and Gary Waller which open this collection, but we know next to nothing about this drama. It might have been written for performance at private theatricals at the Wroths' country estate at Durrants in Enfield but there is no record of such performance.[4] Nor are there other contemporary records to supply context, nor any contemporary, or subsequent criticism of the work. As with much other Renaissance women's writing now being uncovered, we are made to encounter here the thing itself, the bare, unaccommodated text.

Margaret McLaren's useful essay (based only on the incomplete Huntington manuscript) focuses on the intersection and at times conflict of several discourses: courtly Petrarchanism and Neoplatonism, comedic satire, myth and ritual, and what she calls "a special language of avoidance" papering over the increasing powerlessness of women at James's court.[5] Carolyn Swift, using both manuscripts, reads the drama as a dream of female empowerment and autonomy compensating for Wroth's own frustrations in love, and makes the plausible (though I think too restrictive) argument that it rewrites the Philip Sidney–Penelope Rich relationship with a happy ending.[6] I mean to examine here the evidence of deliberate genre transformation to suggest a bolder thesis: that Wroth's drama encodes an implicit feminist politics emphasizing the values of female agency, egalitarianism, female friendship, and community, a politics which subverts both the norms of the genre and of Jacobean society.

Happily, genre affords a useful entrée for Wroth's drama, since this work is carefully positioned within the complex genre systems and codes of the Renaissance literary institution. The few parallels between *Love's Victory* and the manuscript continuation of *Urania* (I:fol.5–8) highlight the difference in genre. Both have a band of shepherds smitten with Love, but in the romance they are royalty and nobility in shepherd guise, led by a brother and sister famed for poetry; in the drama they are true shepherds who share alike in poetry and leadership. There are a few parallel characters—Rustick, Dalinea/Magdalaine, Arcas—though Arcas is a faithful knight in the romance and in the drama a mean-spirited slander-mongering shepherd.[7] *Love's Victory* is much more usefully contextualized in relation to pastoral tragicomedy, a mixed genre especially popular at the Renaissance courts of Italy, France, and England. Comparison with these texts allows us to inspect the literary and political choices Wroth's drama incorporates.

The label itself—pastoral tragicomedy—points up the multiplicity and complexity of the generic codes which can intersect in a given Renaissance text. This new, mixed kind was usually seen as a development from pastoral eclogue. These brief dialogic poems were usually classified as "dramatic" in systems deriving from Plato's and Aristotle's three kinds of imitation or representation.[8] In schemes deriving from the Alexandrian *Canons*, Horace, Cicero and Quintilian, pastoral was classed with epic because written in hexameter, providing a basis for Renaissance claims that it can include or covertly treat great persons and events; the canonical pastoral writers were Theocritus and Virgil.[9] This influential system reinforced the central importance of model texts and authors to Renaissance conceptions of genre.

Pastoral eclogues held an anomalous position in Renaissance systems that identify many particular historical genres (or *kinds*, the Renaissance term) by formal and thematic elements, *topoi*, and conventions. In Put-

tenham's highly politicized system these kinds were arranged hierarchi-
cally according to nobility of subjects and persons treated, and height
of style;[10] pastoral eclogues (though not the most ancient kind of
poetry) are associated with the life and first literary activities of the
lowly, presenting

> in base and humble stile by maner of Dialogue . . . the private and familiar talke
> of the meanest sort of men, as shepheards, heywards, and such like . . . the first
> familiar conversation, and their babble and talk under bushes and shadie trees, the
> first disputation and contentious reasoning . . . the first idle wooings and their
> songs made to their mates or paramours, either upon sorrow or jolity of courage,
> the first amorous musicks, sometime also they sang and played on their pipes for
> wagers . . . no doubt the shepheards life was the first example of honest fellowship,
> their trade the first art of lawful acquisition or purchase. (sigs Eiiv)

Yet he also described eclogue as the creation of sophisticated poets, who
often used it for moral teaching (Mantuan) or for covert political commentary (Virgil):

> The Poet devised the *Eclogue* . . . not of purpose to counterfait or represent the
> rusticall manner of loves and communication: but under the vaile of homely per-
> sons, and in rude speeches to insinuate and glaunce at greater matters, and such
> as perchance had not bene safe to have been disclosed in any other sort, which
> may be perceived by the Eclogues of *Virgill* in which are treated by figure matters
> of greater importance than the loves of *Titirus* and *Corydon*. (Fiiiv–Fiv)

In the Renaissance, pastoral became a mode, interpenetrating works
or parts of works in several genres.[11] We find not only pastoral eclogues
but also pastoral songs, pastoral dramas of various kinds, pastoral funeral
elegies, pastoral entertainments and masques, pastoral romances, pastoral episodes in epics (as in Tasso's *Gerusalemme Liberata* and especially
Spenser's *Faerie Queene* VI). Sidney evidently thought of it as a mode
participating in several genres (eclogue, tale, romance) and emphasized
the uses of pastoral for moral teaching and for covert political commentary, instancing Virgil's First Eclogue:

> Is the poore pipe disdained, which sometimes out of *Moelibeus* mouth can shewe
> the miserie of people, under hard Lords and ravening souldiers? And again by
> *Titerus*, what blessednesse is derived, to them that lie lowest, from the goodnesse
> of them that sit highest? Sometimes under the prettie tales of Woolves and sheepe,
> can enclude the whole considerations of wrong doing and patience.[12]

The politics of pastoral has been much studied recently—by Louis Montrose as a vehicle for Elizabethan courtiership; by Stephen Orgel as a

locus amoenus myth for the Stuart court; and by Annabel Patterson as a means to negotiate multiple and complex stances toward ideology, especially through Virgil's First Eclogue.[13] I suggest that in *Love's Victory* pastoral is adapted to the concerns of a feminist politics.

In the mixture that is pastoral tragicomedy, pastoral is the mode, carrying multiple associations from the long history of pastoral in western literature. The genre, tragicomedy, is a new Renaissance kind, whose emergence into prominence with Tasso's *Aminta* (1580) and Guarini's *Il Pastor Fido* (1590) touched off a storm of controversy.[14] Italian critics complained that the mix of comedy and tragedy violated artistic unity, that the mixture of clowns and kings violated artistic decorum, and that stories of rude shepherds could not instruct sophisticated city dwellers.[15] Guarini, the chief defender and analyst of the new form, declared it to be natural (since nature is full of mixture); defined its specific purpose (to purge melancholy by pleasure); found some warrant for it in antiquity in Aristotle's double plot and in Plautus's *Amphitryo*; praised its comprehensiveness in portraying gods, kings, and shepherds of several ranks and classes; and even proclaimed it the highest kind, best suited to the refined modern age, in that it included all the good features and rejected the excesses of both tragedy and comedy.[16] Denying it to be a crude mixture of comedy and tragedy, he pronounced it a unified and perfect "third thing" using only those elements of comedy and tragedy that can blend together:

> He who composes tragicomedy takes from tragedy its great persons but not its great action, its verisimilar plot but not its true one, its movement of the feelings but not its disturbance of them, its pleasure but not its sadness, its danger but not its death; from comedy it takes laughter that is not excessive, modest amusement, feigned difficulty, happy reversal, and above all the comic order. . . . [Yet] it is still not impossible for the plot to have more of one quality than of another, according to the wish of him who composes it.[17]

In England, Sidney repeated the Italian critics' charges against "mongrell Tragicomedie" that mixes Kings and Clowns, "horne Pipes and Funeralls," though his target seems to be the use of comic scenes in tragedy rather than the new mixed kinds, which he explicitly allowed: "some *Poesies* have coupled togither two or three kindes, as the *Tragicall* and *Comicall*, whereupon is risen the *Tragicomicall* . . . if severed they be good, the coniunction cannot be hurtfull" (sigs. Iv, E3v). In 1610

Fletcher provided a much simplified definition of the kind: "it wants deaths, which is inough to make it no tragedie, yet brings some neere it, which is inough to make it no comedie."[18]

When Lady Mary Wroth wrote *Love's Victory* she may have had only a general awareness of these definitions and controversies. But she certainly looked to the canon of the new kind—Tasso, Guarini, Daniel, Fletcher—to provide what Hans Robert Jauss terms "the horizon of generic expectations"[19] and to suggest a range of generic possibilities and identifying topics, made more obvious as each text responded to its predecessors. All have a five-act structure. Except for Daniel's *The Queen's Arcadia*, all contain lyrical songs and choruses. All contain stock characters: a shepherdess sworn to chastity, a lustful satyr, a libertine or worldly-wise nymph. All use the device of a narrator to describe miraculous escapes from death and the final reunion of lovers. And all present an Arcadia that has declined some distance (small or great) from its Golden Age perfection and that has been infiltrated by characters and values from City and Court.

The chief canonical text was Tasso's *Aminta*, produced for the court at Ferrara in 1573–74, first published in 1580, and instantly popular throughout Europe.[20] If Wroth didn't know it in Italian, an English translation was readily accessible in *The Countess of Pembroke's Ivychurch* (1591) by her aunt's client, Abraham Fraunce. Tasso's style is lyrical throughout, heightened by songs, poignant love complaints, and choruses, the most famous of them extolling the lost Golden Age when love was free and unhampered by notions of chastity and honor. Here the source of trouble is the psyche of the nymph Silvia, whose dedication to chastity and the chase leads her to scorn the devoted and honorable love of the hero, Aminta, who refuses all persuasions (by the libertine Nymph Daphne and the cynic Thyrsis) to take her by force. Saved by Aminta from rape by a lustful satyr, Silvia is reported killed by wolves, prompting Aminta to cast himself off a cliff; but he miraculously survives, Silvia repents, and the lovers are at last united. Cupid in prologue claims his agency in these affairs, undertaken to conquer Silvia's cold chastity; and an epilogue by Venus describes her errant son's power over humankind. There is some local allegory in allusions to personages at the Ferrari court, with Tasso himself shadowed in Thyrsis.[21]

Guarini's *Il Pastor Fido* (1590) was designed for court occasions in

Turin and Mantua.[22] By 1602 twenty Italian editions had appeared, as well as an anonymous English translation set forth with commendatory verses by Samuel Daniel, who may well have introduced Guarini's drama to Wroth.[23] Guarini offers a darker alternative for tragicomedy, an Arcadia which has declined much further than Tasso's from the Golden Age, as his parallel "Golden Age" chorus indicates. Only the subplot reprises the *Aminta* plot and tone—in comic reversal: a shepherd (Silvio) is devoted to chastity and the chase, his lover disguises herself as a wolf to be near him, Silvio shoots her by mistake, then repents, loves her, and cures her wound with herbs. The main plot is much more complex than Tasso's, proliferating violence and threats of death from many sources—the gods, society, human evil. Guarini's perverse characters are worse than Tasso's: a lustful satyr who attempts not only rape but murder, a libertine nymph, Corisca, who will stop at nothing to satisfy her ever-changing desires. A curse by the goddess Diana requires the yearly sacrifice of an unfaithful maiden or wife, or volunteer substitute; it will be lifted only when two descendants of the gods wed, occasioning the forced betrothal of Silvio and Amarillis and thereby threatening the true and mutual love of Amarillis and the titular hero, Mirtillo. Corisca and the lustful satyr trap these lovers together in a cave and slander them as adulterers, the priests prepare to sacrifice Amarillis, and Mirtillo offers himself as a substitute; then come reports of Corisca's confession and Mirtillo's newly discovered divine descent, permitting the reprieve and union of the lovers.

Wroth may have read or even seen Samuel Daniel's *The Queen's Arcadia* (1606), which was presented to Queen Anne and her ladies by the University of Oxford in August 1605, the year Wroth danced with the queen in Jonson's *Masque of Blackness*.[24] Daniel further darkens Guarini's vision, with an Arcadia marred by manifold evils from many sources and lacking the usual songs or choruses that signify pastoral *otium*. Daniel's dedicatory verses to the queen deny any references to matters of state,[25] but so strenuously as in fact to intimate parallels between the great changes the choral figures Ergastus and Meliboeus find when they return to Arcadia and the new mores of King James's court. A licentious traveler, Colax, imports the mores of foreign lands and courts, seducing some nymphs away from their true lovers and slandering others, while his female associate unsettles the nymphs with city fashions, styles, cosmetics, and wanton attitudes. Besides, there is a lawyer who promotes litigation, a doctor who promotes illness, and a religious imposter who undermines established rites and customs. The heroine, Chloris, denies love and her true lover, Amyntas, not from devotion to chastity but from doubt that faithful love can exist. In a version of Guarini's cave trick, Colax attempts to rape and seduce her, and Amyntas, believing her wanton, takes poison; Chloris then admits her love for him and Urania cures him with herbs. In final scenes, Ergastus and Meliboeus reveal all the evils, banish the corrupt foreigners, and urge Arcadians to return to their old ways.

Wroth may or may not have known Fletcher's *Faithful Shepherdess* (c. 1610); this effort to translate a court genre to the private stage (probably Blackfriars) was a disaster.[26] The title and several episodes signal a response to Guarini, lighter in tone but with more overt violence, due to unrestrained passions. Perigot and the titular heroine, Amoret, are faithful, mutual lovers; Amarillis (who also desires Perigot) takes on Amoret's semblance by magic and behaves wantonly; deceived, Perigot stabs Amoret on two occasions, but she responds with unquestioning fidelity and forgiveness. Comic variants of the genre's stock figures include a satyr who is noble and chaste and who rescues nymphs in danger of rape; a libertine shepherdess whose promiscuous solicitations never succeed; and a swain who loves a chaste nymph only for her chastity and is cured when she pretends love to him. The restoration of Arcadia begins as the permanently chaste shepherdess, Clorin, uses her powers to cure both physical wounds and unchaste desires for all the lovers (except for the incurably wicked Sullen Shepherd), and joins them in virtuous love.

Daniel's pastoral drama, *Hymen's Triumph* (1615), was presented at the queen's court in the Strand.[27] As befits a wedding entertainment, it is closer in tone to Tasso than Guarini, incorporating many songs and comic mischances arising from cross-dressing and gender confusion. The prologue identifies the allegorical passions of Envy, Avarice, and Jealousy as enemies of Hymen. The chief source of trouble is paternal avarice, which leads Silvia's father to promise her to a wealthy swain instead of to her true love, Thirsis. Captured and held by pirates for two years and presumed dead, Silvia preserves her chastity, escapes, and returns in male disguise (as Clorindo) to wait out her betrothed's wedding day; betimes, Viola-like, she woos her lover for her mistress, Cloris, and attracts the misguided love of Phillis. A jealous forester who loves Phillis stabs Clarindo and reveals Silvia, Thirsis collapses with grief, both are cured by Lamia, and Silvia's father repents and blesses the union which the chorus celebrates as an ornament to Arcadia.

Wroth's *Love's Victory* appears to draw upon and respond to this entire tradition. In tone it is closest to Tasso, but even more lyrical, with songs and choruses resounding throughout; on Guarini's scale, it stands much closer to comedy than tragedy. Wroth's Arcadia is also closer than Tasso's to the Golden Age. Here, troubles arise chiefly from love's natural anxieties—jealousy, misapprehensions, suspicions, and fears rather than treacherous plots and violence: no near-rapes or near-murders in this work. Moreover, Wroth's drama portrays (beyond anything in this genre) an extended egalitarian community, without gender or class hierarchy, bound together by friendships strong enough to survive even rivalries in love—a community in which friends aid, console, and even sacrifice themselves for each other.

There are four pairs of lovers. Philisses loves Musella but believes she loves his friend Lissius and so prepares to relinquish her and die of grief; he is restored when Musella confesses her love to him. Lissius begins as a scorner of women and love but soon comes to love Simeana (Philisses's sister); their love is threatened by Arcas's slander and Simeana's jealousy, but they are reunited by Musella's good counsel. Silvesta loves Philisses but devotes herself to a life of chastity when she realizes that he loves her friend Musella; accordingly she rejects (until the end) the Forester's faithful love for her—although their names of course predict their final union. In the final act the fickle but not unchaste coquette Dalina is matched with the boorish Rustick—both of them seeking comfort and convenience, not passion or ideal unions. Others exemplify misguided or unrequited love: the foreigner Climeana who is (by Arcadian standards) too bold in wooing Lissius, Fillis who loves Philisses faithfully but hopelessly, and Lacon who so loves Musella. Finally, there is the lone villain, Arcas, who claims to have been rejected by Musella and who takes malicious delight in crossing true love by slander.

In the fifth act Arcas sets in train Guarini-like complications but the expected marvelous escapes are contrived by human wit and natural means. Musella's mother, for "bace gaine" (V.14), arranges her daughter's immediate marriage to Rustick, spurred on by Arcas's slanders about her wanton pursuit of Philisses. Philisses and Musella go to the Temple of Love to pray; they are about to stab themselves in a mutual suicide pact when Silvesta persuades them to die by poison instead of knives and offers them a potion which (apparently) causes their death. Simenea and Silvesta report all this to the rest of the troop, who then repair to Love's Temple, where Venus's priests condemn Silvesta to be burned at the stake. But the Forester offers himself in her stead and (as in Guarini) this substitution must be accepted. Rustick then formally disclaims all right in Musella, and her mother repents the hasty wedding arrangements. At this point the potion wears off, the seeming dead are called forth by Venus and her priests, Silvesta promises to love the Forester (whether other than chastely is left unclear), Rustick matches with the fickle Dalina, and Arcas is punished by public shame.

Love's Victory is marked by conceptual and structural innovations which register an implicit feminist politics. As Richard Cody observes, the genre usually expresses a very different ethos: "The pastoral is as much a man's world as the heroic. Nymph and shepherdess are not personalities but images of women."[28] Wroth, however, emphasizes female agency throughout. In the supernatural realm, Venus, not Cupid, is the dominant presence. Tasso's prologue has Cupid (escaped from Venus) claiming credit for the love complications, whereas in Wroth Venus masterminds the entire enterprise. In the prologue she sends Cupid to foment trials and troubles so as to subject all these lovers more completely to love's power and he agrees to serve "your will and minde" (I.31). At the end of Act I she complains that he still spares half the lovers — "I wowld have all to waile, and all to weepe" (387) — and he promises to effect that, and thereby to do her honor. At the end of Act II, Venus and Cupid appear together in glory, as in a Triumph. At the end of Act III, Cupid brags of his conquests, but Venus is still unsatisfied — "Tis pretty, butt tis nott enough; some are / To slightly wounded" (355–56) — and Cupid promises to cause the lovers still more grief. At the end of Act IV Venus pities the now-humble lovers and (with her priests) urges Cupid to cease the torments. But now Cupid resists, determined to inflict more pain on some before saving them. It is probably significant that when Cupid departs from the sway of

Venus's wishes the Guarini-like complications come into play: Arcas's treachery, the apparent suicide, the threat of a burning at the stake.

At the end of Act V Venus again takes firm charge, managing the entire resolution. She accepts the Forester's offer to die for Silvesta; she claims that the "resurrection" of the lovers was "my deed, / Who could nott suffer your deere harts to bleed"; she terms Silvesta "my instrument ordain'd / To kill, and save her friends" (V.487–88); and she directs her priests to celebrate these events with joyful songs. At the very end Cupid asks her to pass judgment on Arcas and she does so, imposing what he sees as a sentence worse than death — to live on in this society bearing the marks of shame, infamy, and a gnawing conscience.

The emphasis on female agency is also evident in the human sphere. As Musella's father is dead her mother is the familial authority who decides when to enforce the marriage arrangement with Rustick. Moreover, it is chiefly the women who act to resolve problems and to foster friendships and community. To be sure, most of the Arcadian shepherds, male and female, do the offices of friendship for each other — proffering aid and good advice in the tribulations of love, generously giving way to others' better love claims, maintaining friendship despite rivalries in love. They are committed to the principle Philisses enunciates: "Yett when the paine is greatest, 'tis some ease / To lett a freind partake his freind's disease" (I.295–96). Only a few are excluded from this noble ethos: the villain Arcas, and to a lesser degree the insensitive farmer Rustick and the foreigner Climeana, who boldly pursues Lissius despite the better claims of her friend Simeana. Nevertheless, the women's actions and values are dominant and decisive. They are so also in the *Urania* where, as Naomi Miller has shown, values of community and human relationships are central and are promoted chiefly by women.[29]

Male friendship is important in *Love's Victory*, but is somewhat more exclusive in its objects and more limited in its scope than female friendship. Philisses and Lissius are a typical pair of male friends, rather like Pyrocles and Musidorus in the *Arcadia*. Believing that his beloved Musella loves Lissius, Philisses tries to hide the cause of his pain from his friend and relinquish his own claims. Lissius at length prevails in his repeated appeals to their bond of friendship (II.251–310) and their shared confidences result in mutual help: Lissius reveals his new-found love for

Philisses's sister Simeana and encourages Philisses to declare his love openly to Musella; Philisses in turn pledges his good offices with his sister. But other male friendships are less profound. Lissius listens to the Forester's complaint that his beloved Silvesta has withdrawn to the woods after being rejected by Philisses, but these friends are so at odds about love philosophy that their exchange of advice is unhelpful. Lissius — as yet untouched by and scornful of love and women — urges the pursuit of sexual pleasure; the Forester is as yet a strict Neoplatonist who desires to love Silvesta "in truest kind" (I.261), simply in the chaste beholding of her. Rustick also invites but cannot gain love confidences from Philisses, because of the wide abyss in sensibility between them.

The principal female characters are more nearly agreed on the nature and claims of love, more unstinting in the offices of friendship to both women and men, and more active in problem-solving for themselves and each other. Silvesta is the most eminent exemplar of all these traits. Conquering her unrequited love for Philisses by embracing a life devoted to chastity and the chase, she rejoices in her new freedom and independence; she also remains a true friend to both Philisses and Musella. When Musella at length confides her love for Philisses and his failure to declare himself to her, Silvesta finds a solution, hiding Musella where she will hear Philisses's plaints and can respond, reassuring him of her love. Later, Silvesta puts herself at risk of death to rescue them. When she hears of the impending marriage to Rustick, she immediately declares, "It showld nott bee, nor shall bee; noe, noe, / Ill rescue her, or for her sake will dy" (V.176–78). When she offers them the supposed poison draft Philisses praises her as the embodiment of noble friendship:

> Freindship, what greater blessing then thou art,
> Can once desend into a mortall hart.
> Silvesta, freind and priest doth now apeere,
> And as our loves, lett this thy deed shine cleere. (V.250–53)

Venus grants "immortall fame" (V.493) to her deed of friendship, and Musella declares, "in you only was true freindship found" (V.506). At the end, when the Forester matches Silvesta's self-sacrifice by his own offer to die in her stead, she recognizes him as her true soul-mate and offers him her chaste love. Though Venus used her as instrument, Silvesta herself produced the happy resolution — not by magical or supernatural powers (like Fletcher's chaste shepherdess, Clorin), but by her wit, her skill in potions, and her high ideal of friendship.

The other women are also active in their own and their friends' troubles. The coquette Dalina is Simeana's first confidante, advising her not to be won too soon by lovers' protestations. But when they overhear Lissius complain of his love miseries, she counsels pity and a trial of his affections—advice Simeana promptly acts on. Musella is friend and confidante to men and women alike—Lissius, Fillis, Simeana, even Rustick—and is always ready with good sense, warm sympathy, and useful advice. Her most notable accomplishment is the reuniting of Lissius and Simeana, parted by Arcas's slanderous tales about Lissius's infidelity. She first extracts Lissius's story of Simeana's unaccountable scorn and unjust accusations; then she answers all Simeana's jealous charges with cool reason, urging her to overcome "this vild humour of bace jealousie, / Which breedeth nothing butt self misery" (IV.262–63), and to ask pardon of Lissius. At length the ecstatic, reunited lovers praise her as "sole restorer of this joy" (IV.330).

Acting in her own affairs Musella is not always so wise, and she has need of her friends' help. She was arguably too discreet in hiding her love for Philisses, and she clearly misjudged his feelings for her. But she insists on taking responsibility for her choices and actions, despite the power of social constraints and the tyranny of Cupid. Distraught at the news that she must marry Rustick at once, Musella is aided by Simeana's counsels of patience to think through her duties and her options. She sees herself bound by the will of her father who arranged the marriage, and by her mother's commands, "beeing in her hands" (V.45). At length, however, she identifies as the principal bond her own formal consent to that contract, given when she despaired of Philisses's love. Accepting this responsibility empowers her to act: she immediately proposes a visit to the Temple of Venus, where the lovers will either find some means for their union, or die together.

Wroth's representation of a tight-knit, non-hierarchical community linked by bonds of friendship and love is aided by certain structural innovations, the most important of which reaches back to the origins of the genre in pastoral eclogue. Each of the first four acts has at its structural center an eclogue-like game or contest which several members of the community (sometimes called the "troop," or the "flock") play when they withdraw at noon into a shady grove. Even here, female agency is underscored, as in each case Dalina initiates the discussion about game-playing.[30] Each exercise comments on the nature and circumstances of the participants, thereby highlighting thematic and plot issues as well as enhancing the drama's lyrical quality.

In Act I, the game is that most eclogic of activities, a singing match in which the characters sing of their own love experiences. Climeana breaks through the initial impasse over choice of game by singing a love complaint of her wandering eyes and heart; Philisses and Musella propose themselves as judges since they do not have glad hearts for song; Rustick sings a comic blazon of Musella, comparing her parts to farmyard animals and crops; and Lacon sings of initiation into love by Cupid's dart and beauty's sight.

The game in Act II (proposed by Arcas) is fortune-telling: and the characters' chosen fortunes closely anticipate their own futures. Rustick extends the book of fortunes first to Musella, hinting his claim on her: "What shalbee you need nott feare, / Rustick doth thy fortune beare" (II.150–51). Her fortune, read out by Philisses, affirms that though her patience will be much tried, "Fortune can nott cross your will" (161). Philisses's fortune, read out by Dalina, promises that he will suffer much but then obtain his bliss (179). Dalina's lot predicts that her choices in love have and will conform to her nature: "Fickle people, fickly chuse, / Slightly like, and soe refuse" (II.194–95).

In Act III the game, played only by women, is confessions of past loves and passions. Dalina recounts her former coquetry: many lovers wooed her, but she was too fickle to choose any of them, so all at length abandoned her; she now terms that behavior youthful folly and determines to accept the next man who offers. Simeana, without identifying the man, tells of her constancy despite rejection, and her tentative hopes. Fillis follows with her tale of unrequited love for Philisses. Finally, Climeana tells of leaving home and country for a lover who then rejected her; and of her new love for Lissius. A love-debate follows, in which Simeana challenges Climeana's claims and charges her with inconstancy and folly but accepts the love contest with good grace: "But take your course, and win him if you can" (245).

The game in Act IV is riddles, which the characters decide not to expound: in each case they allude to the nature and circumstances of the speaker. Musella begins with a riddle about shunning what is easy but does not please (Rustick) and desiring what can only be gained without pain (Philisses). Dalina's riddle is about seeking what she cannot find in herself (constancy). Philisses riddles about a star whose light he thought to be his own (Musella) and which though clouded is still visible. Rustick betrays his bluntness by repudiating the pastoral wit game altogether and insisting on the superiority of his low georgic interests and talents:

> Truly, I can nott ridle, I 'was not taught
> Thes tricks of witt; my thoughts ne're higher wrought
> Then how to marck a beast, or drive a cowe
> To feed, or els with art to hold a plowe,
> Which if you knew, you surely soone would find
> A matter of more worth then thes od things,
> Which never profitt, butt some laughter brings.
> Thes others bee of body, and of mind. (IV.391–98)

Lissius follows with a riddle alluding to a fog (jealousy) and an unwanted light (Climeana), then two suns (himself and Simeana) who "without envy hold each deere" (424). Fillis's riddle alludes to her disappointment (over Philisses's love) in spring, summer, and autumn.

In Act V the communal dimension is heightened by another structural change. Generic convention calls for the final resolutions—the wonderful escapes of the lovers from danger and their reunion—to be narrated, in the classical manner, rather than represented. Wroth partly follows this convention as the narratives of Simeana and Silvesta report Musella's impending marriage, the suicide attempt in the Temple, Sylvesta's potion, and the lovers' "death." But she adds to this a more dramatic resolution scene with all the company assembled in the Temple of Venus—a scene which opens out to a Kommos-like finale. Here in sight of all, the supposedly dead lovers arise, all pairs of lovers are properly matched, true friendship is honored, and villainy is punished by public shame.

Seen in its generic context Wroth's drama is conceptually and structurally innovative, and often stylistically charming, especially when we imagine (as I think we should) a performance in which the pervasive songs and choruses are set to music. The dialogue, rendered in heroic couplets whose rhymes are neither forced nor obvious, is usually natural and easy. It also manages nice distinctions — as in the following exchange which catches the accents of Lissius's early cynicism:

> Musella   Lissius, I hope this sight doth somthing move
>   In you to pitty soe much constant love.
> Lissius   Yes, thus itt moves, that man showld bee soe fond,
>   As to bee tide t'a woman's faithles bond.
>   For wee showld women love butt as owr sheep
>   Who beeing kind and gentle gives us ease,
>   But cross, or strying, stuborne, and unmeeke,
>   Shun'd as the wulf, which most owr flocks disease. (II.63–70)

Or this exchange, which reflects Rustick's lowness of mind in his low diction, and the power of Philisses's passion in his high rhetoric:

> Philisses   Rustick, faith tell mee, hast thou ever lov'd?
> Rustick   What call you love? I'have bin to trouble mov'd
>   As when my best cloke hath by chance bin torne.
>   I have liv'd wishing till itt mended were
>   And butt soe lovers doe; nor cowld forbeare
>   To cry if I my bag, or bottle lost,
>   As lovers doe who by theyr loves are crost,
>   And grieve as much for thes, as they for scorne.
> Philisses   Call you this love? Why love is noe such thing,
>   Love is a paine which yett doth pleasure bring
>   A passion which alone in harts doe move
>   And they that feele nott this they cannott love.
>   'Twill make one joyfull, merry, pleasant, sad,
>   Cry, weepe, sigh, fast, mourne, nay somtims stark mad. (II.85–98)

Woven into the texture of the heroic couplet dialogue are several generic set-pieces, often with their own distinctive metrical patterns. The hymns of Venus's priests (II.311–42), the prayers of Musella and Philisses to Venus and Cupid (V.188–225), the chant-like fortunes and riddles of Acts II and IV, Philisses's song celebrating Reason guiding Love (II.213–24), and Lacon's love complaint (I.358–74) are all in ocosyllabic couplets. Other set-pieces include the little autobiographical narratives of Act III followed by the love debate between Simeana and Climeana. Scattered throughout are also several kinds of love songs in many different stanzaic patterns: Philisses's love complaint (I.38–62); Lissius's spring song (I.75–80, 85–90); the Forester's complaint-sonnet (I.185–98); Climeana's love complaint (I.311–22); Rustick's comic blazon of Musella (I.335–52); Lissius's song defying Cupid (II.79–85); the para-

gone of Chastity and Love spoken by Silvesta and Musella (III.1–24);
the spring/winter duet of Lissius and Simeana (IV.153–58). This variety
is somewhat reminiscent of Mary Sidney's stanzaic experimentation in
her Psalm versions, and seems clearly meant to display Wroth's technical
skill. We can sample this variety in the following three extracts:

1. CLIMEANA'S LOVE LAMENT

> O mine eyes, why doe you lead
> My poore hart thus forth to rang
> From the wounted course, to strange
> Unknowne ways, and pathes to tread?
> Lett itt home returne againe,
> Free, untouch'd of gadding thought,
> And your forces back bee brought
> To the ridding of my paine.
> Butt mine eyes if you deny
> This small favor to my hart,
> And will force my thoughts to fly
> Know yett you governe butt your part (I.311–22)

2. THE SILVESTA-MUSELLA PARAGONE
   OF CHASTITY AND LOVE

Silvesta   Silent Woods with desart's shade,
                    Giving peace.
              Where all pleasures first ar made
                    To increase.
              Give you favor to my mone
              Now my loving time is gone.
              Chastity my pleasure is.
                    Folly fled
              From hence, now I seeke my blis.
                    Cross love dead,
            In your shadowes I repose
            You then love I rather chose.

Musella   Choice ill made were better left,
                    Being cross.
   Of such choice to bee bereft
                    Were no loss.

Chastitie, you thus commend,
Doth proceed butt from love's end.
And if Love the fountaine was
                    Of your fire,
Love must chastitie surpass
                    In desire.
Love lost bred your chastest thought,
Chastitie by love is wrought (III.1–24)

3. THE LISSIUS/SIMEANA DUET

Love's beginning like the spring,
Gives delight in sweetnes flowing.
Ever pleasant flourishing,
Pride in her brave colors showing.
But love ending is att last
Like the storms of winter's blast (IV.153–59).

What of the political resonance of this pastoral tragicomedy? Wroth's drama may well allude to particular court personages (as does her *Urania*); it probably does figure in some way her own relations with Sir Robert Wroth and Pembroke (and possibly alludes to Philip Sidney and Penelope Rich); but that must be explored in future research. Some connection between Rustick and Sir Robert Wroth is strengthened by Jonson's verse epistle which characterizes him as wholly devoted to country affairs (hunting, hawking, husbandry, sheep, rude country festivals), repudiating such court activities as feasting, masquing, arms, and office-seeking.[31] That portrait is encomiastic, but Jonson later (1619) uses the common pun on Wroth/worth to intimate that his nature is somehow base: "My lord Lisle's daughter, my Lady Wroth, is unworthily married on a jealous husband."[32] Through the portrait of Rustick, Mary Wroth aligns herself firmly with the myth and some of the values of Stuart court pastoral (love, leisure, harmonious community, wit, artful play) in opposition to the plain "country" values often invoked to criticize court extravagance and license.

More importantly, however, Wroth's pastoral drama subverts the patriarchal ideology of the Jacobean court. Her generic alterations evidence a sophisticated knowledge of literary tradition and appear to be used deliberately, to develop an implicit feminist politics which emphasizes a non-hierarchical community, female and cross-gender friendships, and especially female agency in the roles of Venus, Silvesta, Musella, and even Dalina. This female agency is pervasive and positive, not diluted by gestures of containment or critique, a clear challenge to both generic and cultural norms.

Attention to genre affords us some access both to the literary values and the political resonances of this newly discovered and obviously uncanonical work. It invites further speculation about the attraction of pastoral for women writers and readers. And it exemplifies the usefulness of contextualizing such "new" women's texts in literary as well as historical terms.

NOTES

1. All references in text and notes are to act and line number in Brennan's edition.
2. The Huntington manuscript (HM 600) is incomplete, lacking a title page and several passages included in the Penshurst ms.: the beginning exchange between Venus and Cupid (I.1–38) and most of Act V (68–74, 76, 103–end). Brennan, pp. 17–20, concludes that it represents an intermediate stage of composition and is itself the supposedly missing Plymouth Manuscript from which James O. Halliwell published some extracts, in *A Brief Description of the Ancient and Modern Manuscripts Preserved in the Public Library Plymouth* (1853), pp. 212–36. The Penshurst manuscript is complete except for the song of Venus's priests and all the shepherds at the end of Act V.
3. Roberts, *Poems*, p. 38; Brennan, p. 22; see also Margaret [Witten-Hannah] McLaren, "An Unknown Continent: Lady Mary Wroth's Forgotten Pastoral Drama, 'Loves Victorie,'" in *The Renaissance Englishwoman in Print: Counterbalancing the Canon*, ed. Anne M. Haselkorn and Betty S. Travitsky (Amherst: University of Massachusetts Press, 1990), p. 284.
4. That Wroth took an interest in such performances is suggested by the fact that Jonson identified her as a performer in his lost pastoral, *The May Lord*, cast chiefly by the Sidney-Herbert family and faction: "He hath a pastoral entitled *The May Lord*. His own name is Alkin, Ethra the Countess of Bedford's, Mogibell Overbury, the Old Countess of Suffolk an enchantress, other names are given to Somerset's lady, Pembroke, the Countess of Rutland, Lady Wroth." *Conversations with William Drummond of Hawthornden* (1619), *Ben Jonson: The Complete Poems*, ed. George Parfitt (New Haven, Conn.: Yale University Press, 1975), pp. 471–72.
5. McLaren, "An Unknown Continent," pp. 276–94. Lacking access to the complete manuscript, the author cannot take account of the ending, which emphasizes female power rather than powerlessness.

6. Carolyn Ruth Swift, "Feminine Self-Definition in Lady Mary Wroth's *Loves Victorie* (c. 1621)," *English Literary Renaissance* 19 (1989), 171–88.

7. I am grateful to Josephine Roberts for supplying me a typescript of the relevant portions of the manuscript continuation of *Urania*. In the drama the brother is identified as Philisses, in evident allusion to the name under which Sidney shadowed himself in the Eclogues to the *Arcadia*, Philisides.

8. The kinds were: "narrative," in which the poet alone speaks; dramatic, in which the characters alone speak (comedy and tragedy); and mixed, combining the two (Homer's epics). A few Renaissance theorists, notably Minturno, transform the classical triad into something closer to the modern foundation genres — narrative, dramatic, lyric (*L'arte poetica*, Venice 1563 [1564]), p. 3.)

9. In such schemes the major classes of poetry and prose — Quintilian lists epic, lyric, iambic, satire, tragedy, Old Comedy, New Comedy, history, philosophy, and oratory — are defined chiefly by canonical lists of writers. For discussion of this system see James J. Donohue, *The Theory of Literary Kinds: Ancient Classifications of Literature* (Dubuque: Loras College Press 1943); *The Theory of Literary Kinds: The Ancient Classes of Poetry* (Dubuque: Loras College Press, 1949).

10. [George] Puttenham, *The Arte of English Poesie* (London, 1589). Puttenham's system is derived in part from the most important Renaissance genre theorist, Julius-Caesar Scaliger, *Poetices libri septem* (Geneva, 1561), who classifies literally hundreds of historical kinds: divine hymn, ode, epic, philosophical poem, tragedy, eclogue, obsequy or funeral elegy, epigram, etc.

11. The pastoral eclogue had also divided into subgenres, identifiable by subject matter and topics: Sannazaro's piscatory eclogues, E.K.'s differentiation of plaintive, recreative, and moral eclogues in Spenser's *Shepheardes Calendar*. For a useful discussion of genre, mode, and subgenre, see Alastair Fowler, *Kinds of Literature: An Introduction to the Theory of Genres and Modes* (Cambridge: Harvard University Press, 1982).

12. Sir Philip Sidney, *The Defence of Poesie* (London, 1595), sigs. E3v–E4. Sidney derived his eight major "parts, kindes, or species" of poetry from the Alexandrian tradition — "*Heroick, Lyrick, Tragick, Comick, Satyrick, Iambick, Elegiack, Pastorall*, and certaine others" — but he described them by adjectival, modal qualities of tone, attitude, and effect rather than meter or form — the "lamenting Elegiack," the "bitter but wholesome Iambick" (sig. E4).

13. See, e.g., Louis Adrian Montrose, "Of Gentlemen and Shepherds: The Politics of Elizabethan Pastoral Form," *English Literary History*, 50 (1983), 415–59, and Montrose, "'Eliza, Queene of shepheardes,' and the Pastoral of Power," *English Literary Renaissance*, 10 (1980), 153–82; Stephen Orgel, *The Illusion of Power: Political Theater in the English Renaissance* (Berkeley & Los Angeles: University of California Press, 1975); Annabel Patterson, *Pastoral and Ideology: Virgil to Valery* (Berkeley & Los Angeles: University of California Press, 1987), esp. pp. 60–163.

14. At the court of the Estensi in Ferrara a series of literary works gave impetus to the development of pastoral drama: Giraldi Cinthio's *Egle* (1545), Agostino de Beccari's *Il sacrificio* (1554), Alberto Lollio's *Aretusa* (1563), and Argenti's *Lo sfortunato* (1567) point the way toward the full realization of the form in Tasso's *Aminta*. See discussion in W.W. Greg, *Pastoral Poetry and Pastoral Drama* (London: H.H. Bullen, 1906), pp. 153–76.

15. Jason de Nores attacked the tragicomedies of Tasso and Guarini in *Discorso intorno . . . che la commedia, la tragedia, et il poema eroica* (1587), and *Apologia contra l'auttor del Verato* (1590), as did others. See the account of the controversy in Bernard Weinberg, *A History of Literary Criticism in the Italian Renaissance*, 2 vols. (Chicago: University of Chicago Press, 1961), vol. 2, pp. 1074–1105.

16. Italian defenses of tragicomedy include: Cecchi, Prologue, *La Romanesca* (1554); Torquato Tasso, *Discoursi del poema heroico* (Naples [1587]); Battista Guarini, *Il Verato* (Ferrara, 1588), *Il Verato secondo* (Florence, 1593), and *Il Compendio della poesia tragicomica* (Venice, 1599).

17. Trans. and ed. Allan H. Gilbert, *Literary Criticism: Plato to Dryden* (Detroit: Wayne State University Press, 1962), pp. 511, 524.

18. "To the Reader," *The Faithful Shepherdess by John Fletcher: A Critical Edition*, ed. Florence A. Kirk (New York & London: Garland, 1980), pp. 15–16.

19. Hans Robert Jauss, "Literary History as a Challenge to Literary Theory," trans. Elizabeth Bensinger, *New Literary History* 2 (1970–71), 7–37.

20. The *Aminta* was first acted on July 31, 1573, and repeated at the Carnival in Pesaro in 1574, at the request of Lucrezia d'Este. The first edition (Cremona, 1580) lacked the choruses and epilogue; they first appeared complete in the Venice, 1590 edition. It was soon translated into French, German, English, Spanish.

21. See discussion in Greg, *Pastoral Poetry*, pp. 176–94; and "Introduction," *Torquato Tasso's Aminta Englisht*, trans. Henry Reynolds (1628), ed. Clifford Davidson (Fennimore, Wisconsin: John Westburg, 1972). Some critics think Tasso may also shadow his hopeless passion for Leonora D'Este in the characters of Aminta and Silvia.

22. The prologue was written for a performance at Turin, celebrating the marriage of Carlo Emanuele I, Duke of Savoy, to Catherine of Austria, daughter of Philip II of Spain, in 1585; there is some doubt whether this performance actually took place. The first performance which can be established was at Crema in 1596. At Mantua, in November 1598, Duke Vincenzo Gonzaga sponsored a very lavish production. The lavish (20th) edition (Venice, 1602) contained illustrations and notes, together with a treatise on tragicomedy.

23. The English translation (London, 1602) was by an anonymous relative of Daniel's friend and traveling companion, Sir Edward Dymocke; it was much condensed from the original and often inaccurate. Daniel, at one time tutor to the young William Herbert, became masque-writer and groom of the chamber to Queen Anne, and licenser to the Children of the Queen's Revels. See "Introduction," Wilter F. Staton, Jr., and William E. Simeone, eds., *A Critical Edition of Sir Richard Fanshawe's 1647 Translation of Giovanni Battista Guarini's Il Pastor Fido* (Oxford: Clarendon, 1964).

24. The first edition was *The Queenes Arcadia. A Pastorall Trage-Comedie Presented to her Majestie and her Ladies, by the Universitie of Oxford in Christs Church, in August last. 1605* (London, 1606). The work was reprinted in Daniel's *Certaine Small Workes* in 1607, 1609, and 1611, and independently in 1623. The fact that Wroth danced in the Queen's Twelfth-Night masque of 1605 places her among the Queen's inner circle of attendants in that year; she might have been one of the (unnamed) ladies who visited Oxford with the Queen in August.

25. Early in 1605 Daniel was summoned before the Privy Council on suspicion that
     his play *Philotas*, performed and published in 1605, alluded to the Essex rebellion.
     It is not surprising, then, that he strongly denies any reflections here on crowns
     and states—though in terms that themselves invite such comparison:

> And living here under the awfull hand
> Of discipline, and strict observancy,
> Learne but our weakenesses to understand,
> And therefore dare not enterprize to show
> In lowder stile the hidden mysteries,
> And arts of Thrones; which none that are below
> The Sphere of action, and the exercise
> Of power can truely shew.
>
> . . . .
>
> And therefore in the view of state t'have show'd
> A counterfeit of state, had beene to light
> A candle to the Sunne, and so bestow'd
> Our paines to bring our dimnesse unto light.
> For majesty, and power, can nothing see
> Without itselfe, that can sight-worthy be.

26. The play was produced about 1608–1609, probably at Blackfriars, since Jonson's
     commendatory poem refers to a sixpence entrance fee. All the commendatory
     poems by Jonson, Beaumont, and Chapman speak of the play's failure, as does
     Fletcher himself in dedicating the published version to Sir William Aston (II.
     2–3), *The Faithfull Shepheardesse* (London [1610]). It was revived as a Twelfth-
     Night play at court in 1633.

27. *Hymens Triumph. A Pastoral Tragicomaedie Presented at the Queenes Court in the
     Strand at her Majesties magnificent entertainment of the Kings most excellent Majestie,
     being at the Nuptials of the Lord Roxborough* (London, 1615).

28. Richard Cody, *The Landscape of the Mind* (Oxford: Clarendon, 1969), p. 54.

29. Naomi Miller, "'Not much to be marked': Narrative of the Woman's Part in
     Lady Mary Wroth's *Urania*," *Studies in English Literature* 29 (1989), pp. 121–37.

30. Dalina: "Now we are mett, what sport shall we invent / While the sun's fury
     somewhat more bee spent?" (I.300–301); "Mee thinks wee now to silent ar, lett's
     play / Att something while we yett have pleasing day" (II.1–2); "Now w'are
     alone lett every one confess / Truly to other what our lucks have bin, / How
     often lik'd, and lov'd and soe express / Our passions past" (III.125–28); "Heere
     bee owr fellows, now lett us beegin / Some pretty pastime pleasure's sport to
     winn" (IV.351–52).

31. "To Sir Robert Wroth," *The Forest* (#3), in Jonson's *Works* (London, 1616).

32. In his *Conversations with Drummond*, Parfitt, p. 470.

"The Knott Never to Bee Untide": The Controversy Regarding Marriage in Mary Wroth's *Urania*

Josephine A. Roberts

[Marriage] is, of all transactions, the one in which people expect most from others, and are least honest themselves.

Jane Austen, *Mansfield Park*

I

One of the most tangible indicators of a transition in the seventeenth-century ideology of marriage is the debate over the so-called "rule of thumb," in which common law granted a husband the right to batter his wife with a rod no bigger than his thumb. Writing from the 1580s to the 1620s, many Puritan divines called for a gentler means of admonishment that would replace the practice of wife-beating and offered a vision of matrimony as a holy and blessed order.[1] In sermon after sermon, the preachers celebrated a model of marriage as loving partnership and stressed its superiority over the medieval ideal of celibacy. Yet the Puritan assertion of a spiritual equality between men and women coexisted uneasily with a fervent insistence on the absolute, patriarchal authority of husband over wife. In fact, the two conflicting claims of mutuality and patriarchy often occur within the same text. It is by no means clear that the Puritan thinkers were aware of the extent to which their emerging theory of marriage was fraught with contradiction, but it is certain that their sermons and tracts bring into sharp focus the complicated blend of power and subordination that characterized the role of women.[2]

One example is William Heale's *Apologie for Women* (1609), a work written in opposition to William Gager's claim that since wives were worthless and ignorant they deserved harsh punishment. Heale begins by demonstrating that wife-beating violates the true spirit of civil law, the law of God, and the law of Nature. Yet by the middle of his tract, Heale appears to shift gears when he insists upon the various means of correction that husbands may in good conscience use against their wives. He then analyzes the faults of women according to three categories and specifies punishments appropriate to each (with no corresponding attention to male failings). Curiously, at the end of his work, Heale changes perspective once more, this time to offer his own version of the creation myth, with the female as a higher being who enhances and completes the male. Amidst the constantly shifting grounds of his argument, Heale appears oblivious to the collision of conflicting claims; he ends with a paradisal vision of a temple of love in which men and women will coexist in harmony.[3]

If Heale failed to perceive the contradictions, there were other writers of the period, especially playwrights, whose work explored the startling opposition between the rising expectations concerning the role women might play and their subordinate status within the household. Feminist critics of Shakespeare's plays have demonstrated particularly the extent to which the drama served as an arena to debate the changing concepts of marriage.[4] In juxtaposing the plays and their social context, these scholars have recognized the difficulty of discussing women's actual status in marriage because of the absence of eyewitness testimony from women themselves.

Some evidence of women's role in marriage comes from the recent work of social historians, who have attempted to reconstruct the development of the institution through demographic studies of marital patterns and illegitimacy rates, such as pioneered by the work of the Cambridge Group for the History of Population and Social Structures, led by Peter Laslett. Other historians, most prominently Lawrence Stone, have traced the evolution of marital patterns over several centuries to show how the companionate model gradually replaced the concept of the arranged marriage. Critics of Stone's work have pointed out that although he assumes women largely accepted and complied with the institutions, he includes little proof of women's views to support his claims. On the other hand, his opponents admit the difficulty of finding such evidence, especially for the pre–Civil War period.[5]

Perhaps one of the most extensive sources that has yet to be explored is Mary Wroth's vast encyclopedic romance, *Urania*, which depicts a variety of different marital contracts, from the traditional, parentally arranged union to the most clandestine spousals. Wroth offers more than merely a panoramic view of aristocratic marital practices, for she explores the genesis and nature of interpersonal commitment: she questions how, when, and even whether women should enter into exclusively monogamous relationships and how widely such unions need to be acknowledged. *Urania* provides a unique opportunity to study the fictional representation of social institutions during a transitional period in which women's expectations of marriage were rising at a time when their personal freedoms were being held in check.

First, it is necessary to admit that Wroth belonged to an educated, aristocratic elite, and that it is difficult to generalize about the marriage patterns of vastly different social classes. Even among the richest aristocracy, historians have uncovered "a persisting variety of co-existing practises." The arranged marriage, negotiated by parents and friends, was certainly typical of the wealthiest class, which had the most at stake with regard to property and finances. But some members of the upper ranks, such as younger sons, were left relatively free to choose their own marriage partners, and parents varied in their power and willingness to dictate their children's matches.[6] Indeed, the doctrine of parental control showed some weakening in the late sixteenth and early seventeenth centuries, as evidenced by King James's declaration that "parents may forbid their Children an unfitt Marriage, but they may not force their Consciences to a fitt."[7]

The tale of Limena, the first of the interwoven narratives of *Urania*, spotlights the terrible price of obedience to parental authority in the case of a woman who reluctantly agrees to wed a man "her heart so much detested; loathing almost it selfe, for consenting in shew to that which was most contrarie to it selfe" (5). Despite her attachment to Perissus, she "esteem[s] obedience beyond all passions" and marries her father's choice, Philargus, who is an overbearing, jealous man, interested only in possessing his wife "like a Diamond in a rotten box" (7). When Philargus begins to suspect that Limena still loves Perissus, he becomes consumed with jealousy, as his very name suggests (Phil-argus, referring to the many-eyed guardian of Io in Ovid's *Metamorphoses*). Limena defends herself on the grounds that her love for Perissus existed before she even met her husband and that she has always behaved "in a vertuous, and religious fashion" (10). But her husband threatens to kill her in order to extinguish her love, and he conducts a series of tortures — beatings, pinching with irons, and a flaming funeral pyre — to break her will. Limena herself points out that "threatnings are but meanes to strengthen free and pure hearts against the threatners" (10). She succeeds in withstanding the physical and mental abuse of her husband, who on his deathbed belatedly repents of the cruelty that he has shown his wife. Limena's faithful love receives its reward when she at last marries her own choice, Perissus, in a celebrated state wedding (72).

Theoretically, even if aristocratic children began to acquire the power of veto, in actual practice the most severe parental pressure might be exercised on daughters, who often had little alternative to obedience, since spinsterhood was generally less appealing than an unwanted husband. *Urania* is filled with examples of aristocratic women who are the victims of enforced marriages, in which they do not have even the option of refusal. In fact, Wroth paints a very bleak picture of the means — verbal threats, psychological manipulation, and physical coercion — which fathers might use to achieve their daughters' consent. The tale of Limena is emblematic because it sets in opposition the arranged marriage (initiated and enforced by patriarchal authority) with the companionate marriage (undertaken by the mutual consent of the couple) Although showing the eventual triumph of one union over the other, the tale emphasizes the sensational suffering that a woman must undergo in order to have her own choice.

Wroth assembles a variety of different stories which follow the same basic pattern initiated by the tale of Limena. For example, Bellamira reluctantly agrees to marry a nobleman, Treborius, chosen by her parents, even though she is already in love with someone else: "contrary to my soule I gave my selfe to him, my heart to my first love. Thus more then equally did I devide my selfe" (334). Although she escapes domestic violence, she must deal with the psychological strain of concealing her true feelings from those closest to her; unlike Limena, she fails to secure a happy resolution even after the death of her husband (334), but she does maintain her loyalty to her first love. Other similar tales include those of Melasinda, Queen of Hungary, who is constrained by her court council and people to marry Rodolindus in order to preserve peace within her country at the expense of her private happiness (64), and of Lisia, whose parents marry her to a great Lord, but "so dull a piece of flesh, as this or any Country need know" (274).

One of the most fully developed of the tales of enforced marriage is that of Lady Pastora, who is "married to a Knight, but her affections were wedded to her owne choyce" (357). Her beloved is also married to someone else, and the narrator justifies their adultery on the grounds that "few blam'd them, but wish'd they were free, and married together" (357). Just as in the tales of Limena and Bellamira, her husband's death seems to open the possibility of happiness, but she finds herself left alone, abandoned by her first love. Lady Pastora rejects all other suitors: "What could be lost she parted from, content, quiet, honour, rest, reputation, fortunes to succeed, for no match was offered her that was not resolved of refusall, nor at last any, all agreeing her love was so fixed, as it was but vanitie to seeke to remove it" (359). Her determination to insist on her own choice, even if her love is not reciprocated, is so extreme that the narrator calls special attention to it, cautioning that "the relation so rare should have beene taken for an Allegory" (360). Indeed, the repeated pattern of a stoical feminine triumph over enforced marriage is one of the most characteristic elements of *Urania*.

Wroth also includes tales demonstrating more active resistance to parental authority, such as in the tale of Liana, who pleads with her father not to marry her against her will (207). In a dramatic dialogue, her father threatens her with loss of her inheritance, later imprisoning her for six months and torturing her with iron rods. When Liana escapes to be with her love, she discovers him in another's arms and reacts with horror at his betrayal: "Is this thy fervent love's reward? have I got the hate of my freinds, the curse of my parents, and the utter undoing of my selfe, and hopes to be requited with falsehood?" (205). Fortunately, it turns out that she has been deceived merely by appearances, and she is eventually reconciled with her true love, Alanius. The tale's emotional power lies in the moment when Liana believes that her rebellion may have led to absolute ruin as she accuses Alanius of breaking his vow: "you have cut the knot, and I left to joine the pieces againe in misfortune, and your losse of love" (211). The narrator of the tale is Urania, who strongly identifies with Liana, one of her former companions, with whom she shares a belief in the need for feminine self-determination.

While Limena's story demonstrates the risk involved with overt defiance of parental authority, Wroth also includes some tales showing the intervention of women in negotiating marriages; these are particularly prominent in the Newberry manuscript, the second, unpublished part of the *Urania*. When the King of Argos selects a husband for his daughter, her mother quickly expresses disapproval of the match, attempting to prevent it on her daughter's behalf (I.fol.32v). In a later tale, the King of Bulgaria is so proud that he believes no man is good enough for his daughter and rejects all of her potential suitors until at last a court lady intervenes to convince the father that his behavior may lead others to cast aspersions on his child, who then gains the power to make her own choice (II:fol.15). *Urania* thus shows the active involvement of women in matchmaking, a practice that was followed by some of Wroth's closest associates.[8]

Overall, *Urania* tends to highlight the most negative features of arranged marriage, particularly the extent to which consent might be derived by a variety of coercive means. On the other hand, Wroth's repeated attack against enforced marriage does not automatically mean that she approves of marital unions based exclusively on romantic attraction without regard to family, property, or rank. Throughout *Urania*, the narrator warns against "mischievous affection, that affection, mischiefes selfe" (189), which might lead women to make blind choices.

II

In *The Taming of the Shrew* Biondello humorously describes the ease with which it was possible to contract a marriage: "I knew a wench married on an afternoon as she went to the garden for parsley to stuff a rabbit" (IV.iv.99–101). Of the various types of clandestine marriage (by definition involving any irregularity in ecclesiastical law), the most extreme case is the *de praesenti* contract, which often consisted of a simple, oral pronouncement rather than a formal ceremony. As Biondello's example suggests, this type of pledge caused much confusion in seventeenth-century England over exactly what constituted a binding act of marriage. It differed from the *de futuro* contract in that it contained promises made in the present tense rather than the future and thus inaugurated an absolute union, irregular but perfectly legal, that could be broken only by death or entrance into holy orders. The intervention, sanctification, or even presence of civil or ecclesiastical authorities or witnesses was quite unnecessary. The consent of the parties was "the principal Ingredient and most essential Part" of a *de praesenti* contract, according to Henry Swinburne, whose *Treatise on Spousals* offers the most detailed contemporary account of the subject.[9]

Given these conditions, it is easy to imagine how the situation might lend itself to widespread misunderstandings and possible exploitation by either partner. Simply the tense of the verb could determine the difference between a pledge to marry and an absolute, irrevocable union. Since the *de praesenti* contract was an oral agreement, it was difficult to prove its existence in court. Martin Ingram has shown that there was a steady decline in the number of spousal suits that came before the ecclesiastical courts from the fourteenth to the seventeenth centuries. He demonstrated how the church courts gradually became more reluctant to confirm disputed marriage contracts and moved towards recognition of a church wedding as the only satisfactory guarantee of a legally acceptable marriage. By the end of the seventeenth century, the use of *de praesenti* agreements had become relatively rare, as indicated by the editor of Swinburne's *Treatise*, who wrote, "Spousals are now in great measure worn out of use".[10]

One of Wroth's first examples of *de praesenti* marriage concerns the daughter of a rich lord of Cephalonia in love with the younger brother of an Earl (who might expect greater freedom in the selection of a marriage partner than the heir to the estate). However, her parents disapprove of him because of his rank, and disregarding her prior contract, they immediately shut her up in a tower to await her marriage to the wealthy son of the Lord of Zante (34). Wroth's narrator blames the parents for exercising a "cruel & tirannical power over their children"

(35), but the daughter and her beloved outwit their designs; at the wedding feast, the bride escapes in the midst of the performance of a masque, and together they run off to a vineyard where they attempt to hide. Unfortunately, he is killed, and his bride dies two days after, "not sicke in body, but dead in heart" (36). They are buried together outside the walls of a monastery, a symbol of their unsanctified love. The tragic tale illustrates the dangers involved in *de praesenti* marriage, particularly the readiness with which others may deny its existence and validity. A contemporary handbook, *The Lawes Resolutions of Womens Rights* (1632), advises women against "secret sponsion" on the grounds that it is "so little esteemed of, (unlesse it be very manifest) that another promise publique made after it, shall be preferred and prevaile against it." The editor, T.E., warns even more strongly against elopement when he points out that a "woman in her frenzy may cut her husbands throat, and it is no forfeiture of Dower; but if she make an Elopment (which is a mad tricke), Dower is forfeited."[11]

Wroth shows how some characters sought to avoid the disadvantages of *de praesenti* marriage by arranging a private ceremony, attended by witnesses. In the Newberry manuscript the daughter of the Tartarian King falls in love with the second son of the King of Frigia, but her father adamantly opposes her union with a second son (I:fol.4). She agrees to a private wedding, held before fourteen friends and servants. Wroth's contemporaries would have described this as a clandestine marriage because it did not follow the ecclesiastical requirements of the calling of banns and the issuing of a license; the canons of 1604 further stipulated that the wedding must take place between 8 A.M. and noon in the church at the place of residence of one of the pair, although the upper classes could evade these canonical restrictions on time and place by obtaining a special license. Even if these requirements were not met, the marriage would still be upheld by the church if there were no impediments. Preachers, however, strongly advised against private ceremonies, as William Gouge argues in *Of Domesticall Duties* (1622): "Contrary are clandestine mariages, such as are made in private houses, or other secret places, or in Churches without a sufficient number of witnesses, or in the night time, or without a lawfull Minister of the word. . . . There is little hope that such mariages should have any good successe".[12] Such is the outcome of Wroth's tale, for after the daughter of the Tartarian king bears her husband two daughters, he is slain in a civil war, and she is left destitute: "I lost all my freinds for him, my owne blood hating mee to death" (I:fol.4).

One further restriction specified by the ecclesiastical canons was to forbid anyone under the age of twenty-one to marry without parental approval, although English common law did not agree in these age limitations.[13] Wroth includes a tale involving a girl of fourteen, Allarina, who falls in love, but conceals her feelings for five years, while her beloved is married to someone else. Later she contracts a *de praesenti* marriage with the young man, but he soon abandons her, and she is left without the support of family or friends: "my parents have I left, and they displeased have rated mee, for my immoderate love, and all to be requited with gaine, at last of fowle disdaine, for fervent truth?" (184). Allarina, determined to become a "vasall to Diana," takes the new name Silviana, together with a vow of chastity, and reappears much later in the *Urania* after she is reconciled to her former love. Although Pamphilia charges her with breaking her vow, she defends herself by undertaking a traditional seventeenth-century ecclesiastical wedding with all of the trimmings: crowned with roses, she is led between two brideknights to the church for solemnizing the union (410). What began as a secret *de praesenti* contract ends in a highly conventional, public ceremony.

Perhaps Wroth's most detailed account of *de praesenti* marriage occurs in the Newberry Library's soon-to-be published manuscript continuation of the romance, when the central couple, Pamphilia and Amphilanthus, exchanges vows in a private ceremony held before five witnesses: Urania, Selarina, Antissius, Allimarlus, and Polarchos (I:fol.14v). Wroth shows that the couple hastily decides to wed when Amphilanthus becomes jealous over the arrival of Rodomandro, the Tartarian king, who seems interested in courting Pamphilia. To reassure Amphilanthus of her devotion, Pamphilia agrees to exchange vows shortly before he plans to leave for Candia. The narrator makes clear that they are engaging in a *de praesenti*, rather than *de futuro*, contract because she states that the ceremony was "nott as an absolute marriage though as perfect as that, beeing onely an outward serimony of the church; this as absolute beefore God and as fast a tiing, for such a contract can nott bee broken by any lawe whatsoever" (I:fol.14v). Significantly, they do not exchange any kind of rings or tokens; in middle-class spousals, frequently the lovers would break a piece of silver, a six pence or two pence, with each keeping half.[14] Pamphilia has only Amphilanthus's word that they have knit "the knott never to bee untide" (I:fol.14v), an image used in the Protestant tracts on marriage.[15] The narrator observes that "after the Contract ther was les outward cerimony, butt more truly felt hapines then beefor" (I:fol.14v).

Pamphilia soon begins to hear rumors that Amphilanthus has betrayed her with the Queen of Candia, and she has a dream in which he is led away in black to be married (I.fol.38v). Meanwhile, the queen deceives Amphilanthus into believing that Pamphilia has been unfaithful. He at first refuses to believe the lies, maintaining that Pamphilia is "by deere affection tyed in strictest bands" (I:fol.49v), but he eventually decides to throw off "his contract" (I:fol.50). The queen urges him to wed the Slavonian king's daughter in order to strengthen his empire and enlarge it in the east, but her real motive is that she has grown bored with him: he is now "stale, and she thought fitter for marriage then to bee a servant" (I:fol.49). The wedding ceremony is itself clandestine, held in a private location without ecclesiastical sanction, and Amphilanthus sends the bride away immediately after the ceremony without consummating the marriage. When her parents begin to question the legitimacy of the proceedings (II:fol.36), Amphilanthus agrees to undergo a second wedding, which Rodomandro actually attends as one of the witnesses — a situation fraught with heavy irony (II:fol.42v).

On her own part, Pamphilia resists all thought of marrying someone else and denies Amphilanthus's accusations that she is engaged ("assured" is the seventeenth-century term) to Rodomandro (II:fol.18v). Pamphilia is very much aware that Amphilanthus has broken more than simply a promise, but she is doubtful where that leaves her. Contemporary legal authorities, such as Henry Swinburne, seem also to have found such a situation vexing and problematic. In *Of Spousals*, Swinburne specifically considers the case of a woman whose secret contract was broken when her partner publicly married another woman. He determines that the first marriage is still valid, but he is less certain about her course of action. If she attempts to recover him for her husband "but prevaileth not for want of sufficient proof, may she with safe Conscience Marry another Husband?" He answers cautiously in the affirmative: "It seemeth that she may, for having indeavoured to the utmost of her power, nor able to continue any longer; It were not only against Law, but against Reason and Equity, that she should be bound to an impossibility." Admittedly, Swinburne does consider the other alternative, that if she is subject to the man, she could be considered "bound unto him while he liveth, nor is delivered, until the Man be Dead." It is to Swinburne's credit that he does not seem to be particularly convinced by the harsher, subjugating argument because he finally affirms the woman's right to wed again. At the same time, he repeats his belief that the prior *de praesenti* contract generally takes precedence over any subsequent marriage.[16]

When Amphilanthus accuses Pamphilia of an engagement with Rodomandro, she is quick to deny it with the added claim that "noe child, especiall the female, ought to marry without the fathers consent first demaunded" (II:fol.18v). She seems to overlook the fact that she undertook her own *de praesenti* contract without her father's knowledge, but Pamphilia may also be reflecting on the rashness of her vows (and reminding Amphilanthus of the risk that she took for his sake). Significantly, in arranging her second marriage, she very carefully follows all of the proper procedures, so that Rodomandro must go to her father first to ask for his consent, which he grants, but only on the condition that it is Pamphilia's will; as Rodomandro agrees, "force can never bee companionated with love" (II:fol.21), a view that the *Urania* amply illustrates. Yet when courting Pamphilia, he makes clear that he does not expect romantic involvement; he asks only that she allow him to be her companion in solitude. He will watch her while she reads her books: "Love your booke, but love mee soe farr as that I may hold itt to you that while you peruse that, I may joye in beeholding you" (II:fol.21v). She agrees to this proposal, but the marriage is still "against her owne minde, yett nott constrain'd" (II:fol.22).[17]

Although the wedding follows the conventional forms, Pamphilia indicates her inward resistance to it through a series of conspicuous details. She wears a black dress, which she explains as a sign of mourning for her dead brother, Philarchos. Traditionally, seventeenth-century brides wore their hair down, crowned with a garland of flowers; Shakespeare refers to a "new untrimmed bride" (*King John*, III.i.209). Even

Frances Howard, divorced from Robert Devereux, third Earl of Essex, wore her hair down in token of virginity at her marriage to Robert Carr.[18] Yet Pamphilia wears her hair up, a decision that puzzles the rest of the wedding guests (II:fol.22v). At the last minute, Amphilanthus volunteers to serve in the ceremony as a bride-knight, a role typically designated for unmarried men. When he is questioned about his marital status, Amphilanthus replies that he is not married (II:fol.22v). To his mother, the Queen of Naples, Pamphilia confides that this is a blatant lie, but she permits him to accompany the rest of the party. She is somewhat awkwardly escorted by three bride-knights to "the most undesired wedding when her hart was longe beefor maried to a more beeloved creature" (II:fol.22v). In her misery, Pamphilia unburdens her heart to only one person, the Queen of Naples, for "she onely was the true secretary of her thoughts" (II:fol.23). Even though the Queen seems discreetly aware of the relationship between her son and her niece, Pamphilia still conceals from her the knowledge of their secret marriage.[19] Near the end of the Newberry manuscript the lovers are reconciled in a purely platonic relationship (II:fol.60v), but the memory of their *de praesenti* marriage is not entirely lost: Urania refers to Pamphilia as Amphilanthus's "truest wife," and she recalls how "longe beefore their harts had binn linked, nay bound together" (II:fol.51).

Significantly, Urania and Pamphilia are strongly associated as either the narrator or audience of tales concerned with secret spousals. For example, Limena tells Pamphilia a story in which she claims "you shall see your selfe truly free from such distresse, as in a perfect glasse" (189). Her tale describes how Alena gives her heart to Lincus, only to discover his repeated betrayal. She continues to love him despite his unfaithfulness, a fact that Limena emphasizes at the end of her narration: "And to satisfie you, I have given you this short example of true love, faigned I confesse the story is, yet such may be, and will be lovers Fates" (191). Pamphilia later befriends an unnamed lady who describes how she exchanged *de praesenti* vows "privately made to me, and for greater satisfaction given before witnesses for marriage" (420). Pamphilia also tells the tale of Lindamira as a mirror of her own life, a technique followed by Urania's narrative of the secret spousals of Liana, who is dressed in the habit of a shepherdess, Urania's own former disguise (205). When Lady Pastora prepares to relate her story, Steriamus sees her from afar and mistakenly thinks that she is Urania (356). The carefully defined focus on secret marriage in the tales associated with Pamphilia and Urania certainly raises the question of the extent to which they may be autobiographical.

III

Whether or not Wroth actually contracted a *de praesenti* marriage with her lover, William Herbert, third Earl of Pembroke, is very difficult to determine. The correspondence of the Sidney family indicates that Wroth had known her first cousin Pembroke from childhood and that she often stayed at Baynards Castle, the London home of the Pembrokes. As Gary Waller suggests in his essay, her father, Sir Robert Sidney, took special interest in his nephew, "young Lord Harbert," whom he viewed as an important political and financial ally. Because of Pembroke's strained relations with his own aging father, he seems to have turned to his uncle for advice on a range of matters, and their friendship continued until Sidney's death. Pembroke's younger brother, Philip, actually lived for a time in the Sidney household, and William visited three or four times a week.[20]

Dating from 1540, marriage between first cousins was technically allowable by English law, but there is not much evidence of close kinship marriages in the seventeenth century.[21] An even greater obstacle was the tremendous discrepancy in wealth between the two families. Sir Robert Sidney, who spent ten years in the service of the crown as Governor of Flushing, was perpetually in need of funds; in fact, he turned to his nephew to provide a dowry of a thousand pounds for Mary.[22] On the other hand, Pembroke's estate consisted of vast holdings of property, a fortune which his family certainly expected his marriage would enhance. Yet Pembroke himself showed considerable independence in the face of pressures to marry. As his biographers have shown, he seems to have expressed very little interest in the steady stream of potential brides which his family paraded before him from 1595 onward; the names of at least four young women appear in the surviving correspondence. Instead, he conducted his well-known affair with the courtier Mary Fitton, who bore his child. When he steadfastly refused to marry her—resisting once more the dictates of his elders—he was finally sent to Fleet Prison for a brief period in 1601.

At the death of his father, Pembroke acquired some measure of independence in negotiating his own marital situation. With the aid of his old tutor, Hugh Sanford, he began discussions with Gilbert, seventh Earl of Shrewsbury, for the hand of his eldest daughter, Mary Talbot, who was coheir with her two sisters to immense wealth. The progress of the negotiations was very slow, and the Shrewsburys doubted whether Pembroke was actually interested in the match since the prospective bridegroom devoted so much time to financial wrangling.[23] It is very possible that some of his delay may have been due to a prior love commitment to his cousin Mary, but we have no written evidence that might prove this. What we do know is that in 1603 Mary's family betrothed her to Robert Wroth, son of a wealthy Essex landowner. Sanford renewed the negotiations with the Shrewsburys in September 1603, which eventually led to Pembroke's wedding on November 4, 1604, less than three months after Mary Wroth's marriage. The proximity of dates could of course be simply coincidental, but the evidence suggests that both of these arranged marriages had unhappy beginnings. Not long after the ceremony at Penshurst, Robert Wroth met his father-in-law in London to complain about his wife's carriage towards him. In the case of Pembroke, Rowland Whyte, Sidney's confidential advisor, wrote in May 1605 to the father of the bride, the Earl of Shrewsbury, to urge him to ignore rumors: "And let me assure your Honours that my Lady Pembroke is very much respected by all her Lord's friends, she worthely deserving it. It may be the indiscretion of some that love tattling may buzz out the contrary, which occasions this protestations [sic] of mine to your Honour."[24] It is clear from the Sidney correspondence that Mary Wroth's relationship with Pembroke continued after her marriage, for he was a visitor at her home, Loughton Hall, and participated in many of the same family and court gatherings.[25]

In the end, the written records do not provide a final answer to the question of whether Wroth exchanged *de praesenti* vows with Pembroke. In *Urania* Pamphilia describes how Amphilanthus's tutor, Forsandurus (probably an anagram for Hugh Sanford), deceives both parties into believing that they have become engaged to others. Only on his deathbed does Forsandurus confess that he has been bribed by the Queen of Slavonia to marry Amphilanthus to her eldest daughter (II:fol.52v). Since Sanford played such a prominent role in arranging both of the marriages of Pembroke and Wroth, it is very possible that he could have intervened in some way to preserve what he believed were Pembroke's best interests. But it must be admitted that, of all the various tales with the greatest concentration of autobiographical detail, only Pamphilia's account in the Newberry manuscript provides a description of their *de praesenti* wedding.

It is quite conceivable that the story is pure fabrication, a fantasy designed to justify her own charges of betrayal against Pembroke. As Jane Austen acutely observed, there is a human tendency in matters of the heart to expect more from others than oneself; perhaps Wroth so strongly wished to believe in a vow of the present tense, rather than the future, that she fashioned the episode accordingly. But in the Newberry manuscript, she makes clear that Amphilanthus is not alone at fault for breaking his vow, for Pamphilia also agrees to marry someone else. The problem, then as now, is that the whole agreement depends solely upon an unwritten bond of mutual trust. Clearly, the account of the secret marriage may also be a way of claiming legitimacy for the two children Wroth bore to Pembroke after the death of her husband. She omits them from the story of Pamphilia's life, although natural sons and daughters play an important role in other tales in the Newberry manuscript.

Wroth's own arranged marriage must have provided her with ample opportunity to explore the pitfalls associated with the institution and to measure it against other alternatives. The dedicatee of the *Urania*, Susan Herbert, Countess of Montgomery (Wroth's closest friend), had her own share of experience with secret marriage. In 1601, she vowed to her uncle and guardian, Sir Robert Cecil, that contrary to rumors, "I will never match with any without your consent."[26] Yet three years later, William Herbert wrote to Shrewsbury to confess that he had just learned "after long love, and many changes, my brother on Friday last was privately contracted to my Lady Susan, without the knowledge of any of his or her friends." Despite the validity of a *de praesenti* contract, there seems to have been some pressure to hold a public church wedding to solemnize the union. The event, held December 27, 1604, was lavish, as reported by Sir Ralph Winwood, who delighted in an account of the various festivities, including the appearance of James I in the couple's bedroom the next morning: "No Ceremony was omitted of Bride-Cakes, Points, Garters, and Gloves, which have been ever since the Livery of the Court; and at Night there was sewing into the Sheet, casting off the Bride's left Hose, with many other petty Sorceries."[27] What is significant about the entire episode is the freedom with which the lady contracted herself and the fact that she seems to have cast aside concern with the financial negotiations. Her independent behavior, much like Wroth's own, suggests that she came to believe in the right to initiate her own spousals, rather than to depend upon patriarchal control.

Mary's brother Robert, the eventual heir to the Sidney estates, apparently contracted his own secret marriage with Lady Dorothy Percy, the daughter of Henry Percy, ninth Earl of Northumberland (the Wizard Earl, who was imprisoned in the Tower). She was privately married to Sidney in 1616 "without her father's knowledge," but possibly with "her mother's connivance," and the union was not publicly announced until the following year.[28] Wroth perhaps hints at the unusual circumstances in her account of Rosindy's misadventures in *Urania*, when the young knight overcomes his rival Clotorindus and exchanges vows with Meriana, Queen of Macedon (133).

Other members of Wroth's aristocratic circle seem to have acted with similar freedom. Christiana, daughter and heir of Edward, Lord Kinloss, contracted a secret marriage with William, eldest son of Lord Cavendish of Hardwick in 1608. The Earl of Arundel, Pembroke's brother-in-law, wrote to the Earl of Shrewsbury to describe "how the matter hath been so secretly carried as it was never heard of until it was done." Later, the Countess of Devonshire became one of Pembroke's close friends, with whom he dined on the last evening of his life; he shared his love poetry with the countess, who supplied a manuscript of Pembroke's poems for the edition published posthumously in 1660.[29]

Another example is that of the powerful courtier, Lucy Harington, Countess of Bedford. Although her own marriage was highly conventional, she played an important role as a matchmaker for others, often defying parental will. The countess's enjoyment of her role is suggested in a letter to her intimate friend, Lady Jane Cornwallis, when she describes the strategy involved in matchmaking: "Sir Robert Chichester's scurvie dealing hath broken up the match betwixt his daughter and my Lo. of Arran, which drives me to play my game another way than I had layed my cards." But perhaps the best example of her match-making occurs in the case of Sir John Smith, sole heir to his father, who fell in love with Lady Isabella Rich in 1618. Chamberlain records how, "without his fathers consent or privitie," the young man married her in a secret wedding, where the countess and other ladies served as witnesses, and the Earl of Pembroke gave the bride away. Chamberlain was particularly shocked by the involvement of Pembroke, now Lord Chamberlain: "which is thought a strange thing that so great a man and a counsaillor shold give countenance to such an action as robbing a man of his only child, a youth of 18 yeares old (for he is no more), and sure I have seen the time that such a matter could not have been so caried." Chamberlain's alarm is understandable — given the conflicting marital practices in the early seventeenth-century — but secret marriage was certainly a frequent enough occurrence among the aristocratic elite to which Pembroke, Bedford, Montgomery, and Wroth belonged.[30]

Even if Pembroke willingly participated in arranging love matches without regard to parental authority, when it came time to provide for his own estate he took a very different approach. Near the end of his life, when it became apparent that he would have no surviving heir by his wife, he assigned his estate in 1626 to his seven-year-old nephew, Lord Charles Herbert. To achieve a political *rapprochement* with his rival Buckingham, he helped arrange a marriage between his nephew and four-year-old Mary Villiers, daughter of the Duke of Buckingham. Their eventual marriage in 1634 brought with it a handsome portion of £25,000, but Philip Herbert was forced to return it when his eldest son died suddenly of smallpox in Florence shortly after the wedding. Ironically, Pembroke's masterfully arranged marriage did not secure happiness for anyone, least of all his brother, who had to scrap his plans for remodeling Wilton.[31]

In spite of the numerous instances of *de praesenti* contracts among members of the social circle to which Wroth belonged — pledges of which she could hardly have been ignorant — it would be a mistake to establish a simple referential correspondence between any of them and the tales in her romance. The very multiplicity of secret spousals among the characters of *Urania* suggests a process of meditation and progressive, experimental alteration of form that quickly moves beyond an element-by-element adherence to material "reality." The marital adventures of Pamphilia are autobiographical mainly in the sense that they permit the author consciously and unconsciously to reorder herself, and through this ongoing struggle to narrate herself in the conditional or subjunctive mode, as she could have, should have, or might have been.

IV

As a witness of early seventeenth-century court society, Wroth was in an ideal position to analyze the multiplicty of practices and behavior. Although she was certainly not an unbiased observer, she was in a sense an outsider—her bearing of illegitimate children (at least in the eyes of others) and her debt-ridden condition meant that she came to occupy a marginal position at court and was acutely aware of social stigma. As we have already seen, the marital patterns of her closest friends were indeed contradictory, with a number of secret spousals set alongside more traditional arranged marriages.

Yet *Urania* is fiction, and whatever evidence it has to offer must be understood also in relation to its literary character. For example, one of the most important sources of Wroth's romance is the fourteenth-century *Amadis de Gaule*, which she may well have read in either a French or English translation.[32] Secret marriage serves as one of the central motifs of *Amadis*, for the title character, the product of an unsanctified union, is abandoned at birth by his mother; when he grows up, he also contracts a secret marriage with his beloved Oriana, which must withstand numerous separations and misunderstandings. Because Wroth drew upon *Amadis* for a number of key episodes, particularly the Throne of Love (39–41), she was doubtless familiar with its account of secret spousals. The recognition that *de praesenti*, as opposed to *de futuro*, marriage depended upon the simple tense of the verb was also incorporated into numerous pedagogical works, such as Erasmus's *Colloquies*. In one of the most appealing dialogues, "Courtship," Pamphilus pleads with Maria to "say just three words—I am yours," but she cleverly avoids committing herself before gaining parental approval.[33] Finally, *de praesenti* marriage became an important source of plot complication in early seventeenth-century drama, with Webster's *Duchess of Malfi* and Shakespeare's *Measure for Measure* as two of the most outstanding examples. Wroth indeed had ample precedent to incorporate secret spousals as a highly popular literary device.[34]

One feature, however, which sets Wroth's romance apart from the preceding works is her emphasis on precise, realistic detail in describing both the parentally controlled and *de praesenti* contracts. Her work contains a broad spectrum of different types of unions, even within the category of arranged marriage. A recent debate in the journal *Past and Present* highlighted the difficulty of generalizing about the institution itself, for it is clear that whereas some seventeenth-century parents negotiated contracts purely for financial gain without consulting their offspring, other parents became involved only after their children had taken the first initiative.[35] Wroth successfully presents both the most blatant examples of parental coercion, as well as the more cooperative models of "multilateral consent."[36] One area in which *Urania* appears to contradict the research of Stone and others concerns female expectations regarding marriage. Social historians have largely assumed that women complied with arranged marriage by anticipating relatively little affection or fidelity from their husbands. In fact, Stone particularly stated that "the only period in which the double standard was seriously questioned was in the 1630's and 1640's."[37] On the contrary, *Urania* is filled with many examples of women who believe in the primacy of a meaningful love bond and are not content to remain in unfulfilling relationships. They act decisively, as in the case of Liana or Lady Pastora, to assert their own right to happiness. In fact, Wroth's emphasis on *de praesenti* marriage seems to coincide with her affirmation of the importance of a genuine bond of love that needs no outside institutions to confirm it. It is true that her tales of secret spousals frequently involve great risk to the women involved, but in some sense they choose to place themselves in the most vulnerable state as a means of expressing the extremity of their devotion. Against Stone's view that social relations of the period tended to be cool and unfriendly is the positive portrait in *Urania* of the network of women who mutually support and assist each other. Pamphilia and Urania function together to listen sympathetically to other women who have been willing to test the limits of social propriety through their own independently contracted marriages. To be sure, *Urania* paints the other side of court life as well—for example, the treachery, slander, and sinister manipulation that brings down fragile reputation—but Wroth provides her female characters with an alternative to the competitive quest for power and favor.

Among the upper classes, marriage was undergoing a crisis of enormous proportions in the seventeenth century. Stone has estimated that between 1595 and 1620, nearly one-third of the older peerage was involved in serious marital difficulties.[38] The turmoil may be partly reflected in Wroth's portrayal in *Urania* of the various problems associated with arranged marriage—parental coercion, domestic violence, adultery, and frustrated expectations. But Wroth does not appear to advocate abolishing the entire institution of marriage. In the Newberry manuscript a character named Fancy rejects marriage on the grounds that she does not want to endure the "bawling of bratts, monthes keeping in, housewyfery, and daries, and a pudder of all home made troubles" (I:fol.12v). Despite her claim to total independence, Fancy soon begins to wonder how she will "indure the winter of my age." She comes to recognize the economic reasons for an alliance, even if she insists on the need to retain her own power of choice. Wroth's portrait of marriage within *Urania* is complex in that she stresses the importance of a woman's quest for a truly companionate relationship, but without ever calling into question the economic rationale that allowed arranged marriage to continue for centuries more.

The problems of marriage that Wroth raised in *Urania* were to become the central concerns of later women writers, beginning with Margaret Cavendish, Duchess of Newcastle. In her play *The Bridals*, she portrays three couples, two of whom undergo elaborate arranged marriages, while the third couple, Sir Mercury Poet and Lady Fancy, exchanges simple *de praesenti* vows: "I do consent to be your Wife. / For without you, I have no life."[39] Although problems quickly surface between the first two sets of newlyweds, the play ends happily with a scene of reconciliation between the third couple and their parents, who give their consent after the fact. The dangers of arranged marriage also became an important issue in Aphra Behn's fiction, but her most acerbic treatment occurs in *The Pleasures of Marriage* (1682), in which like Wroth she exposes the underside of domestic arrangements, tracing the various miseries associated with the negotiation of the match through to the birth of the first child.

Near the end of the Newberry manuscript, one of the characters, the daughter of the Duke of Sabbro, calls attention to the fact that few women were able to speak out about their most private relationships: "Itt is the infinite misfortune . . . that Planett like governs the commune natures of all woemen to love, and wurse that they can nott relate the truthe of their lives and fortunes, butt wee must bee the blasers of our owne shame, in illustrating our fond passions" (II:fol.59). In a sense, Wroth's preoccupation with marriage in *Urania* necessarily involves emblazoning her own shame (especially through the autobiographical tales), but in doing so she provides us with a vivid portrait of the highly conflicting practices of the early seventeeth-century court society, and she initiates a concern with marriage that is to stand at the foreground of women's fiction from its earliest beginnings to Austen.

NOTES

1. For background on the Puritan ideology of marriage, see William and Malleville Haller, "The Puritan Art of Love," *Huntington Library Quarterly* 5 (1941–42), 235–72, and Linda T. Fitz, "'What Says the Maried Woman?': Marriage Theory and Feminism in the English Renaissance," *Mosaic* 13 (1980), 1–22. Not all Puritans opposed wife-beating, as Fitz notes, pp. 3–4.

2. R. Valerie Lucas argues that the Puritan preachers used rhetorical strategies to secure acceptance of patriarchal authority in "Puritan Preaching and the Politics of the Family," in *The Renaissance Englishwoman in Print: Counterbalancing the Canon*, ed. Anne M. Haselkorn and Betty S. Travitsky (Amherst: University of Massachusetts Press, 1990), pp. 224–40, whereas Mary Beth Rose maintains that the Puritans failed to recognize the contradictions inherent in their theory of marriage: *The Expense of Spirit: Love and Sexuality in English Renaissance Drama* (Ithaca: Cornell University Press, 1988), pp. 130–31. Marianne Novy describes the opposition between patriarchy and mutuality as ideals of marriage in *Love's Argument: Gender Relations in Shakespeare* (Chapel Hill: University of North Carolina Press, 1984), p. 4.

3. William Heale, *An Apologie for Women, or An Opposition to M^r D^r G his assertion, who held in the Act at Oxforde. Anno 1608. That it was lawfull for husbands to beate their wives* (Oxford: Joseph Barnes, 1609). James Grantham Turner identifies Heale's opponent as William Gager: *One Flesh: Paradisal Marriage and Sex-*

ual Relations in the Age of Milton (Oxford: Clarendon Press, 1987), pp. 1–3, 111–13. Heale refers to Sidney's *Arcadia* for models of companionate marriage (pp. 14, 15, 19, 34).

4. See, for example, Carol Thomas Neely, *Broken Nuptials in Shakespeare's Plays* (New Haven: Yale University Press, 1985), p. 9. Lisa Jardine, *Still Harping on Daughters: Women and Drama in the Age of Shakespeare*, 2nd ed. (New York: Columbia University Press, 1989), pp. 42–43, challenges Juliet Dusinberre's assumption that the status of women improved as a result of the Protestant ideology of marriage: *Shakespeare and the Nature of Women* (London: Macmillan, 1975). In fact, Ian Maclean, *The Renaissance Notion of Women* (Cambridge: Cambridge University Press, 1980), p. 85, emphasizes the profoundly conservative effect of the Protestant paradigm in perpetuating views of women's inferiority in the areas of theology, ethics, politics, and law.

5. For criticism of Stone's work, see Alan Macfarlane's extended review in *History and Theory* 18 (1979), 103–26; Barbara Harris, "Marriage Sixteenth Century Style: Elizabeth Stafford and the Third Duke of Norfolk," *Journal of Social History* 3 (1981), 371–82; and Lois G. Schwoerer, "Seventeenth-Century English Women Engraved in Stone?" *Albion* 16 (1984), 389–403.

6. Keith Wrightson, *English Society, 1580–1680* (New Brunswick: Rutgers University Press, 1982), p. 79; Ralph Houlbrooke, *The English Family, 1450–1700* (London: Longman, 1984), p. 88.

7. BM Harl. MS 7582, fol. 53v. Lawrence Stone cites this passage among others to show the gradual weakening of the authoritarian control by parents over the marriages of their children, but he argues that parental authority lasted longest in the richest and most aristocratic circles: *The Family, Sex and Marriage in England, 1500–1800* (London: Weidenfeld and Nicholson, 1977), p. 184.

8. For discussion of the role women played in negotiating marriage contracts, see Margaret J.M. Ezell, *The Patriarch's Wife: Literary Evidence and the History of the Family* (Chapel Hill: University of North Carolina Press, 1987), pp. 18–35.

9. Henry Swinburne, *A Treatise on Spousals or Matrimonial Contracts* (London: R. Clavell, 1686), sig. A3. The canonical distinction between *sponsalia per verba de futuro* and *sponsalia per verba de praesenti* was established in the twelfth century and remained virtually unchanged until Lord Hardwicke's Marriage Act of 1753, which ruled that only church weddings, nor verbal spousals, were legally binding. See Sir Frederick Pollock and F.W. Maitland, *The History of English Law Before the Time of Edward I*, 2 vols. (Cambridge: Cambridge University Press, 1895), II, p. 368; G.E. Howard, *A History of Matrimonial Institutions*, 3 vols. (Chicago: University of Chicago Press, 1904), I, pp. 308–20; and Chilton L. Powell, *English Domestic Relations, 1487–1653* (New York: Columbia University Press, 1917), p. 3–21.

10. Martin Ingram, "Spousals Litigation in the English Ecclesiastical Courts, c. 1350–c. 1640," in *Marriage and Society: Studies in the Social History of Marriage*, ed. R.B. Outhwaite (New York: St. Martin's, 1981), p. 42; Swinburne, *Treatise on Spousals*, sig. A2ᵛ.

11. *The Lawes Resolutions of Womens Rights: or The Lawes Provision for Woemen* (London: John More, 1632), pp. 53, 144.

12. Stone, *Family*, p. 32; William Gouge, *Of Domesticall Duties, Eight Treatises* (London: W. Bladen, 1622), p. 205.

13. For the 1603 canon, see E. Gibson, *Codex Juris Ecclesiastici Anglican* (London: Clarendon, 1761), 421, cited by Ann Jenalie Cook, "Wooing and Wedding: Shakespeare's Dramatic Distortion of the Customs of His Time," in *Shakespeare's Art from a Comparatist Perspective*, ed. Wendell M. Aycock (Lubbock: Texas Tech Press, 1981), p. 85. Alan Macfarlane points out that according to English common law, men over fourteen and women over twelve could get married without parental consent, a situation that differed markedly from French law, where as late as 1907, a son under twenty-five and a daughter under twenty-one could not marry without parental approval: *Marriage and Love in England: Modes of Reproduction 1300–1840* (Oxford: Basil Blackwell, 1986), p. 127.

14. G. R. Quaife, *Wanton Wenches and Wayward Wives: Peasants and Illicit Sex in Early Seventeenth Century England* (New Brunswick: Rutgers University Press, 1979), p. 60.

15. Heale, for example, describes marriage as "a Gordian knot that may not bee loosed by the sworde of death" (*Apologie*, p. 10).

16. Swinburne, *Treatise on Spousals*, pp. 199, 201, 202, 223.

17. See Lamb's discussion of the passage in this volume.

18. Sir Sidney Lee, ed. *Shakespeare's England*, 2 vols. (London: Oxford University Press, 1912), II, p. 146; *The Letters of John Chamberlain*, ed. Norman McClure, 2 vols. (Philadelphia: American Philosophical Society, 1939), I, p. 495.

19. See Hannay's essay for discussion of Wroth's portrait of the Queen of Naples, who is most probably based on the Countess of Pembroke.

20. HMC, De L'Isle and Dudley, II, p. 456.

21. MacFarlane, *Marriage*, pp. 247–49.

22. HMC, De L'Isle and Dudley, II, p. 127.

23. Edmund Lodge, *Illustrations of British History*, 3 vols., 2nd ed. (London: John Chidley, 1838), III, p. 35. One of the letters from the Talbot collection that Lodge omitted from his edition is a two-page list of Pembroke's objections to certain terms proposed by Shrewsbury with regard to Mary's portion (III, p. 97).

24. HMC, De L'Isle and Dudley, III, p. 140; Lodge, *Illustrations*, III, pp. 151–52.

25. HMC, De L'Isle and Dudley, III, 414; IV, 44.

26. HMC, Salisbury (Cecil), XI, p. 581. Lady Dorothy Moryson later wrote to Cecil (Feb. 3, 1601/2), asking on behalf of her son for his permission to seek Lady Susan's favor: HMC, Salisbury (Cecil), XII, p. 43.

27. Lodge, *Illustrations*, II, p. 100; Thomas Birch, ed., *The Court and Times of Charles the First*, 2 vols. (London: H. Colburn, 1848), II, p. 73.

28. Edward Barrington de Fonblanque, *Annals of the House of Percy, From the conquest to the Opening of the Nineteenth Century*, 2 vols. (London: Richard Clay, 1887), II, pp. 341–42. See HMC, De L'Isle and Dudley, V, 407, for Sir Francis Darcy's letter of July 20, 1616, concerning the match; Chamberlain, *Letters*, records learning of the marriage in March, 1617 (II, p. 57).

29. Lodge, *Illustrations*, III, p. 232; Birch, *Court*, II, p. 73.

30. *The Private Correspondence of Lady Jane Cornwallis, 1613–44*, ed. Lord Braybrooke (London: S. & J. Bentley, Wilson, & Fley, 1842), p. 79; Chamberlain, *Letters*, II, p. 187.

31. Lawrence Stone, *The Crisis of the Aristocracy, 1558–1641* (Oxford: Clarendon Press, 1965), p. 61.

32. Nicholas de Herberay translated the Spanish *Amadis* into French in 1540. An English translation by Anthony Munday of the first four books of the romance appeared in 1619 and was dedicated to the Earl and Countess of Montgomery, the dedicatee of the *Urania*. In the preface, the translator expresses his gratitude to the countess for allowing him to consult her personal copies of the romance. As early as 1595, when Wroth's father, Sir Robert Sidney, expressed interest in *Amadis*, Rowland Whyte asked Pembroke to help him obtain a copy: "I have written to Lord Herbert to have that Spanish *Amadis de Gaule* you speake of sought out" (HMC, De L'Isle and Dudley, II, p. 422).

33. *The Colloquies of Erasmus*, trans. Craig R. Thompson (Chicago: University of Chicago Press, 1965), p. 97.

34. Shakespeare's treatment of the marriage contracts in *Measure for Measure* has generated a large body of conflicting criticism. See, for example, such studies as Davis P. Harding, "Elizabethan Betrothals and *Measure for Measure*," *Journal of English and Germanic Philology* 49 (1950), 139–58, and Ernest Schanzer, "The Marriage-Contracts in *Measure for Measure*," *Shakespeare Survey* 13 (1960), 81–89.

35. Miriam Slater argued that the arranged marriage predominated as a method of expanding and preserving property accumulations in "The Weightiest Business: Marriage in an Upper-Gentry Family in Seventeenth-Century England," *Past and Present* 72 (1976), 25–54. Sara Heller Mendelson disputed her findings by casting doubt on the use of a relatively small sample of letters and cited opposing evidence to suggest a growing interest in companionate marriage: *Past and Present* 85 (1979), 126–35. What the debate reveals is the extent to which multiple marital patterns occurred among the early seventeenth-century gentry.

36. Martin Ingram, "The Reform of Popular Culture? Sex and Marriage in Early Modern England," in *Popular Culture in Seventeenth-Century England*, ed. Barry Reay (New York: St. Martin's Press, 1985), p. 136.

37. Stone, *Family*, p. 505.

38. Lawrence Stone, "Marriage Among the English Nobility in the 16th and 17th Centuries," *Comparative Studies in Society and History* 3 (1961), 202.

39. Margaret Cavendish, Duchess of Newcastle, *Plays Never Before Printed* (London, 1668), p. 60.

PART THREE

Rewriting the Renaissance

Designing Women:
The Self as Spectacle
in Mary Wroth and Veronica Franco

Ann Rosalind Jones

Why read Mary Wroth, a Jacobean courtier, and Veronica Franco, a Venetian courtesan, together? Because both demonstrate a multi-media process through which women poets could rewrite unstable social positions by drawing on the visual arts privileged in their cultural milieux: the portrait in enamel and oil in Italy, the masque and the stage play in Jacobean London. Through verbal appropriation of elite spectacle, the Italian and the English poet construct themselves as public figures empowered by their relation to male artists and to modes of representation beyond poetry.

How were these women socially disadvantaged, and by what arts did they construct legitimate public selves? Franco's profession as a *cortigiana onesta* (*onesta* in the sense of "honored," that is, prosperous and highly placed) was simultaneously elevated and perilous. The city of Venice tolerated courtesans in practice, as a tourist attraction, source of taxes, and protection for the purity of aristocratic marriage. Thomas Coryat, reporting on his 1608 visit to the city, wrote that without courtesans, Venetian gentlemen "thinke the chastity of their wives would be the sooner assaulted, and so consequently they should be capricornified (which of all the indignities in the world the Venetian cannot patiently endure) were it not for these places of evacuation."[1] Guido Ruggiero argues that the city permitted prostitution as a hedge against male homosexuality and as a practical means of placing young women lacking dowries into a sexual caste system that assigned them at least temporary security.[2] Nonetheless, the profession was highly risky. Courtesans could be arrested at any time; frequent proclamations imposed controls upon their dress, places of residence, and public appearances.[3] Many were accused of witchcraft and pilloried by satirists, and all depended on the good will of clients who were bound to them neither by law nor custom.[4]

Yet Veronica Franco resisted being paralyzed by the masculine gaze that regulated the behavior and representation of women in Venice, whether it belonged to city officials empowered to arrest and fine women of her station or to the painters and engravers who used courtesans as models for erotic images. In her *Rime*, published in Venice in 1574, and her *Lettere* (1580), Franco elaborated a technique of verbal self-portraiture through which she inscribed compliments to powerful artists into texts designed to serve her own interests. In fact, although the courtesan lacked the guild support that successful Venetian artists could count on, her profession, like theirs, depended on patronage: both kinds of work required learning as well as physical skill, the ability to flatter connoisseurs, and the use of fame to justify high fees. Like the painter, the courtesan constructed herself as a cultural luxury. What elevated her above the common prostitute was her literacy, her knowledge of classical mythology, her familiarity with philosophical questions — including aesthetic theory and debates in the arts. Franco systematically cultivated men in the Venier academy, an association of scholars, musicians, poets, and connoisseurs led by Domenico Venier, the oldest son of the well-known patrician family.[5] This symbolic capital, this carefully publicized link to high culture, was the courtesan's investment against being defined — and paid — merely as "a place of evacuation," as Coryat so bluntly put it. For artist and courtesan alike, a successful career depended on intellectual as well as material skill, and also on compliment and persuasion — on glorification of the mighty, and of oneself through association with them.

Such requirements were also central to the career of a courtier, whether a male advisor to a prince, the master of his revels, or, like Mary Wroth, a lady-in-waiting to a queen. In fact, Wroth was a fallen courtier when her romance was published in 1621, far less prosperous than she had been from 1604 to 1614 as a companion to Anne of Denmark, wife of James I.[6] After 1614, déclassée as a result of her husband's death and bankruptcy, and attacked as the mother of illegitimate children, Wroth spent her time visiting better-established friends, petitioning the king for tax relief, and composing *Urania*, in which her contemporaries recognized that she was writing attacks on certain courtiers as well as inviting sympathy for two heroines whose misfortunes paralleled her own: Pamphilia, a princess neglected by her beloved Amphilanthus, and Lindamira, a noblewoman exiled by false rumors from her queen and court.[7] I will concentrate here on Wroth's sonnet sequence, *Pamphilia to Amphilanthus*, to argue that Wroth makes Pamphilia's situation as unrequited lover the subject of laments that were strategic attempts to rewrite her disgrace and to put an end to her exclusion from court society. Whereas Franco uses the visual arts to construct a prestigious reputation for herself, Wroth uses them to reconstruct hers. She draws upon pastoral lyric, Jonsonian masque and playhouse tragedy to plead indirectly for a return of royal favor and to demonstrate that she deserves it. Representing her heroine's exile as heroic renunciation, she stages Pamphilia's captivity as a spectacle through which she resists her own disappearance into the categories of failed courtier and silenced woman.

FRANCO'S *RIME*: THE ARTS OF COMPLIMENT

Although Franco could hardly claim the purity that Wroth so consistently attributes to Pamphilia, the courtesan manages her own social instability by writing direct compliments to the great, compliments which reflect the prestige of kings, patrons, and painters back onto her. In her letters and poems, she takes concrete art objects—a portrait miniature of herself, a full-scale portrait by Tintoretto, a nobleman's country villa—as topics through which she exhibits her verbal and erotic skills. A first instance is a letter she composed after the young Henri de Valois, soon to be Henri III of France, secretly visited her during his stay in Venice in 1575. Franco's interest lay in making that visit public in order to advertise her status as the choice of a royal client. She also wrote the prince two sonnets on the subject of his acceptance, as he was departing, of an enamel portrait miniature of her. Like the portrait, Franco offers her sonnets as presents of herself to the king—

presents that dramatize her power to be the bestower, not merely the recipient, of gifts.

The compliment to the king and to Franco begins with the prose epistle in which she dedicates her *Lettere* to him. Franco equates the memory he left in her heart, "the living image" of his virtue and valor, with the *ritratto* (the portrait) he took away with him. She claims the exchange as the catalyst for her own high literary ambition: Henri's generosity challenges her, as a poet, to do justice to him. In spite of the small scale and rough surface of the work (it is *stretto e rozzo*), she asks the king to accept it as a sign of her "immense desire" to celebrate him beyond all earthly limits. Thus she relates her text to a miniaturist's reduction of the full-scale, three-dimensional figure of a sitter into a small frame. Yet she implies that such spatial compression can do justice to what is represented, even intensify an artist's subject matter: "just as the whole world can be depicted on one small sheet of paper, I have in these short verses done a sketch . . . of my gratitude."[8] The word Franco uses for sketch is *disegno*, which means, in draughtsman's vocabulary, a "design," a "drawing," a "plan." More generally, it connotes a "scheme" or "plot"—the Elizabethan English equivalent was a "device."[9] This second meaning points to Franco's double strategy here: her thanks to the king for accepting her dedication is also a reminder to the readers of her *Lettere* of her privileged relationship to a royal client. Of such designs reputations are made.

Franco's two sonnets carry out the laudatory aesthetic she promises in her dedication: she composes a set of variations on the theme of immensity enclosed in a small space. Classical mythology is one source of such imagery, particularly Jove's sexual adventures—a topic frequently exploited by Venetian painters in their canvases of mortal women seduced by the king of the gods: Danae, Semele, Europa. In Franco's first sonnet she compares the king to Jove, disguised in human form so as not to dazzle mortal eyes. By narrating her own dazzlement when he abandoned his disguise, she implicitly links herself to Semele, mortally overwhelmed when Jove appeared to her as a flash of lightning: "Benche si sconosciuto, anch'al mio core / tal raggio impresse del divin suo merto, / ch'n me s'estinse il natural vigore"[10] (And though I did not recognize him, upon my heart / he shone such a ray of his divine virtue / that my inborn strength was overcome). Franco uses the paradox of immensity in a small space in order to point out the class-crossing novelty of the king's presence in her house and also to hint at the contrast between her full bodily presence and the portrait that records it in miniature. The sonnet moves from praise for the king to praise for the courtesan, who turns the ending focus of the poem onto the enamel image of herself: "Di ch'ei, di tanto affetto non incerto, / l'imagin mia di smalto e di colore / prese al partir con grat'animo aperto" (So, not doubting the depth of my feelings, / he took my image, in enamel and paint / away with him in a gracious, open-hearted spirit). The poem is quintessentially Venetian in the grandiosity of its praise and its use of classical myth to glorify the present. Yet however Franco elevates the king, her published narrative of his visit has a leveling effect: this prodigy, after all, came to her in the body of a customer seeking sexual pleasure and left as the recipient of her portrait. Moreover, she takes him as a pretext for her own literary self-preservation. As he puts a permanent image of her into circulation by accepting her portrait, so she immortalizes herself in the sonnet.

Her second sonnet to Henri opens with another gift-giving formula, through which her generosity and beauty become the subject of the poem. In a parallel to a long-running debate about whether painting or sculpture is the superior art, Franco's poem sets up an implicit contest between painting and poetry.[11] In Franco's version, the living body of the courtesan and her motive of praising the king seem to exceed the frame of the enamel. The portrait freezes and diminishes the woman, but the desire she claims, to eternalize Henri, expands both of them to more than life size. Franco implies, in fact, that the miniature does not do justice to her living, breathing devotion:

> Prendi, re per virtù sommo et perfetto,
> quel che la mano a porgerti si stende:
> questo scolpito e colorato aspetto,
> in cui 'l mio vivo e natural s'intende.
>   E, s'a esempio si basso e si imperfetto
> la tua vista beata non s'attende,
> risguarda a la cagion, non a l'effetto.

> Take, oh, king, sum of virtue and perfection,
> what my hand reaches out to offer you:
> this carved and colored version of myself,
> in which my living, real appearance is represented.

And if such a lowly and flawed image
is not what your blessed gaze expects,
consider my motive rather than the result.

In the last lines of the sonnet, Franco balances the king's public triumphs with her efforts as a poet to do him justice. Again, the poet takes the upper hand over the painter. Franco claims that the king can see her desire to praise him "expressed" in her portrait—but this desire is actually expressed not in the face painted by the male miniaturist but in the language of the woman's poem: "cosi 'l desio, di donna in cor sofferto, / d'alzarti sopra 'l ciel dal mondo fore, / mira in quel mio sembiante espresso e certo" (See, then, the desire, felt in a woman's heart, / to raise you above the earth and beyond the skies / expressed and affirmed in this likeness of me).

Franco's most direct response to a particular artist involves similar strategies of self-praise through praise of a public man. She links herself specifically to Jacopo Tintoretto in a letter (21) thanking him for the full-size portrait he has recently completed of her. Franco names "signor Tentoretto" explicitly in the first sentence of her letter, to demonstrate her familiarity with one of the most distinguished painters of the city. Tintoretto's portrait of Franco has not been identified. Lynne Lawner conjectures that it might have been a "Flora" or one of several paintings from his workshop that resemble each other.[12] Her argument is less than conclusive, but she makes an important point about the formulaic quality of the Floras painted by Tintoretto and his followers: they used classical mythology to produce these paintings "in series, as commodity items" (101). Throughout her *Rime*, Franco, too, draws on classical conventions of representation to produce herself as a commodity item. But she does so by means of an intricate rhetroic that sets her apart from the silent models in the canvases of Tintoretto and his followers.

Franco's letter to Tintoretto reproduces the strategy of her sonnet to Henri III: she praises the painter to the skies in return for the evidence of her desirability that he communicates to her public. She begins by invoking the debate between the ancients and the moderns, siding against those who argue that recent times have produced no equals to Apelles, Zeuxis, or Praxiteles and ending with a dazzling compliment to Tintoretto: "I have heard gentlemen deeply versed in antiquity and most expert in these arts say that in our era . . . there are painters and sculptors who must not only be equalled to the ancients, but acknowl-edged to surpass them, as Michelangelo, Raphael, Titian and others have done, and as you do today" (*Lettere*, 34). This is a strategy of glory by association: Franco links herself to the gentleman connois-seurs, presumably members of the Venier academy, at the same time that she links Tintoretto with the master painters of central Italy and with his great Venetian precedessor. She goes on to say that his painting of her combines magical accuracy with irresistible seductiveness, a com-pliment that claims the man's pictorial skill as a guarantee of her own beauty: "I swear to you that when I saw my own portrait, the work of your god-like hand, I hesitated a moment, wondering whether it was a painting or rather a hallucination appearing before me through some trickery of the devil." Then, in a witty denial that the image has succeeded in making her fall in love with herself, Franco leaves open the possibility that other viewers might be less able to resist it: "not, certainly, to make me fall in love with myself, as happened to Narcissus, for, thank God, I don't think myself so lovely that I fear having any reason to go insane over my own beauty, but if it has some other pur-pose, what do I know of it?" So the topic of the painting allows her two maneuvers at once: to praise the painter's accuracy and to declare her own modesty in regard to the beauty he has captured. In her con-clusion, she promises Tintoretto that no writer will ever be able to do justice to his talent: "And I, certain not to succeed in such a great undertaking, lay down my pen." But if Franco has not done justice to Tintoretto in this ingenious encomium, she has certainly done justice to herself.

Whatever the courtesan poet's contest with painters may have been, her use of them in the sonnets to Henri and the letter to Tintoretto demonstrates that her relations with artists were actually more col-laborative than competitive. Given the parallels between the two pro-fessions, it would be surprising never to find Franco writing in support of artists. And indeed, in the final poem of her *Rime*, she eulogizes a patron of the arts through a combination of classical and Christian compliment which spectacularly serves her interests as well as those of his builders and decorators. Capitolo 25, a long idyll or country-house poem, is written in praise of Marcantonio della Torre, a prelate of Verona whose villa still stands at Fumane, in Valpolicella.[13] Much of the poem repeats the conventions of pastoral description as they were also used to compliment aristocrats in England.[14] Franco's skill as an artist in words is evident in her praise of the villa and its landscape as signs of Neoplatonic enlightenment—an argument that allows her to construct an ennobling role for her patron and for herself as participant in Fumane's ideal wonders.

Capitolo 25 opens with a staging of memory. Franco represents herself as recalling Della Torre's estate so vividly that she gives it a second existence. As she dramatizes the shift from recall to representation, she compares herself to an artist drawing and painting a landscape: "I take my pen in eager hand, . . . / and . . . depict / the place as truthfully as I can . . . ; / . . . inspired by my great longing, / without art I draw and paint what I know" (*Rime*, 338). In the elaborate description that ensues, however, Franco attributes the villa's beauty to art more than to nature: heavenly order, "the source of art in all lovely things," has shaped the landscape. Her detailed enumeration of the villa's ornaments draws concrete terms from the contemporary decorative arts into a compliment both to the man who has built the estate and the visitor who appreciates its value:

> The polished marble and glowing porphyry,
> cornices, arches, columns, reliefs and friezes,
> figures, perspective views, gilt and silver,
>   are of such variety and such great value,
>   that no other palaces attain that height,
>   though built by ancient emperors and kings. (136)

Franco then turns to the owner of the villa, to elevate him from collector to Christian and Platonic hero. Della Torre had assembled a series of portraits of prelates, whom Franco describes with appreciative awe: "Because this heavenly dwelling / is like paradise itself, it encloses / the faces of such saintly and pious men" (342). Thus she praises Della Torre's taste and affirms her respect for the spiritual power of his colleagues. The poet then moves to a Platonizing celebration of the spiritual effect of Della Torre's artfully ordered landscape. She uses the word *convito*, with its overtones of "banquet" or "symposium," to sum up his "prodigious feast" for the senses, which she presents as a stimulus to higher intellectual contemplation:

Thus, in the power of the infinite,
without ever being satisfied, we rest,
so closely is our thought united with the highest good.
   And we feel this endless longing
for an express purpose: that, philosophizing,
we may experience the divine intellect. (280)

Franco concludes the passage by positioning Della Torre as the mediating figure through whom divine artistry is translated into earthly form. The poet places the patron — of gardeners, architects, painters, sculptors and courtesans — in immediate proximity to the divine, although she writes this sanctification of the collector into a secular literary genre, the praise of the country house. She adopts a classical genre that coincides with her actual relationship to Della Torre, as visitor to his rural retreat rather than the churches of Verona — but she expands the form to place her patron in the company of Virgil's Maecenas as well as Plato's illuminated philosopher. Franco gains twice over from this lavish performance: she advertises her status as a guest of the country elite and as a poet able to do justice to the refined pleasures provided by artists of all kinds at Fumane, whom she represents as a chorus of *ingegni* ("geniuses," "talents"), co-creators who, like her, elevate Della Torre to semi-divine status. The poem transforms commissioning art from an economic matter of employing cultural workers into a process of constructing oneself as a secular god.

In each of her texts on the visual arts, then, Franco employs a range of high-cultural vocabularies to affirm her status as *cortigiana onesta*. A more socially critical reading of these three episodes could stress, instead, the exploitation any courtesan underwent as paid sexual performer. As a trophy of Henri's Venetian tour, as the model for a painter whose name, rather than hers, identifies their shared work, as a collector's item temporarily lodged at Della Torre's estate, the courtesan was positioned as a commodity, an object of exchange among men. But in her writing she positions herself as a subject of discourse, as a manipulator of visual languages rather than a passive model for them. Her profession, her practice in effective poses and strategic compliment, trained her in the wit necessary to attain the status of a literary woman; and her association with the artists of Venice gave her a vocabulary she could use to their common advantage.

WROTH'S PAMPHILIA: CAPTIVITY AS THEATER
IN THE MASQUE OF LOVE'S COURT

Two obvious differences between Franco and Wroth are the directness
of the courtesan's appeal for favor and her erotic warmth, which contrast strikingly with Pamphilia's resolutely ascetic constancy. Yet Wroth's
strategies are nonetheless similar to Franco's. When her sonnets were
published at the end of *Urania* in 1621, they would have reminded her
readers of her history as a performer in two visual spectacles of James's
court, Ben Jonson's *Masque of Blackness* and *Masque of Beauty*. Her
references to blackness and night intertwine her poetic structures with
Jonson's script and Inigo Jones's designs. As a poetic parallel to their
Neoplatonic architecture, Wroth's corona of sonnets to Love links her
to the king and to his court artists. Occasionally, as well, she draws
on more popular dramatic spectacle — tragedy, as it figures the spectacularly suffering bodies of women — to add intensity to her complaints.
On the literal level, Pamphilia is deprived of Amphilanthus's love; but
on a figurative level where loss of social status is displaced into amorous
loss, Wroth may well have constructed her persona to reclaim the affection of her sovereigns and the respect of their courtiers.

Like Franco, Wroth also adopts conventions of pastoral, although
she uses them not to celebrate the owners of country houses but to
establish an unimpeachably chaste speaking position for Pamphlia. Re-
gendering Petrarch's self-representation as lover isolated in the Vaucluse,
a rural setting far from his lady, Wroth assigns her heroine the physical
separation from the beloved through which women poets throughout
Europe recruited Petrarchism as an ideologically safe mode for women
(no proximity meant no threat to chastity). The figure of Amphilanthus is virtually absent from Wroth's sequence: never named, rarely
described, and only occasionally addressed. But she also adopts a specifically English stance of isolation. The primary setting of *Pamphilia
to Amphilanthus* is a rural vacuum from which characters modeled on
the courtiers Wroth actually associated with are significantly excluded.[15]
Pamphilia makes a merit of her rejection of social life, dismissing the
activities of her companions, through whom she implicitly criticizes
the trivial amours of courtiers and the frivolous occupations of country
life. Here and when she refers explicitly to the court, she does so in

a dismissive vein which belongs to a prestigious Jacobean discourse: the theory and practice of melancholy.

Roy Strong has traced a fascinating line of descent for this posture through Elizabethan and Jacobean portraiture. He points out that Ficino elevated the melancholy temperament into a sign of genius in quattrocento Italy; later in England, Richard Burton rephrased the link between the depressive humor and divine *furor* in *The Anatomy of Melancholy*: "melancholy men of all others are most witty" because they are susceptible to "divine ravishment, and a kind of *enthusiasmus* . . . which stirreth them up to be excellent Philosophers, Poets, Prophets, &c."[16] Strong points out details of costume and landscape shared by portraits and woodcuts from the 1590s to the 1610s: the reclining figure of Edward Herbert in a forest, foregrounded against a group of hunters in the distance; Isaac Oliver's *Unknown Young Man* in black, crossing his arms and turning his back to the gardens and arcades of a palace; the title page to Burton's *Anatomy*, in which a bearded sage shields his eyes against a castle garden laid out behind him; an anonymous portrait of the young John Donne, with the folded arms and wide-brimmed black hat that signaled the melancholy intellectual (335–37). Strong's point holds for poetry as well as painting: melancholy connoted disdain for social contact and worldly entertainments. Yet the portrait of the melancholic requires allusions to the pleasures of woods and country houses in order to affirm the contrary disposition, just as pastoral depends on the invocation of corruption in cities and courts.

Wroth uses this technique of exclusion via inclusion throughout her sonnets. Cupid, in an early song, warns lovers to "fly" the court: "Ther no true love you shall espy" (P14). Pamphilia's melancholy is typified in sonnet 23, in which she defines her state of mind by contrasting it to elite distractions that she transcends:

> When every one to pleasing pastime hies
> Some hunt, some hauke, some play, while some delight
> In sweet discourse, and musique shows joys might
> Yett I my thoughts doe farr above these prise . . .
> When others hunt, my thoughts I have in chase;
> If hauke, my minde att wished end doth fly,
> Discourse, I with my spiritt tauke, and cry
> While others, musique choose as greatest grace.
> O god, say I, can thes fond pleasures move?
> Or musique bee butt in sweet thoughts of love? (P26)

By purifying Pamphilia of the trivial pursuits associated with court and country house, by raising her thoughts above daylight sports to nocturnal self-examination, Wroth affirms her heroine's merit.[17]

Another way Wroth's fixation on the court to which she no longer belonged is figured is her frequent apostrophes to allegorical figures rather than human beings. Pamphilia invokes mythological figures and personified abstractions such as Venus and Jealousy far more often than she calls to her wandering beloved or to friends and onlookers. To make a virtue of necessity, Wroth represents her exile from court as a test that proves her heroine's mettle. Like an anchoress purifying her soul in a cave, Pamphilia embraces her solitude by choice. Wroth emphasizes, through negation, her sacrifice of the sunshine of social life to the dark night of the constant woman's ascesis.

One of the personifications Wroth invokes most often is Night, figured as a feminine figure allowing uninterrupted melancholy reverie. But Night also had a specific historical connotation for Wroth. One of her first triumphs at court was her appearance, in 1605, as one of twelve Ethiopian maidens led by Queen Anne in Jonson's *Masque of Blackness*. In the masque, Wroth blacked her arms and face, wore a rich orientalizing costume, and played the part of "Baryte," carrying a hieroglyphic image of an urn twined with grape leaves. According to Jonson's allegorical commentary, her appearance was intended to symbolize the solidity and fertility of earth among the other elements.[18] She performed again as a "daughter of Niger" in Jonson's *Masque of Beauty*, in which the dark skins of the African women are contrasted to the fair beauty of Albion's daughters, protected by the brilliant but clement English monarch, whom Jonson represents as a beneficent sun king. So Pamphilia's dark visions would have been received as reminders of Wroth's past glories at Whitehall and of her loyalty to the king glorified in such performances.[19] Sonnets on blackness in *Pamphilia to Amphilanthus*, then, recall its author's earlier relation to blackness as a theme of self-display in court pageantry and reinforce it with the coloring of rural melancholy.

But blackness is also associated with benign female power in this sequence. In fact, the speaker's speeches to Night construct the most sustained relationship imagined in the sequence. Unlike Amphilanthus, Night can be counted on for regular appearances and sustaining company.[20] The dignity of her outer appearance is taken as a sign of her moral clarity and purificatory power, qualities Wroth claims for Pamphilia as well by framing Night as her heroine's mirror image (Sonnet 25):

> Truly poore Night thou wellcome art to mee:
>   I love thee better in this sad attire
>   Then that which raiseth some mens phant'sies higher
>   Like painted outsid[e]s which foule inward bee;
> I love thy grave, and saddest lookes to see,
>   Which seems my soule, and dying hart intire,
>   Like to the ashes of some happy fire
>   That flam'd in joy, but quench'd in miserie: (P17)

The sonnet ends with the implication that Night has lenitive power in the political as well as the psychic world. She is represented as the mediator of daytime justice, promising relief not only to lovers but to other categories of the oppressed as well:

> I love thy count'nance, and thy sober pace
>   Which evenly goes, and as of loving grace
>   To uss, and mee among the rest oprest
> Gives quiet, peace to my poore self alone,
>   And freely grants day leave when thou art gone
>   To give cleere light to see all ill redrest.

This poem certainly raises the possibility that Night is a figure for Queen Anne, through whom Wroth imagines regaining court approval. If the link is there, it is made via a complex intermeshing of individual wish and public symbol: the poet offers her pastoral isolation as evidence that she possesses a higher set of values, values which nonetheless look toward the court precisely by distinguishing Pamphilia from her peers there (although it is interesting that she also includes herself in the group of the oppressed, presumably others equally deprived of favor). By implying that Pamphilia's willingness to suffer as a captive of love demonstrates that she deserves to have her love requited, Wroth rewrites the isolation of a banished woman as the precondition for the ending of that isolation.

Pamphilia is more than an image of passive suffering, however. To affirm her heroism, Wroth represents her self-sufficiency as a public spectacle. The political vocabulary in such poems is more than metaphorical conceit: the loss of which Pamphilia complains is not only the loss of love but the loss of just estimation, of prestige in a world of power and self-display from which she implicitly demands better treatment. Wroth's dramas of torment are not acts of self-punishment for her trans-gression of sexual codes;[21] rather, these self-exposures position Pam-philia as a martyr in order to put her tormentors in the wrong. Sonnet 13, addressed to Amphilanthus, typifies her rhetoric of submission and blame. She appeals to the man as a captive of war would appeal to a conquering general needing to be recalled to the *noblesse oblige* of kings:

> An easy thing itt is to shed the blood
> > Of one, who att your will, yeelds to the grave;
> > Butt more you may true worthe by mercy crave
> > When you preserve, nott spoyle, butt nurrish good. (P15)

This kind of chivalrous rhetoric, by which obligations are imposed on the superior figure, operates in several sonnets.

But Wroth also draws on more concrete contemporary vocabularies of torment. One of the most startling metaphors she employs is the rack, the stretching device used to extort confessions. It first appears in sonnet 36, in which Pamphilia speaks to her heart as the only wit-ness of a love that must be kept secret: "What torments thou hast suffered . . . / thou tortur'd wert with racks which longing beares, / Pinch'd with desires which yett but wishing reares" (P41). A heart stretched on a rack is a bizarre and frightening conceit, not entirely diminished by the aphoristic final couplet that contrasts Pamphilia's fidelity to the pretence of lesser lovers: "For know more passion in my hart doth move / Then in a million that make show of love."

The political dimension of the metaphor is extended in a much bleaker later poem, sonnet 4 of the second series of sonnets, which narrates Pamphilia's struggle against jealousy. Here the rack concretizes the vulnerability of the lover by paralleling it to the terror of a political prisoner: "Cruel suspition, O! been now at rest, / Lett dayly torments bring to thee some stay" (P66). Wroth uses the vocabulary of torture not to construct a metaphysical conceit, whereby a state of mind is elaborated in terms belonging to a totally different realm. Rather, she breaks down the opposition between unrequited love as a private dilemma and the pursuit of favor as a public one: her figures for internal anxiety correspond to her social entrapment as bankrupt widow exiled from court. She compares suffering on love's rack to confinement in a narrow prison cell:

I ame by care sufficiently distrest,
> Noe rack can stretch my hart more, nor a way
> Can I find out for least content to lay
> One happy foote of joye, one step that's blest; (P66)

She concretizes the scene of imprisonment further through two allegorical figures: Suspicion and his servant and go-between, Jealousy, jailers who frustrate Pamphilia's search for tranquillity. The scene set up in the sonnet remarkably resembles the prison scene in Webster's *Duchess of Malfi*. Wroth constructs a contrast between Pamphilia's innocence and the brutality of her guards, and she appeals for sympathy in the stunned wonder of Pamphilia's comment on her entrapment:

Butt to my end thou fly'st with greedy eye,
> Seeking to bring griefe by bace jealousie,
> O in how strang a cage am I kept in?

In sonnet 42, Wroth stages Pamphilia's mistreatment as an explicitly theatrical scene, soliciting the sympathy of witnesses she imagines as the audience at an execution, then in a playhouse. The poem opens with an eerie scene of public dismemberment. Wroth condenses the Neoplatonic conceit whereby each lover's heart lodges in the other's breast into a quasi-surgical formula (line 7) that sums up her loss of this reciprocity as a result of Amphilanthus's absence:

If ever love had force in humaine brest?
> If ever hee could move in pensive hart?
> Or if that hee such powre could butt impart
> To breed those flames whose heat brings joys unrest.
Then looke on mee; I ame to thes adrest,
> I, ame the soule that feeles the greatest smart;
> I, ame that hartles trunk of harts depart
> And I, that one, by love, and griefe oprest. (P48)

In the tercets, Wroth directs the gaze of her audience away from the fragmented body of Pamphilia to the blind figure of Love, who, like Amphilanthus, ignores her appeals. She sets up only one possible response for her observers: the pitiful response the god and the man withhold from her. Pamphilia declaims the poem in the posture of a tragic heroine, but she is also an orator using public space to denounce injustice:

Non[e] ever felt the truth of loves great miss
   Of eyes, till I deprived was of bliss;
   For had hee seene, hee must have pitty show'd:
I should nott have bin made this stage of woe
   Wher sad disasters have theyr open showe
   O noe, more pitty hee had sure beestow'd.

This claim to the status of martyr positions Pamphilia as public sign, pointing to the cruelty of her oppressors. The woman calls upon the gaze of a public to make a case for her innocence and merit, and she invokes a tragic setting to reinforce that innocence through direct, even aggressive control of audience perspective.[22]

Expiatory and accusatory motives are also implicit in Wroth's much praised *corona,* the "crowne of [fourteen] Sonnets" written as a paean to pure love. Here Wroth offers proof that she has reformed by means of an elaborate synthesis of myth and Christianized Neoplatonism that shares many of the terms of Jonson's *Masque of Beauty* (and of Franco's poem in praise of Della Torre). J.D. Gordon points out, in Jonson's masque, the displacement of Venus and Cupid by a purified King of Love;[23] Wroth's narration of a symbolic procession through royal chambers further recalls the masques; and she draws on a pictorial convention of Neoplatonism in her assurance to true lovers (which resembles Bembo's advice in Book 4 of *The Courtier*) that their internal images of the beloved are more accurate and durable than any merely material portrait:

Love will a painter make you, such, as you
   Shall able bee to drawe your only deere
   More lively, parfett, lasting, and more true
   Then rarest woorkman, and to you more neere. (P83)

If Wroth's word-painting in the "Crowne of Sonetts" was intended to regain her position at court, however, she knew how risky such attempts were. One way of reading the conceit of Love's labyrinth, which opens and closes the corona, is as a figure both elegant and sinister for the entrapping anxiety of courtiers in quest of favor. Wroth's technique for attracting and controlling the readers and rulers of her Jacobean milieu is to demonstrate Pamphilia's innocence as shepherdess and her fealty to a king of love whom she shows her readers how to serve in the corona's series of lessons on how to "bee in [love's] brave court a glorious light" [P79, 80]. Yet even after her ostensibly liberatory definition of true love, Pamphilia ends by returning to the labyrinth established as the setting in the corona's first sonnet: "In this strang labourinth how shall I turne?"

The sequence, then, does not resolve the problems of frustrated desire and banishment from a once friendly court. Franco's rural landscape is a much more benign place than Wroth's royal labyrinth. But Wroth's appropriation of available discourses of pastoral and tragedy allowed her to claim a sympathetic hearing for the complaint of the woman courtier. Her poems clearly register early modern restrictions on feminine speech; their voices are relatively restrained, their anger is repressed. Yet this repression produces some of the most violently original scenarios and soliloquies in the sonnets, which juxtapose the high spirituality of Neoplatonism with a painful physicality.

Franco's self-representation is the product of a different culture and class, of welcomed participation in the Venetian academy and a city that tolerated her profession: more glamorous, more confident, written less in protest than in self-embellishment. Wroth, already the target of censure in the Stuart court, was far more strictly bound by demands for proper womanly speech and deference to authority. Yet however Pamphilia's chaste constancy appears to conform to expectations for proper womanly behavior, Wroth uses that appearance as initial justification for lyrics that in fact oppose injunctions to feminine silence and invisibility. Like Franco, she hybridizes visual and pastoral vocabularies to her own advantage. Her appeals to men and women in power are less direct than Franco's, but she moves past such indirection in the vividness of her self-portrait of woman as stoic heroine and victim denouncing her persecutors. *Pamphilia to Amphilanthus* turns what might appear to be a masochistic dwelling on loss against the subject position assigned to women in male-authored spectacle. Rather than disciplining her body to the group parade of the twelve daughters of Niger or to the role of a silent Baryte bearing emblems, Pamphilia produces a noisy interior monologue that demands attention. And her images of captivity suggest ingenious resistance rather than submission to royal choreographies. In all the senses of the densely signifying word *disegno*, Veronica Franco and Mary Wroth were designing women.[24]

NOTES

1. Thomas Coryat, *Coryats Crudities* (London, 1611; rpt. Glasgow: MacLehose, 1905), I:58.

2. Guido Ruggiero, *The Boundaries of Eros: Sex Crime and Sexuality in Renaissance Venice* (Oxford: Oxford University Press, 1985), p. 153. For an earlier study, see Arturo Graf, "Veronica Franco: una cortigiana fra mille," in *Attraverso il Cinquecento* (Turin: Loescher, 1888). More recent studies include Paul Larivaille, *La vie quotidienne des courtisanes en Italie (Rome et Venise: XV et XVI siècles)* (Paris: Hachette, 1975) and Rita Casagrande della Villaviera, *Le cortigiane veneziane nel Cinquecento* (Milan: Longanesi, 1968). Popular surveys in English include Georgina Masson, *Courtesans of the Italian Renaissance* (London: St. Martin's Press, 1976), and Lynne Lawner, *The Lives of the Courtesans* (New York: Rizzoli, 1987).

3. For citations of anti-courtesan edicts, see Casagrande di Villaviera, *Cortigiane*, pp. 64ff., 79ff. 106ff.

4. For a discussion of Franco's trial for witchcraft, see Margaret Rosenthal, *The Honest Courtesan: Veronica Franco as Citizen and Writer in Sixteenth-Century Venice* (Chicago: University of Chicago Press, 1991), ch. 4, and Alvise Zorzi, *Cortigiana veneziana: Veronica Franco e i suoi poeti* (Milan: Camunia, 1986), ch. 2.

5. For an overview of this academy, see Margaret Rosenthal, "Veronica Franco: The Venetian Courtesan's Defense," *Renaissance Quarterly* 42 (Summer 1989), and Lina Bulzoni, "L'Accademia veneziana: splendore e decadenza di una utopia enciclopedica," in *Università, accademie e società in Italia e Germania dal Cinquecento a Settecento*, ed. Laetitia Boehm and Ezio Raimondi (Bologna: Mulino, 1981), pp. 117–67.

6. For Wroth's biography, see Roberts's introduction to the *Poems*.

7. Roberts discusses *Urania* as a *roman à clef*, *The Poems*, pp. 28–36. For an interpretation of the romance as both critique and concession to Stuart constraints on women, see Carolyn Ruth Swift, "Feminine Identity in Lady Mary Wroth's Romance *Urania*," *English Literary Renaissance* 14 (1984), 328–46. Elaine Beilin takes Pamphilia's constancy as the theme of the romance, which, she argues, Wroth contrasts to "the inconstancy and deviation from reason" of the male characters, in *Redeeming Eve: Women Writers of the English Renaissance* (Princeton: Princeton University Press, 1987), p. 217. See also Naomi J. Miller, "'Not much to be marked': Narrative of the Woman's Part in Lady Mary Wroth's *Urania*," *Studies in English Literature* 29 (1989), 121–37, and Maureen Quilligan, "Lady Mary Wroth: Female Authority and the Family Romance," in *Unfolded Tales: Essays on Renaissance Romance*, ed. George M. Logan and Gordon Teskey (Ithaca: Cornell University Press, 1989), pp. 257–80, as well as the essays in this volume by Lamb, Miller, Roberts, and Weidemann.

8. Veronica Franco, *Lettere*, ed. Benedetto Croce (Naples: Ricciardi, 1949) p. 7.

9. For the term "device" and the relation between Elizabethan portrait miniatures and sonnets, see Patricia Fumerton, "'Secret' Arts: Elizabethan Miniatures and Sonnets," *Representations* 15 (Summer 1986), 57–97.

10. Veronica Franco, *Rime*, ed. Abdelkader Salza, in *Scrittori d'Italia*, vol. 52 (Bari: Laterza, 1913), p. 353.

11. On the poetry/painting debate in Italy, summed up in Leonardo da Vinci's *Para-*

gone (*Comparison of the Arts*), see the brief discussion in D. H. Craig, "A Hybrid Growth: Sidney's Theory of Poetry in *An Apology for Poetry*," in *Essential Articles for the Study of Sir Philip Sidney*, ed. Arthur Kinney (Hamden, Conn.: Archon, 1986), 113–34. Bernardo Tasso argues, as Franco does, for the superiority of poetry in a sonnet to Titian, "Ben potrete con l'ombre e coi colori," conceding that painterly technique can render the still beauty of a woman but cannot represent her grace in action (Sonnet 327, *Rime*, ed. Pierantonio Serassi [Bergamo, 1749]).

12. Lawner, *The Lives of the Courtesans*, pp. 58, 205 n.12.

13. For an argument that this poem transforms the Petrarchan stance of victimization by love, see Sara Maria Adler, "Veronica Franco's Petrarchan *Terze Rime*: Subverting the Master's Plan," *Italica* 65 (Autumn 1988), 223–25.

14. For the social purposes of English country-house poetry, see Don Wayne, *Penshurst: The Semiotics of Place and the Poetics of History* (Madison: University of Wisconsin Press, 1984).

15. For a study of dedications and poetic exchanges that suggest how socially engaged Wroth remained even after she left the court, see May Nelson Paulissen, "The Love Sonnets of Lady Mary Wroth: A Critical Introduction," Ph.D. diss. University of Houston, 1976, ch. 2.

16. Cited by Roy Strong, "The Elizabethan Malady: Melancholy in Elizabethan and Jacobean Portraiture," *Apollo Magazine* 79 (1964); rpt. in *The English Icon: Elizabethan and Jacobean Portraiture* (London: Routledge & Kegan Paul, 1969), p. 352.

17. See also Masten's and Fienberg's discussions of this poem in their essays in this volume.

18. For detail about the masques, see Roberts, pp. 12, 13 n.28. For an analysis of the scripts, see D.J. Gordon, "The Imagery of Ben Jonson's *Masques of Blacknesse and Beautie*," in *The Renaissance Imagination: Essays and Lectures by D.J. Gordon*, ed. Stephen Orgel (Berkeley: University of California Press, 1975; rpt. 1980), pp. 134–56. For the masques' costumes, see Stephen Orgel and Roy Strong, *Inigo Jones: The Theatre of the Stuart Court* (London & Berkeley: Sotheby Parke Bernet and University of California Press, 1973), I, color plates, figs. 1 and 88.

19. For dedicatory poems to Wroth suggesting that she continued to be associated with the masque, see Roberts, pp. 16–22, and Paulissen, "Love Sonnets," p. 15.

20. For more discussion of the role of Night as a female friend to Pamphilia, see Naomi J. Miller, "Rewriting Lyric Fictions: The Role of the Lady in Lady Mary Wroth's *Pamphilia to Amphilanthus*," in *The Renaissance Englishwoman in Print: Counterbalancing the Canon*, ed. Anne M. Haselkorn and Betty S. Travitsky (Amherst: University of Massachusetts Press, 1990), pp. 295–310.

21. Len Tennenhouse, in *Power on Display: The Politics of Shakespeare's Genres* (London: Methuen, 1986), argues that male-authored representations of women in physical torment reveal aristocratic anxiety about the loss of control over women in kinship alliances (ch. 3: "The Theater of Punishment: Jacobean tragedy and the politics of misogyny"). Although his analysis is limited to male playwrights, his generic focus suggests one source for the imagery of Wroth's "torture" sonnets.

22. See also Masten's and Fienberg's discussions of sonnet 42 in this volume.

23. Gordon, "Imagery," p. 145.

24. Indiana University Press has kindly granted permission to publish portions of this essay which also appear in my recent book, *The Currency of Eros: Women's Love Lyric in Europe, 1540–1620* (Bloomington: Indiana University Press, 1990).

Engendering Discourse:
Women's Voices in Wroth's *Urania*
and Shakespeare's Plays

Naomi J. Miller

It is not the fashion to see the lady the epilogue," comments Rosalind at the end of *As You Like It*. She proceeds to deliver the epilogue apparently as "she" likes it nonetheless, before concluding with an acknowledgment that she is no lady after all, but a boy playing a woman's part. Lady Mary Wroth's prose romance, *Urania*, countered prevailing literary fashions in achieving the distinction of being the first published work of fiction by an Englishwoman in the Renaissance. As Sir Philip Sidney's niece and literary successor in the genre of the prose romance, Wroth adopts and revises many of the literary principles and assumptions of her fashionable uncle. At the same time, as a Jacobean woman writer acquainted with the drama of the period, from court masques to plays, Wroth fashions her characterizations in dramatic terms quite distinct from the narrative tradition of the prose romance.[1] In this essay, I examine Wroth's construction of women's voices in *Urania* in relation to the discourse of Shakespeare's female protagonists. My comparison of Wroth and Shakespeare across generic lines makes evident some of the fissures of gender ideology within both narrative and dramatic genres in early modern England.[2] The comparison illumines not only Wroth's subversion of generic boundaries but also the restrictions on feminine speech which mark even the most vocal of Shakespeare's heroines. By contrast to Shakespeare, Wroth reveals her ability to fashion "the woman's part" from a consciously female perspective, using her narrative to explore the ways in which questions of gender can empower or subvert verbal constructions of identity.

Wroth's interest in dramatic productions while active in the Jacobean court is evidenced by her participation in performances of Jonson's *The Masque of Blackness* (1605) and *The Masque of Beauty* (1608), as well as by her attendance at numerous other masques.[3] While the significance of Wroth's role in the masques to her representation of women is addressed elsewhere in the volume by the essays of Ann Rosalind Jones and Heather Weidemann, I wish to suggest here that Wroth's female characters, as both speaking and acting agents, encode a potential revision of the silent, passive masquers identified in Suzanne Gossett's recent essay on women in the masques.[4] In the present essay I focus, however, not on the Jacobean masques, where women remain voiceless, but rather on the male-authored feminine discourse of Shakespeare's plays as a basis for comparison.[5] As I have elsewhere compared Wroth's constructions of female agency and identity with those of male authors ranging from Sidney and Spenser to Montemayor and d'Urfé, I have limited the scope of the present essay to the comparison with Shakespeare.[6] By "over-reading" Shakespeare with Wroth, to borrow Carol Thomas Neely's language, I hope to establish not an assertion of influence so much as a scrutiny of difference, considering the implications of gender in constructions of discourse in order to contribute to the "reengendering" of the Renaissance envisioned by Neely.[7]

Recently, scholars have called attention to the social and rhetorical obstacles confronting Renaissance women who attempted to write within genres structured by male categories and dominated by masculine discourse.[8] Many of the feminist pamphlets of the period take a defensive stance in seeking to refute the stereotypes presented by misogynistic treatises.[9] Wroth, however, chooses not to portray women only reactively, in relation to patriarchal norms, but rather to construct, in *Urania*, a culture defined *by* women's voices. Writing out of a tenuous and largely disregarded "subculture" of women's voices in her own Renaissance society, Wroth nevertheless elevates the authority of feminine discourse in her narrative.

In constructing that discourse, Wroth incorporates theatrical elements not common to the genre of prose romance, which have not been fully taken account of by previous critics.[10] In place of the stylized discourse and narrated summaries of conversations which Sidney, for example, relies upon to convey the communication between Pamela and Philoclea, Wroth includes extensive passages of spoken dialogue which give dramatic immediacy to the voices of her female characters. Significantly, several pivotal scenes occur in "theaters," which are depicted as dramatic sites of contestation and enchantment (321ff.), while portions of the narrative are described as "acts" in the ongoing drama of the protagonists' fortunes (II:fol.42v). Although Wroth draws heavily upon the prose romance tradition for outlines of plot and characterization, *Urania* is informed by a sense of theatrical moment and dramatic speech. Some of the most prominent dramatic scenes and elements of characterization in Wroth's work even yield echoes of Shakespeare, but echoes transformed: Shakespearean moments re-viewed and re-formed to reveal a woman's vision of romance.

Urania opens in traditional prose romance fashion, with a pastoral character in lamentation. Wroth's protagonist is not a shepherd mourning the rejection or absence of his beloved, however, as in Montemayor's *Diana*, d'Urfé's *Astrée*, or Sidney's *New Arcadia*, but rather a shepherdess lamenting the question of her identity as a woman. Having just discovered that the shepherds who raised her are not her real parents, and that her origins are unknown, Urania cries out to herself: "Of any misery that can befall woman, is not this the most and greatest which thou art falne into?" (1). The plight of Urania, and of another of Wroth's "lost shepherdesses," Veralinda, can be linked more directly to Shakespeare's Perdita than to the lamenting male shepherds of the prose romance tradition, yet Wroth heightens the tension of unknown identity beyond the example of Perdita by insisting upon the relevance of gender. Shakespeare's "shepherdess" remains unaware of her own ignorance of her origins until the moment of reunion with her royal family at the conclusion of the play, and thus she has neither the time nor the opportunity to question the significance of gender to her familial and social roles. By positioning Urania's lament at the beginning of her narrative, Wroth establishes both the power of gender to shape discourse and the importance of self-awareness as a starting point for female constructions of identity.

A more direct parallel to *The Winter's Tale* occurs in the unpublished manuscript continuation of *Urania*, when the "shepherdess" daughter of the ruler Leonius marries the young prince Floristello, just as the "shepherdess" daughter of Shakespeare's Leontes marries the young prince Florizel. However, in the parallel examples of the royal shepherdess and prince just cited, it is the present friendship of the young lovers' mothers which contextualizes their bond in *Urania*, in contrast to the past rivalry of the lovers' fathers which contextualizes the bond in *The Winter's Tale*. Wroth's "lost shepherdess" is the daughter not only of Leonius, but more significantly of Veralinda, while the prince Floristello is the son of Urania. The friendship between these two female protagonists influences their children, as well as other characters, more directly than do the roles played by their husbands. Thus when Floristello reflects upon the pastoral appearance of his beloved, he recognizes that "her spiritt is as high as an Emperess" (I:fol.32), remembering that his own mother Urania once appeared to be a shepherdess. Veralinda's daughter, meanwhile, lives up to her mother's assertion that a woman can "bee the Emperess of the world, comaunding the Empire of [her] own minde" (I:fol.40v), by her confident demeanor even when she believes herself to be only a shepherdess. Shakespeare's plays often address conflict with fathers in the absence of mothers which affects bonds of friendship (Rosalind/Celia) as well as love (Desdemona, Perdita/Florizel).[11] Wroth rewrites that familial dynamic in her own work to emphasize connections both with and of mothers.

The potential implications of gender difference for the discourses of Shakespeare and Wroth may be glimpsed in light of recent feminist studies on gender and identity formation. Nancy Chodorow's influential analysis of the sociology of gender, in particular, suggests that while masculine identification processes stress differentiation from others, feminine identification processes stress relationship to others, especially continuity of identities with mothers.[12] This is not to say that the bonds between mothers and children in Wroth's narrative remain free of tension, but rather to recognize that Wroth restores to mothers not only a discourse of their own, but also a significant influence upon the identity formation of their offspring.[13]

Furthermore, Wroth disrupts the gendered hierarchy which in Shakespeare's plays prioritizes male bonding over female friendship.[14] Louis Montrose has suggested, in his exploration of gender in Elizabethan culture, that "men make women, and make themselves through the medium of women," using *A Midsummer Night's Dream* as one of his examples. According to Montrose, the examples of male and female doubling in that work result in "the maidens remain[ing] constant to their men at the cost of inconstancy to each other," while the marriages at the end "dissolve the bonds of sisterhood at the same time that they forge the bonds of brotherhood."[15] In fact, the marriages at the end of many Shakespearean comedies place women primarily in relation to men rather than to each other, as the "counter-universe" of female friends, to use Carole McKewin's term, is subsumed under the patriarchy.[16]

Assuming the dominance of patriarchal structures in Wroth's narrative as well as in her society, critics of *Urania* have often focused on questions of victimization in examining Wroth's female characters.[17] Yet Wroth develops the relationships among her characters not only before but also after marriage, and highlights examples of female friendship without subordinating them to parallel examples of male friendship. By re-viewing and revising the conventions of narrative romance to emphasize women's speech in dramatic terms, Wroth undermines the strictures of female silence and passivity so much emphasized in Renaissance directives for women. While translating from social into literary terms the precariousness of the female position in Jacobean society, Wroth nevertheless affirms the resilience rather than victimization of the female character.

The female conversations in Shakespeare's comedies in particular have prompted feminist critics such as McKewin to praise Shakespeare's mimetic skill in "creating the sound of women's voices placing themselves in a man's world."[18] Some critics have pointed to the interaction between Shakespeare's female friends as suggestive of a female "subculture" in contrast to the dominant male order.[19] In *Urania*, however, Wroth explores the nature not of a female "subculture" but a female culture, to create the sound not simply of women's voices in a man's world, but of a world of women's voices.

On a general level, some of the lively and dramatic interchanges between Wroth's female protagonists recall the verbal wit of Shakespeare's comic heroines. When one of Wroth's female characters, known as the "Merry Marquess," warns another that "husbands are strange things if nott discreetly handled," and proceeds to compare husbands to horses which must be kept on a tight rein (II:fol.24v), her sally suggests the independence and humor of a Beatrice or a Rosalind. At the same time, the comment by the Merry Marquess ironically reverses the common Renaissance comparison between horses and wives.[20] Not only does Shakespeare's Antigonus threaten to confine his wife, were she false, as he would his mares in stable (*WT*, II.i.133–35), but even Hermione refers with acceptance to the Renaissance conceit of wives being ridden by their husbands (*WT*, I.ii.94–96). When the Merry Marquess warns women to guard against the potential tyranny of husbands lest they "like horses gett the bitt beetweene their teeth, and run the full race, or course of their owne humour, and the wives slaverye" (II:fol.24v), Wroth's character re-forms the metaphor from a woman's perspective. In this instance, Wroth's narrative exhibits affinities with the sixteenth-century feminist admonitions of Jane Anger, who compares male lovers to horses and warns women not to trust them, "for although a jade may be still in a stable when his gall backe is healed, yet hee will showe himselfe in his kind when he is travelling."[21] Such examples illuminate the revisionary nature of Wroth's relation to the governing metaphors of her culture, if not necessarily establishing specific Shake-spearean plays as sources. Summoning up a misogynist metaphor only to subvert its terms, Wroth uses the very language of patriarchy to undermine male assumptions of dominance.

The sisterly sharing of fortunes and misfortunes in love in Wroth's narrative often takes the form of extended dramatic dialogues not commonly found in other prose romances, but comparable to the conversations of Beatrice and Hero, Rosalind and Celia, and even of such later Shakespearean women as Desdemona and Emilia, Hermione and Paulina. While it can be argued that the conversations between Pamela and Philoclea, particularly in the *New Arcadia*, provide an antecedent in prose romance for the intimate exchanges between Wroth's female characters, in fact the interaction of the Arcadian sisters consists less of a mutual interchange than a frequently one-sided discourse where Pamela confides in Philoclea, who draws parallels between their situations in her mind rather than in direct response to her sister. The mutuality of the conversations shared by Wroth's female characters, on the other hand, relies upon the voicing rather than sublimation of thoughts and emotions.

At the same time, Wroth re-forms the "heroine/confidante" pattern governing many of the close female friendships in Shakespeare's plays, to establish more equality of role and voice in the bonds joining Urania, Veralinda, and Pamphilia. The hierarchical separation between heroine and confidante in Shakespeare's plays encodes, and in the process enforces, the hierarchical dynamic governing the relation between man and woman, husband and wife, in which love consists of accepting service on the one hand, and offering it on the other. Even when the women share a comparable social rank, in most scenes one of them serves primarily as voice, the other as interpreter or echo. Beatrice's voice, for example, often overrides that of her friend Hero, while when Hero does give voice to her thoughts on Beatrice, it is in her hearing rather than to her face. Urania and Pamphilia speak *with* each other rather than simply to or for each other, not only offering their own thoughts aloud but responding directly to each other's narrations. And when Wroth's female friends are rulers, as in the cases of Urania, Pamphilia, and Veralinda, their discourse becomes an occasion for sharing, rather than delegating, authority.

On Shakespeare's stage, women's voices often acquire their greatest resonance when addressed to men — Beatrice demanding that Benedick "Kill Claudio," for example, or Rosalind instructing Orlando that men have died, but not for love — or achieve their greatest pathos when silenced by men, as in the cases of Desdemona and Hermione. In Wroth's romance, the most witty or impassioned speeches by women are often addressed to other women. In constructing these speeches along dramatic lines, Wroth subverts the narrative conventions governing women's speech in the prose romance, while remaining unconstrained by the cultural expectations limiting the range of dialogue between female characters on the stage.

Wroth's emphasis upon mutuality rather than hierarchy in female friendship may reflect her own experiences as a Jacobean noblewoman: surviving letters and diaries written by women of the period attest to close personal friendships among women of the courtly class to which Wroth belonged.[22] The importance of female friendship as a context for as well as a subject of Wroth's romance is signaled also in her choice of title: *The Countesse of Mountgomeries Urania* honors Susan Herbert, one of Wroth's closest friends. Where the friendships of Shakespeare's women often take shape in relation to male tyranny, whether of fathers (*As You Like It*), lovers (*Much Ado About Nothing*), or husbands (*Othello, The Winter's Tale*), the sisterly bonds of Wroth's women consistently predate, coexist with, and outlast their fluctuating relationships with the men in their lives.

Wroth departs notably from the pattern of Shakespeare's comic heroines in rejecting the use of male disguise as a catalyst which allows women to transcend the social limitations of their gender.[23] Assuming new roles through cross-gender disguise, Shakespeare's heroines acquire at the same time new voices which allow them to cloak feminine desire with masculine discourse.[24] On the other hand, as Jonathan Goldberg points out, in a play "it is not necessarily a sign of power to have a voice, not necessarily a sign of subjection to lose it."[25] Describing the plight of many women in love with reference to theatrical conventions, Wroth observes that "an Actor knowes when to speake, when to sigh, when to end: a true feeler is wrapped in distempers, and only can know how to beare" (314). When the female protagonists in *Urania* gradually learn to command voices of their own in love, the "unfeigned" power of their speech is highlighted by the narrative frame. Wroth's female characters must learn both "when to speake" and "how to beare," how to speak without feigning and when to bear without speaking, how to claim the power of acting without relinquishing the authority of feeling. Here the difference in genres allows Wroth to emphasize her own distinctions between the "counterfeit" discourse of playacting, where speech alone does not necessarily "engender" power, and the deliberate counterbalancing of speech and description in her narrative, where undisguised "voicing" of affection and desire empowers feminine discourse.

The issue of counterfeit discourse underlies both writers' treatments of communication between young lovers. Just as Rosalind presumes to instruct Orlando in the art of love, Pamphilia addresses the subject with Amphilanthus. But where Rosalind denies her passion, proclaiming in her disguise as a boy that her playing of the woman's part is mere "counterfeit" (*AYLI*, IV.iii.166–82), Pamphilia responds to Amphilanthus's observation that she "counterfeit[s] loving . . . well" with a boldly direct affirmation of her love (266). In representing Pamphilia as direct and not feigning, Wroth disrupts male Renaissance conventions associating women with inconstancy and pretense.[26] Less constrained by social "fashions" than Shakespeare's women, Wroth's female protagonists speak with the authority of their own voices. Furthermore, while Rosalind, as Ganymede, serves as the interpreter of Orlando's stilted poems rather than as the author of any poems of her own, Wroth attributes the power of successful poetry to the woman in love.[27] And while Orlando carves Rosalind's name upon trees in the forest (*AYLI*, III.ii), Pamphilia is the one who carves Amphilanthus's name in cipher upon an oak tree (270). By reversing the gender of the carver, Wroth underscores the enabling effects of love upon the woman as writer rather than simply reader, inscriber rather than inscribed.

A comparison of climactic moments of both jealousy and friendship from *Urania* and *Othello* suggests how Wroth places significantly more emphasis than does Shakespeare on the active rather than passive nature of the woman's part. The parallels — such as Wroth's choice of the island of Cyprus, associated at the time not only with Venus but also with Othello and Desdemona, as the theatricalized setting for Pamphilia and Amphilanthus's first love and final reunion — only underscore the magnitude of difference. In one particularly notable scene from *Urania*, Wroth stages the entrance of Pamphilia into her own bedroom to find her lover, Amphilanthus, flung upon the bed in the throes of jealousy. Grieving that his breath should be spent on sighs "for noe cause," Pamphilia inquires "what is the cause" for this unease when her heart is so clearly his, while he responds to her assurances by asking "is itt soe my onely soule" (I:fol.14). This exchange recalls, in both language and content, the scene in which Othello, consumed by jealousy, comes upon Desdemona in her bed, exclaiming: "It is the cause, it is the cause, my soul. / Let me not name it to you, you chaste stars. / It is the cause" (*Othello*, V.ii.1–3). By contrast to this pivotal Shakespearean scene of male jealousy, Wroth situates the male lover in the supine position upon the bed, and represents the effectiveness of female discourse in breaking down the masculine barrier of jealousy through direct communication.

Amphilanthus excuses his jealousy by explaining "thatt while we are butt lovers I am suspitious, love never having the true heigth of zeale in love till the knott never to bee untide bee tied, therfor knitt that, and noe more shall you see mee suspect" (I:fol.14v). Instead of arguing with his construction of the situation, Pamphilia replies: "butt for the knott you demaund, I ame reddy to ty that with all sincerity, affection, and obedience requisitt for my part to performe" (I:fol.14v).[28] By appropriating for herself a conventional feminine position of obedience, Pamphilia preempts and thus disarms the disciplinary strategies enacted by the jealous male lover. At the same time, her acknowledgment of the nature of this part as a "performance" suggests her ability to distinguish between the constancy which she chooses to define her identity and the obedience which she enacts to calm Amphilanthus's jealousy. By knowing both "when to speake" and "how to beare," Pamphilia successfully deflates her lover's defensive posture without compromising her constancy or self-confidence. Encoded within her apparent submission, then, is a resistance to masculine assumptions of authority.

Furthermore, in the larger narrative of *Urania*, it is not Amphilanthus's jealousy but Pamphilia's constancy which takes center stage and which ultimately prevails. In the face of Amphilanthus's unfounded bursts of jealousy and frequent absences, Pamphilia comes to terms with the tensions between her role and her identity largely through her shared conversations on the nature of constancy with Urania and Veralinda. By defining her constancy in relation to her love, rather than in defensive response to a jealous lover, Pamphilia is enabled to decenter the punitive absences of that lover through an empowering re-vision of her own subjection to love. Pamphilia's resolve to maintain her constancy, whether in the presence or absence of Amphilanthus, safeguards the continuity of her discourse from the instability of changeable male response. At the same time, Wroth provides more than one articulation of women's relation to love, counterpointing Pamphilia's dedication to constancy with Urania's emphasis on female agency. In Wroth's narrative, the presence of two women produces two voices, not a single female perspective on love. Thus Urania actually criticizes Pamphilia's "bondage" to love, asserting that women must not let "want of courage and judgement make us [love's] slaves," and advising Pamphilia that even the virtue of constancy is not absolute, but rather socially constructed with "limits to hold it in" (399–400).

Subsequently, Wroth refocuses the concept of constancy itself to address not simply male-female love relationships, but specifically female friendships:

> For never was ther greater, nor Constanter love beetweene woemen, then bee-
> tweene thes towe most excellent Ladys, continuing to ther ends, beeing for itt
> called the matchles loving Ladys, as a rare thing to see that parfection in woemen,
> especially one to an other soe permanent, soe as while the warrs might bee cruell,
> and curst, yett they might in sweet conversation injoye one the other. (I:fol.39v)

Acknowledging the cultural myth of women's inconstancy to one another
in order to refute it, Wroth constructs the friendship between Pamphilia and Veralinda with an emphasis on the importance of their "conversation" in opposition to the violence of "warrs" staged by men.

Both Shakespeare and Wroth interrogate gender-specific assumptions through examples of private discourse shared among women
friends. Emilia's longest conversation with Desdemona, for example, is
marked by bold challenges to a gendered hierarchy of emotions, in such
questions as: "have not we affections, / Desires for sport, and frailty,
as men have?" (*Othello*, IV.iii.100–101). Pamphilia and Veralinda discourse in a similar vein upon the frailty of Amphilanthus:

> Those days are past, my deere Veralinda, cride Pamphilia, and hee is changed, and
> proved a man; hee was ever thought soe, sayd Veralinda . . . you were, and are
> the discreetest of your sex, yett you would have impossibilities; you say Amphilan-
> thus is a man, why did you ever know any man, especially any brave man, con-
> tinue constant to the end? . . . all men are faulty, I would nott my self have my
> Lord Constant, for feare of a miracle . . . say he hath left you, lett him goe
> in his owne pathe, tread nott in itt, an other is more straite, follow that, and
> bee the Emperess of the world, comaunding the Empire of your owne minde;
> (I:fol.40–40v)

One notable difference, however, is that while Shakespeare's Emilia defines women in relation to men's faults—"The ills we do, their ills instruct us so" (*Othello*, IV.iii.103)—Wroth's Veralinda asserts the possibility that women may choose a path of their own. A specifically female
precedent for Wroth's representation of male inconstancy can be found
in the feminist pronouncements of Jane Anger and Joane Sharp on the
nature of men.[29] Furthermore, Wroth diverges from the "heroine/
confidante" hierarchy governing the relationship between Desdemona
and Emilia to convey a greater mutuality of friendship between her female characters. Finally, while both Emilia and Desdemona are ultimately silenced, for all their courage, at the hands of their husbands,
Wroth's female protagonists demonstrate the potential not only to endure, but to prevail.

Page from the manuscript continuation of *Urania*,
showing Wroth's characteristic hand.

(Courtesy of the Newberry Library, Chicago)

The closest that Shakespeare comes to representing the quality of female endurance explored by Wroth is in his late romances. Both Pamphilia and Hermione suffer the jealousy of male tyranny with a certain stoicism. Aware that her years of separation from Amphilanthus have taken their toll, Pamphilia muses: "Can he smile on these wrincles, and be loving in my decay?" (482). Her feminine perspective on their separation can be compared to Leontes's protest to Paulina upon beholding the statue of his wife in *The Winter's Tale*: "But yet, Paulina, / Hermione was not so much wrinkled, nothing / So aged as this seems" (V.iii.27–29). Having been cast off by her husband without cause, Hermione has aged through the intervening years only to be "reborn" into a reunion with the repentant Leontes. However, in Wroth's treatment of undeserved rejection it is not Pamphilia but Amphilanthus who is described as figuratively frozen in stone by his act of abandonment, so that his feelings of repentance "wrought in him, like drops falling on soft stones, they weare in to them at last, though in the beginning touch and slide off" (556). In *The Winter's Tale*, Leontes responds to the statue of Hermione reflexively by invoking stone-like comparisons for both himself and Perdita, while in Wroth's romance the stone-like associations are exclusive to the male. Furthermore, while Hermione's statue-like passivity constitutes acquiescence to her husband's authority not only to reject her but effectively to silence her for sixteen years, Pamphilia refuses to wait out Amphilanthus's inconstancy in silent passivity, asserting instead the continuity of her discourse both as a woman and as a ruler.

In both *Urania* and *The Winter's Tale*, male-female conflict is triangulated by the presence of a defender of female honor, a woman's voice to challenge masculine authority. When Amphilanthus attributes his sorrow to "inconstancie in [Pamphilia] and ingrat[it]ude in mee," Urania responds tartly: "I beeleeve the latter . . . for Pamphilia is above all worldly nations fixt, and onely fixt to you, therfor what have you dun?" (II:fol.52). Although Urania's frank speech recalls the no-nonsense approach of Paulina, her position as Amphilanthus's sister, and a ruler in her own right, enables her to address him from a position of political equality rather than subordination, while her friendship with Pamphilia similarly remains free of the social hierarchy separating Paulina and her queen. Thus Wroth elevates the woman's role in the political structures of the community, while stressing the mutuality of female companionship.

In the latter part of *Urania*, Wroth conjoins the mutuality of friendship and love, and transforms some of the boundaries distinguishing masculine and feminine behavior and discourse. Florizel and Lindavera come together more as equals than as wooer and wooed, while Pamphilia and Amphilanthus now prove able to move beyond some of the gender-specific expectations which previously bound them. In *As You Like It*, Rosalind maintains gendered expectations of behavior by remarking: "I could find in my heart to disgrace my man's apparel and to cry like a woman; but I must comfort the weaker vessel" (*AYLI*, II.iv.4–6). Amphilanthus, on the other hand, weeps much more copiously than Pamphilia in the second portion of Wroth's narrative, while the "feminine" comparisons which Wroth uses to describe him — hands more delicate than those of a lady, and behavior "as if hee had bin bred in a ladys chamber" (II:fol.2) — parallel his increased capacity for friendship and mutual bonding. Instead of cloaking her women in masculine disguises which provide them artificial entry into a world of patriarchal discourse, Wroth depicts a male character coming to terms with feminine qualities not as weaknesses but as strengths within himself, and learning to appreciate the friendship not only of male comrades but also of women.[30] No longer approaching Pamphilia solely as a lover, Amphilanthus becomes her loving friend as well.

At the same time, Wroth subverts cultural and literary norms to emphasize the increasingly articulate voices of the women in her fictive society. In one late scene, Wroth depicts a circle of friends, including both Pamphilia and Amphilanthus, staying up into the night and sharing reminiscences about their youth, "the flowering time of their first lovings, every one, nott nice, butt truly telling their infinitely suffering passions" (II:fol.57v). Pamphilia initially suffered love as a "true feeler" who "only can know how to beare" (314), but by the end of *Urania* she has learned to "truly tell" her passions, to speak with her own voice. And unlike Rosalind at the conclusion of *As You Like It*, who confesses that s/he is an actor after all, Pamphilia need not excuse any lack of "fashion" in speaking as she likes.[31] With the encouragement of female friends such as Urania and Veralinda, Pamphilia moves beyond the dependency of her "first loving" to realize her capability, as a woman, to command her mind's "Empire" and to claim the authority of her own discourse.

However vocal initially, Shakespeare's female characters often lose their voices, effectually if not literally, by the endings of their plays. Desdemona and Hermione can be silenced by their husbands because both women function primarily not as speakers, but as listeners, as the recipients and interpreters of male speech. Even Beatrice and Rosalind move from speeches of their own to the relative suppression of women's discourse predicated by Shakespeare's dramatic denouements: Beatrice's mouth is literally "stopped" by Benedick's kiss (rather than the other way around), and Rosalind disavows her woman's voice in the epilogue by calling attention to the male actor who speaks it. Wroth's women, however, not only are not reduced to silence as the romance progresses but instead are increasingly empowered to construct their identities through the authority of their own speech. Instead of looking to Amphilanthus, Pamphilia looks to herself to articulate her avowed constancy as a woman. And once Urania matures through her initial search for self-definition, she becomes a touchstone for other characters seeking to define, that is to give voice to, their identities.

Even as Wroth "dramatizes" women's voices within a narrative genre, she re-fashions some of the gender-specific expectations which mark women's speech, and silence, in the dramatic genres of Shakespeare's plays as well. By privileging female bonding and representing mutuality rather than hierarchy as a viable basis for communication in friendship and love, Wroth feminizes the discourse of romance. She translates Shakespeare's "subculture" of female friendship into a governing force in her own narrative, re-forming Shakespeare's focus on patriarchal tensions with her own emphasis on matrilineal bonds and shared women's speech.[32] The multiplicity and variety of women's voices in *Urania* resists an essentialist interpretation of the nature of femininity in early modern England, inviting rather our renewed awareness of the constructed nature of every voice. Through her narrative of "the woman's part," Mary Wroth conveys the potential for women, both as friends and as lovers, to command not one but many voices of their own.

Carol Neely's call for a "reengendering" of the Renaissance requires not only critical juxtapositions of male and female writers in early modern England, "overread[ing] men's canonical texts with women's uncanonical ones," but also attention to the role of "gender" in "engendering" discourse. The *Oxford English Dictionary* distinguishes between two gender-specific definitions of the term "engender": "of the male: to beget," and "of the female: to conceive, bear." For the male, in biological terms, engendering is a single act, precipitating consequences but not necessarily responsibility. For the woman, the act of engendering is an ongoing and manifold process, from conception, through "bearing" the gestation, to birth. When Margaret Homans explores the significance of sexual difference to the act of writing in her study of nineteenth-century women writers, *Bearing the Word*, she suggests how women writers' attempts to reclaim their own experiences as paradigms for writing collide with their acknowledgment of a dominant cultural myth of language which presumes their silence.[33] The tension between "when to speake" and "how to beare" in silence, identified early in *Urania*, modulates later on, particularly for Pamphilia, into the challenge of how to bear speech, how to give birth to female discourse in the face of patriarchal constraints.

The engendering of discourse for women writers depends upon gender distinctions "begot" by male writers, but reconceived by women "bearing the word" in a different voice. Mary Wroth foregrounds the gender-specific nature of speech in her narrative, writing against the "fashion" which Shakespeare's Rosalind appears to transgress but in fact enforces. When women's voices are constructed and spoken by men, gender distinctions are frequently marginalized, subsumed into a discourse where men have the last word. By contrast, women's voices in *Urania* encode female resistance to assumptions of masculine authority. The "reengendering" of any period, from early modern England to the present, must begin with our awareness not only of the oppositional strategies but also of the "engendering" potential of female-authored discourse. Mary Wroth's *Urania* gives early and gendered voice to the concerns of such discourse.

NOTES

1. For more detailed consideration of Wroth's relation to the prose romance tradition, see Naomi J. Miller, "'Not much to be marked': Narrative of the Woman's Part in Lady Mary Wroth's *Urania*," *Studies in English Literature* 29 (1989), 121–37, and Margaret [Witten-Hannah] McLaren, "Lady Mary Wroth's *Urania*: The Work and the Tradition," Ph.D. diss., University of Auckland, 1978, ch. 1.

2. Janet Todd, *Feminist Literary History* (New York: Routledge, 1988), p. 136, discusses in theoretical terms how attention to genre "makes discernible otherwise hidden ideological constraints."

3. Roberts, *Poems*, pp. 12–15.

4. Suzanne Gossett, "'Man-maid, begone!': Women in Masques," *English Literary Renaissance* 18 (1988), 96–113.

5. It is quite possible that Wroth witnessed court performances of such plays as *Othello* in 1604 and *The Winter's Tale* in 1611. Andrew Gurr, *Playgoing in Shakespeare's London* (Cambridge: Cambridge University Press, 1987), pp. 57–63, 167, documents the large number of "ladies" in attendance at Shakespeare's plays during the early seventeenth century, as does Richard Levin, "Women in the Renaissance Theatre Audience," *Shakespeare Quarterly* 40 (1989), 165–74.

6. See "'Not much to be marked'," esp. pp. 123–24, 126ff.

7. Carol Thomas Neely, "Constructing the Subject: Feminist Practice and the New Renaissance Discourses," *English Literary Renaissance* 18 (1988), 5–18.

8. See Jonathan Goldberg, "Shakespearean inscriptions: the voicing of power," in *Shakespeare and the Question of Theory*, ed. Patricia Parker and Geoffrey Hartman (New York: Methuen, 1985), pp. 134–35, and Gary Waller, "Struggling into Discourse: The Emergence of Renaissance Women's Writing," in *Silent but for the Word: Tudor Women as Patrons, Translators, and Writers of Religious Works*, ed. Margaret Patterson Hannay (Kent, Ohio: The Kent State University Press, 1985), pp. 238–56.

9. Katherine Usher Henderson and Barbara F. McManus, *Half-Humankind: Contexts and Texts of the Controversy about Women in England, 1540–1640* (Urbana: University of Illinois Press, 1985), p. 48.

10. McLaren, "Lady Mary Wroth's *Urania*," 170–95, makes a case for the influence of "late Elizabethan and Jacobean spectacular theatre" upon Wroth's motifs and settings, without attending to her dialogue and action. Carolyn Ruth Swift, "Feminine Identity in Lady Mary Wroth's Romance *Urania*," *English Literary Renaissance* 14 (1984), 336–37, 344–46, draws only brief comparisons between some of Wroth's and Shakespeare's female characters, concluding that Wroth's women appear trapped and victimized by contrast to the strong heroines of Shakespeare. See Weidemann's essay in this volume for further analysis of Wroth's vision of "femininity as theater."

11. Coppelia Kahn, "The Absent Mother in *King Lear*," in *Rewriting the Renaissance: The Discourses of Sexual Difference in Early Modern Europe*, ed. Margaret W. Ferguson, Maureen Quilligan, and Nancy J. Vickers (Chicago: University of Chicago Press, 1986), pp. 33–49, addresses the significance of absent mothers in the patriarchal families headed by Gloucester and Lear.

12. Nancy Chodorow, *The Reproduction of Mothering: Psychoanalysis and the Sociology of Gender* (Berkeley: University of California Press, 1978), pp. 169, 176, 207. Chodorow predicates her theory upon the presence of a female primary caretaker during a child's early years, a situation which predominated even in courtly circles in the Renaissance, through the use of wet nurses.

13. While critics have alluded to the significance of Worth's close, if ambivalent, relationship with her father, less noted is the fact that she preserved a strong and affectionate bond with her own mother. From her childhood, when her nine-months-pregnant mother refused to be separated from the eight-year-old Mary, who had the measles, to her adulthood, when she retired to her mother's company at Penshurst to recover from a miscarriage, Mary Wroth was able to count on the loving presence of her mother, in contrast to the frequent absences, abroad or at court, of her father. See De L'Isle MS, U1475: Rowland Whyte to Robert Sidney, 12 November 1595, C12/23; Robert Sidney to Barbara Sidney, 8 August 1608, C81/159, and 28 August 1608, C81/160.

14. See Eve Kosofsky Sedgwick, *Between Men: English Literature and Male Homosocial Desire* (New York: Columbia University Press, 1985), pp. 18, 28–48, on the subordination of "femaleness" to patterns of male homosocial desire in Shakespeare's sonnets.

15. Louis A. Montrose, "'Shaping Fantasies': Figurations of Gender and Power in Elizabethan Culture," *Representations* 1 (1983), 69. Similarly, Peter Erickson, *Patriarchal Structures in Shakespeare's Drama* (Berkeley: University of California Press, 1985), observes that "ties between men remain central" (pp. 4–8) and that "men originally divided are reunited . . . but women undergo the reverse process" (p. 36), while Janet Adelman, "Male Bonding in Shakespeare's Comedies," in *Shakespeare's "Rough Magic": Renaissance Essays in Honor of C.L. Barber*, ed. Peter Erickson and Coppelia Kahn (Newark: University of Delaware Press, 1985), p. 81, suggests further that "the breach in bonding felt as potentially tragic when it occurs between men is felt as negligible or even as deeply comic when it occurs between women."

16. Carole McKewin, "Counsels of Gall and Grace: Intimate Conversations Between Women in Shakespeare's Plays," in *The Woman's Part: Feminist Criticism of Shakespeare*, ed. Carolyn Ruth Swift Lenz, Gayle Greene, and Carol Neely (Urbana: University of Illinois Press, 1980), pp. 122–23.

17. See Swift, "Feminine Identity," 329, and McLaren, "Lady Mary Wroth's *Urania*," 253–55.

18. McKewin, "Gall and Grace," p. 117. See also Simon Shepherd, *Amazons and Warrior Women: Varieties of Feminism in Seventeenth-Century Drama* (Sussex: Harvester Press, 1981), p. 159, on the nature of the "separate female group" created by the presence of female companions in Shakespeare's later comedies.

19. Lenz, Greene, and Neely, eds., introduction to *The Woman's Part*, p. 5.

20. Jeanne Addison Roberts explores that comparison at some length in "Horses and Hermaphrodites in *The Taming of the Shrew*," *Shakespeare Quarterly* 34 (1983), 159–71.

21. "Jane Anger her protection for Women" (1589), reproduced in *First Feminists: British Women Writers, 1578–1799*, ed. Moira Ferguson (Bloomington: Indiana University Press, 1985), p. 71.

22. See *The Private Correspondence of Lady Jane Cornwallis, 1613–44,* ed. Lord Braybrooke (London: S & J. Bentley, Wilson, & Fley, 1842), pp. 22–173, and *The Diary of Lady Anne Clifford,* ed. Vita Sackville-West (New York: Doran, 1923).

23. See Marianne Novy, "Shakespeare's Imagery of Gender and Gender Crossing," ch. 10 in *Love's Argument: Gender Relations in Shakespeare* (Chapel Hill: University of North Carolina Press, 1984), pp. 188–202.

24. Catherine Belsey, "Disrupting sexual difference: meaning and gender in the comedies," in *Alternative Shakespeares,* ed. John Drakakis (London: Methuen, 1985), pp. 166–90, focuses on the tensions attending the disguised heroine's attempt "to speak from a position which is not that of a full, unified, gendered subject."

25. Goldberg, "Shakespearean inscriptions," p. 130.

26. Henderson and McManus, *Half Humankind,* pp. 47–53, summarize such popular Renaissance stereotypes.

27. For more discussion of Pamphilia's voice as a poet, see Naomi J. Miller, "Rewriting Lyric Fictions: The Role of the Lady in Lady Mary Wroth's *Pamphilia to Amphilanthus,*" in *The Renaissance Englishwoman in Print: Counterbalancing the Canon,* ed. Anne M. Haselkorn and Betty S. Travitsky (Amherst: University of Massachusetts Press, 1990), pp. 295–310, and Masten's and Fienberg's essays in this volume.

28. See Roberts's essay in this volume for a discussion of the nature of the *de praesenti* contract into which Pamphilia and Amphilanthus enter at this time.

29. "Jane Anger" (see n. 21) and Joane Sharp, "A Defence of Women" (1617), reproduced in *First Feminists,* ed. Ferguson.

30. Contrast with Sedgwick's analysis, *Between Men,* pp. 36, 45–47, of feminization as a degeneration of masculine identity in Shakespeare's sonnets.

31. The Shakespearean collapsing of categories dividing women and actors, which Wroth resists, is further illuminated by Jean E. Howard's essay, "Renaissance antitheatricality and the politics of gender and rank in *Much Ado About Nothing,*" in *Shakespeare Reproduced: The Text in History and Ideology,* ed. Jean E. Howard and Marion F. O'Connor (Methuen: London, 1987), pp. 163–87, which demonstrates that the antitheatrical tracts construct women and actors "interchangeably, in the same rhetoric of contamination and adulteration."

32. See Alison M. Jaggar, *Feminist Politics and Human Nature* (Totowa, N.J.: Rowman and Allan Held, 1983), p. 270, on the role of "womanspace" in allowing women to "nurture each other and themselves" within a patriarchal culture.

33. Margaret Homans, *Bearing the Word: Language and Female Experience in Nineteenth-Century Women's Writing* (Chicago: University of Chicago Press, 1986).

PART FOUR

In Different Voices

Mary Wroth and the Invention
of Female Poetic Subjectivity

Nona Fienberg

The nature of women's writing was clearly at issue early in the seventeenth century. Remember Rosalind's response to Phoebe's verses: "I say she never did invent this letter, / This is a man's invention and his hand" (*AYLI*, IV.ii.28–29). She insists that "women's gentle brain / Could not drop forth such giant-rude invention" (IV.iii.34–35). While Rosalind as Ganymede speculates about how a woman's writing might sound, the work of feminist scholars confirms the range of women writers. Yet as scholars have reexamined the writings of Vittoria Colonna, Veronica Gambara, Marguerite de Navarre, and Margaret More Roper, they have reconstructed a history of the invention of female subjectivity that Renaissance women writers themselves worked to recover. When Mary Wroth writes *Pamphilia to Amphilanthus* (1621), the first sonnet sequence in English written from the point of view of a woman, she demonstrates her poetic invention. As Margaret Hannay showed in the opening essay of this collection, Wroth situates her texts in the line of her aunt, Mary Sidney, Countess of Pembroke, by interweaving references to Sidney's literary reputation and her poetry. In addition, Wroth creates a fictional audience of women readers and writers. This female community testifies to the mythological, allegorical, and historical traditions of women in the making of culture, while it is also generative of that creativity.

In sonnet 38 of *Pamphilia to Amphilanthus*, Wroth's speaker describes a woman's marginal relationship to the dominant culture. But her question also suggests the need for an audience to confirm her contributions to poetic invention: "What pleasure can a bannish'd creature have / In

all the pastimes that invented arr / By witt or learning" (P44).[1] The
"pastimes" of "witt or learning" as the court culture would define
them have been "invented" by men. While her question expresses the
pain of her banishment, earlier in the sequence sonnet 23 provides an
alternative perspective on her social isolation. In sonnet 23, Wroth's
speaker engages in the process of inventing herself:

> When every one to pleasing pastime hies
>   Some hunt, some hauke, some play, while some delight
>   In sweet discourse, and musique showes joys might
>   Yett I my thoughts doe farre above thes prise. . . .
> When others hunt, my thoughts I have in chase;
>   If hauke, my minde att wished end doth fly,
>   Discourse, I with my spiritt tauke, and cry
>   While others, musique choose as greatest grace.
> O God, say I, can thes fond pleasures move?
> Or musique bee butt in sweet thoughts of love? (P26)

Not the pastimes of the court "invented" by men, but her own invention, the pleasures of her inward self, shape her sonnet. In the third
quatrain, the speaker redefines terms that allow her to create her own
subjectivity. Instead of the courtly hunt, she will chase her thoughts.
Instead of accepting the court's definition of hawking, discourse, and
music, the speaker appropriates those terms into her interior landscape.
Instead of praising the beloved, she praises and values her own "thoughts."
Such a re-evaluation of courtly values offers liberation. Instead of being
the object seen or spoken of, she declares herself "free from eyes" and
discoursing with "my spiritt." Still, the couplet's turn to questions
and to the authority of God in her struggle marks the extent to which
the speaker's internalizing of courtly values undermines the apparent
confidence of the quatrains' assertions.[2]

Surely the speaker's retreat from the public court world into an inward, private world is familiar. Derived from Petrarch's self-making
in his *Canzoniere*, the turn inward becomes part of the sonnet tradition
in the line of Wyatt, Sidney, Spenser, Shakespeare, and perhaps Donne.[3]
Yet the female authorship of *Pamphilia to Amphilanthus* marks the work's
difference and its danger. Since Petrarch's songs and sonnets, the poet's
turn to an interior self had been valorized by the humanist tradition.
By means of his learning, the poet as humanist justified his preoccupa-
tion with himself as subject. Through Virgil and Ovid, through re-

discovery of the classics, male poets created voices of authority in poetry. In Petrarch's love poetry, however, the male poetic corpus is substantiated at the cost of the dismemberment of Laura, his beloved. As Thomas Greene argues in demonstrating Donne's self-discovery in his elegies, "for males at any rate the habit of transforming the object of desire, and especially her body, into a symbol seems virtually irresistible."[4] To Greene's speculation that the love poetry of a female poet might escape this process, Wroth's poetry provides one clear answer: no blazons scattering the parts of her beloved, no fetishizing of a veil, a foot, an eyebrow, and thus no self-creation out of the scattered parts of the beloved. But if the women of the English Renaissance won only limited access to the classical learning through which the humanist poets validated their self-exploration, and if Wroth rejected reification of the beloved, then what are the materials out of which she invented female poetic subjectivity? In articulating the process of transforming herself from object to subject, Wroth speaks of the pleasures of the self.

Wroth's authorship and 1621 publication of *The Countess of Mountgomeries Urania* offers a partial answer. By writing a secular text and by publishing the fine folio volume of her romance with its accompanying songs and sonnets, Wroth transgresses the boundaries of sacred writings that had largely contained women writers in English.[5] Her collection violates the courtly codes of coterie transmission of aristocratic poetry and disrupts male conversation with female discourses. Wroth knows, I believe, the danger of "dismemberment," exclusion from membership in her community, that her writing and publication challenge. She knows the codes of her courtly world. In writing her poetry she negotiates between the violation she risks and the work she values.

Wroth gives that danger narrative form in the dynamic exchange between the theatrical spectacles of the Jacobean court masques, tilts, and barriers, and the secret cabinets where the women of the court keep their portrait miniatures, their love sonnets, and their intimate writings. In the past, the public life and heroic action in a chivalric sense attested to worth in the court world. In the early decades of the seventeenth century in England, a new definition of value in interiority begins to emerge, to which Drayton ironically attests, "nothing is esteemed in this lunatic age but what is kept in cabinets."[6] Although the authorities in Wroth's court society came to view the increasing emphasis on the private world strictly in terms of conspiracy and cabal, Wroth places new value on female subjectivity and invites her readers to contemplate the consequences.

While the disparity between public shows and private secrets could inform Ben Jonson's gossip that "my lady Wroth is unworthily married on a jealous husband," his play upon Wroth's name becomes—for Wroth herself, in *Pamphilia to Amphilanthus*—a means of creating female poetic subjectivity. Wroth thematizes the danger of writing and publishing in her social position through serious play upon her name. The contemporary regulation of women's lives in marriage sought to preclude the value of female subjectivity, but Wroth asserts her "worth" in her writing. Her name holds both a public standing and a private, interior measure of value. Each time she writes her own name, it is also her husband's. She doubts her "worth," questions her "work," and detaches herself from what she has "wrought." So Wroth's praise of her "true worth" in sonnet 13 may also encode the financial indebtedness in which her husband's death left her (P15). The name bespeaks her husband's family, but neither her literary ancestry nor her love. In writing about cultural conditions which would impose female silence, Wroth both risks punishment and challenges those conditions. Our cultural work, to recover the female subjectivity she invents, begins with Wroth's inscribing of Pamphilia as a reader and writer of her self.

Reading and writing serve as critical moves in the creation of female subjectivity in the central moment of *Urania*. A crucial act of reading and self-invention lies at the heart of the romance. Even as Pamphilia and Amphilanthus struggle to declare their love, Wroth's heroine retreats into her private chambers to read a romance which recounts "the affection of a Lady to a brave Gentleman." Although they "equally loved," his manhood demands that he "exceede a woman in all things," including his "inconstancie," and so "hee left her for a new" (264). Pamphilia is reading a book very like *Urania* itself, the story of her constant love for the inconstant Amphilanthus. To read, and to recognize in her reading the story of her self, is Pamphilia's occasion for self-discovery.

The moment recalls analogous events of self-discovery in the creation of male subjectivity, like Augustine's reading of the pertinent Bible passage at the conversion scene in the *Confessions*, or Petrarch's reading of Augustine when he recalls himself to interiority on the peak of Mount Ventoux. But the differences in Wroth's interior world help to mark her position in cultural history as an inventor of female subjectivity. Pamphilia is reading neither the Bible nor the confessions of a Church father. The value of her subjectivity is not measured by the judgment of spiritual authority. Her reading is not prompted by a voice of admonition, either external as when Augustine hears a voice call "take it and read," or internal as in Petrarch's guilt in his pleasures in the view from the mountain. Instead, we may imagine Pamphilia reading the very text in which Mary Wroth has inscribed her as a character. Pamphilia's turn inward is, thus, validated by a woman writer, whose plots of women's self-discovery turn not on admonitions from male authorities but on the women reading, speaking, and writing stories of themselves.

This scene of Pamphilia as a reader of her self is followed immediately by a scene which marks the social danger of her writing. When Amphilanthus returns from his adventures to Pamphilia's side, he asks for her verses. She admits him to the privacy of "her Cabinet." Step by step, Amphilanthus appropriates Pamphilia's private, inward places:

> When they were there, she tooke a deske, wherein her papers lay, and kissing them, delivered all shee had saved from the fire, being in her owne hand unto him, yet blushing told him, she was ashamed, so much of her folly should present her selfe unto his eyes. (266)

Amphilanthus wonders at the emotion she reveals "in her owne hand," in her own poetry. She blushes and he kisses her. In the same box Amphilanthus discovers Pamphilia's picture, "drawne by the best hand of the time." With increasing physical intimacy, Pamphilia allows Amphilanthus to enter her private cabinet, then to read her own verses, then to kiss her, then to handle her portrait miniature, and finally to claim it as a love token. Amphilanthus's discovery of Pamphilia's physical self depends upon her own self-discovery as a subject, first through reading her own story, and then through her writing. But the cabinet, the box, the verses, and the miniature which had been Pamphilia's inward places have become a site of appropriation, even violation. Amphilanthus's intrusion into her secret cabinets is architectural, but it is also somatic.

Her body responds not in fear, but in embarrassment. Pamphilia adopts Amphilanthus's evaluation of her verses in her blushes and in her shame. She has become the work, the artifact he now claims as an object for his pleasure.

In the romance the intimate encounter between the two lovers has greater narrative value than Pamphilia's loss. Thus, although the text of *Urania* has unfolded many lyrics written by female characters, in this encounter readers are not privy to Pamphilia's poems. Once Amphilanthus has opened Pamphilia's desk, her poetry, like her body, becomes an object of his speculation. The poetry disappears into Amphilanthus's eyes. But the songs and sonnets which follow *Urania* suggest a different measure of value. When Pamphilia's poetry is finally revealed to the readers of *Urania*, Amphilanthus's shocking transgression mediates the intrusion of Pamphilia's female discourses into the world of print.[7]

Wroth's *Urania* establishes a female subjectivity which finds its center in reading and in writing. But the romance pressure toward adventure turns outward, where the sonnets turn inward, toward invention. Also, unlike *Urania*, where women's participation in the material world is given such concrete form as Pamphilia's embroidering of a waistcoat, *Pamphilia to Amphilanthus* banishes the signs of women's material culture. In the songs and sonnets there is no needlework, no housecleaning, no childrearing, no supervising of servants, no cookery, preserving, surgery, physic, tailoring, and no hospitality.[8] Wroth's avoidance of such signs of women's culture proves politically telling. King James sought to enforce the power of his state machinery through policing material culture. In the year of Wroth's publication of *Urania* he instructed the clergy to "inveigh vehemently against the insolencies of our women, and their wearing of broad brimmed hats, pointed doublets, their hair cut short or shorne, and some of them stilletoes or poniards."[9] James's attempts to enforce the boundaries of dress in the formation of gender roles constitute part of the fiction of a state where only men are producers. Wroth, however, asserts her value as a producer through the writing of her own hand.

Thus, in *Pamphilia to Amphilanthus* the work wrought by a woman's hand is the poetic lines themselves. Like the interior world the portrait miniature creates, Wroth's poetry creates a world of interiority, where everyday life is deferred and excluded. Instead of the pull of adventure of public life, Wroth finds freedom in the imaginative sanctuary of reading and writing. But she also writes of the dangers of oppression and pain posed both by that retreat and by the public world. For all her efforts to banish those signs of her contingent being, subject to the enforcement of the state, the absolutist court powers compel her to withdraw her book from circulation. Those Jacobean attempts to suppress female authorship are reinscribed in some contemporary formulations of the history of consciousness.

Since Wroth's invention of female poetic subjectivity in *Pamphilia to Amphilanthus* contributes to our understanding of self-fashioning in the Renaissance, it is important to distinguish her materials from those Stephen Greenblatt has described in his use of the term. In *Renaissance Self-Fashioning*, Greenblatt posits a theatrical sense of selfhood and self-making that proves compelling in his discussion of the participants in a court dominated by men.[10] He demonstrates that self-fashioning takes place in language, that the self is fashioned in relation both to the sources of authority and to those defined as alien to a culture, and that achieved identity is always vulnerable to subversion or loss. Nevertheless, questions remain about the adequacy of Greenblatt's work as a model for female expressiveness. Not only does his model exclude women from participation in a masculinist stage-play world, it also appropriates women's own discourse as a product of the dominant culture. Remember Amphilanthus's appropriation of Pamphilia's verse. How, then, does a woman, who has been ascribed the roles of object of vision and of speech, write herself as the subject who sees and who speaks?[11]

In her poetry, Wroth invents a different authority of origin from that the court validates.[12] Wroth's speaker declares herself as a subject not in a theatrical sense, but in a private accounting like that which might take place in devotional or financial secret cabinets. For example, in sonnet 42, the metaphor of "this stage of woe / wher sad disasters have theyr open showe" (12–13) contrasts with the contemplative manner of the octave:

If ever love had force in humaine brest?
    If ever hee could move in pensive hart?
    Or if that hee such powre could butt impart
    To breed those flames whose heart brings joys unrest.
Then looke on mee: I am to thes adrest,

> I, ame the soule that feeles the greatest smart;
> I, ame that hartles trunk of harts depart
> And I, that one, by love, and griefe oprest. (P48)

In summoning the eyes of the beloved to look on "mee," the "I" of the speaker calls upon an inward self that "this stage of woe" with its "open showe" cannot reveal. The subjunctive verbs of the opening quatrain lead the reader to an inward, imagined state of possibility, which reveals the speaker's "I." In contrast, the "o" sound of the rhymes in the final four lines reject "this stage of woe" as hollow:

> For had hee seene, hee must have pitty show'd;
> I should nott have bin made this stage of woe
> Wher sad disasters have theyr open showe
> O noe, more pitty he had sure beestow'd.

The stage of woe becomes a site of violation, and of exposure to misreading. The subjunctive inwardness of the opening quatrain offers an alternative derived from the secret cabinet of spiritual or economic accounting, but translated into the making of the female "I."[13]

How does Wroth's invention of female poetic subjectivity differ from what Joel Fineman has described as the invention of poetic subjectivity in Shakespeare's sonnets?[14] The "perjured eye" of Shakespeare's sonnets praises a subject about whose shattered image he must lie. In sonnet 59, when he is "laboring for invention," Shakespeare's speaker must "beare amisse / The second burthen of a former child." Only so monstrous a birth remains possible to the speaker, so exhausted is the rhetoric of praise. Wroth too acknowledges the exhaustion of epideictic poetics in sonnet 7 in the second half of her sequence. Her opening quatrain asserts:

> An end fond jealousie alas I know
> Thy hidenest and thy most secrett art
> Thou canst noe new invention frame but part
> I have allreddy seene, and felt with woe. (P69)

Like Shakespeare's speaker, Wroth's identifies the problematics of poetic invention. She knows her "eye" to have been "perjured" by "fained show." But Wroth rejects that tired subject for invention: "thy flattery, and thy skill, / Which idly made mee to observe thy will; / Thus is my learning by my bondage bought." Instead of paying obeisance to the male "will" which impels Shakespeare's speaker, Wroth subverts that observation. Wroth's speaker finds the words that Petrarch's Laura, Sidney's Stella, and Shakespeare's Dark Lady had been denied. In declaring "Thus is my learning by my bondage bought." she is, through the poetics of the Petrarchan tradition, asserting her freedom to rewrite that tradition.

Wroth thematizes her resistance in her most physically and politically explicit sonnet. In sonnet 35, Wroth creates in the shape of the sonnet a body which unlike both the body politic and her own body does not betray her. Male appropriation of birth to provide metaphors for poetic creation, like Shakespeare's monstrous birth and Sidney's comical "great with child to speak and helpless in my throes," constitutes a poetic commonplace. For a woman to write a poem about birth, however, as Wroth does in sonnet 35, is to reclaim her body as her own. In this poem about miscarriage, Wroth gives a new and natural meaning to a wrenched and overused convention:

> Faulce hope which feeds but to destroy, and spill
>   What itt first breeds; unaturall to the birth
>   Of thine owne wombe; conceaving butt to kill,
>   And plenty gives to make the greater dearth. (P40)

Only late in her marriage to Robert Wroth and the year before his death did she bear their one child, a son, James, who may have, had he lived, spared his mother the financial difficulties of her later years. She may, perhaps, be writing from the pain of her body's betrayal. The opening quatrain carries a powerful conviction of an internal deception. When Wroth moves from her natural body to the body politic in the second quatrain, she broaches dangerously political territory:

> Soe Tirants doe who faulsly ruling earth
>   Outwardly grace them, and with profitts fill
>   Advance those who appointed are to death
>   To make theyr greater falle to please theyr will.

By the third quatrain, she explicates the analogy between the "faire showes" tyrants employ to deceive those they would kill and the hopes that delude those who rely on appearances. Not love, but physical and political betrayal, and biological and social oppression impel this sonnet. Just as a woman's body may betray itself, so does the body politic betray those it contains. But the tyrant's "will" places him in control. In contrast, in the most interior places, "thine owne wombe," the speaker acknowledges that she is not in control. That involuntary self-hood is privileged in the closing sestet:

> Thus shadow they theyr wicked vile intent
>> Coulering evill with a show of good
>> While in faire showes theyr malice soe is spent;
>> Hope kills the hart, and tirants shed the blood.
> For hope deluding brings us to the pride
> Of our desires the farder downe to slide.

The "faire showes" of tyrants reveal "the pride / Of our desires." The speaker, on the other hand, contains secrets beyond mere human will, with the power implicit in such secrets.

While Wroth's rewriting of Petrarchan poetics accounts for her debt to her uncle, Sir Philip Sidney, her aunt, Mary Sidney, Countess of Pembroke, helps her to claim female origins for her poetic authority. In Mary Sidney's work, Wroth might well have found an alternative Petrarchan tradition more suited to her poetics. Wroth announces her debt to the visionary Petrarch of the *Trionfi* in the liminal sonnet of the sequence. In so doing, she places herself in a line of women writers that extends from Queen Elizabeth through the Countess of Pembroke, for whom the *Triumphs* provide an invitation to female poetics. Queen Elizabeth's translation of *The Triumph of Eternity* is eclipsed in importance to Wroth, however, by her aunt's translation of *The Triumph of Death*. Wroth found, in that vision where Laura at last declares her love for Petrarch, the familial and female precedent for her poetry's open declaration of female desire. While Wroth's debt is not a verbal one, in the opening vision of her sequence she speaks as a woman who loves, like Laura in *The Triumph of Death*. The sonnet translates both the visionary Petrarch and the visionary Dante of the *Vita Nuova* into the making of her poetic subject:

> When nights black mantle could most darkness prove,
>> And sleepe deaths Image did my sences hiere
>> From knowledge of my self, then thoughts did move
>> Swifter then those most swiftnes need require:
> In sleepe, a Chariot drawne by wing'd desire
>> I sawe: wher sate bright Venus Queene of love,
>> And att her feete her sonne, still adding fire

To burning hearts which she did hold above,
Butt one hart flaming more then all the rest
    The goddess held, and putt itt to my brest,
    Deare sonne, now shutt sayd she: thus must wee winn;
Hee her obay'd, and martir'd my poore hart,
    I, waking hop'd as dreames it would depart
Yett since: O mee: a lover I have binn. (P1)

In this, the first of the 103 poems of *Pamphilia to Amphilanthus*, Wroth announces her poetic intentions. The danger of her enterprise is suggested by the 558-page prose and poetry "preface" to the sequence. By envisioning her opening sonnet in implicit response to the opening visionary sonnet of Dante's *Vita Nuova*, Wroth is challenging the Italianist world. Where Dante saw a man feeding Dante's own burning heart to his beloved lady, Wroth sees a flaming heart held by Venus, then shut within the visionary speaker's breast. The vision which makes a lover and a poet of Dante constitutes a similarly metamorphic moment for Wroth: "Yett since: O mee: a lover I have binn." Like the poetry of Dante and Petrarch, Wroth's poetry investigates her origins as a poet. But her answers are complicated by the male legacy of female silencing. How can she create a language for female desire?

This liminal sonnet both poses the problems she must engage and begins to suggest her solutions. Her vision responds on the one hand to Dante's and Petrarch's. But on the other hand, by enclosing the flaming heart within her breast, the speaker lays claim to her own body. Moreover, the vision of woman's desire is generated through a female community, including Mary Sidney, the translator of Laura's declaration of female desire in *The Triumph of Death*.

This opening poem of the sequence also rewrites Wroth's own text. Self-referential in two ways, Wroth announces herself as a reader and writer of her own work. First, the frontispiece of the published volume frames with a classical triumphal arch an expansive landscape with, at its center, a statue of Venus holding a flaming heart. Then, in Urania's early wanderings, she comes upon a Palace on a Hill, on which stands a white marble statue of Venus "in her left hand holding a flaming Heart"(39). Venus's statue directs the spectators' attention to the figure of "*Constancy*, holding in her hand the Keyes of the Pallace." From allegorical engraved frontispiece, through prose and poetry in the romance, to the opening sonnet, Wroth leads readers on a journey inward.

Analogously, Wroth creates an inwardness out of Mary Sidney's public legacy of writing. Much as Wroth's rewriting of the male invention of subjectivity depends upon her reclamation of her name, similarly her use of the traditions of female writing reclaims the ideology of the name. Wroth's romance heroine's name, Urania, alludes to Edmund Spenser's praise in "Colin Clout's Come Home Again" of Mary Sidney, Countess of Pembroke. He calls her: "Urania, sister to *Astrofell*, / In whose brave mynd, as in a golden cofer, / All heavenly gifts and riches locked are."

For Wroth, that "golden cofer," like Pamphilia's locked cabinet, contains verses in a woman's own hand: Mary Sidney's poetry. In weaving Mary Sidney's verses from her elegy, "The Dolefull Lay of Clorinda," into her own text in song 2 of *Pamphilia to Amphilanthus*, Wroth reveals a female origin for herself as a reader and writer. Mary Sidney distances her lament for her brother's death through the pastoral voice of the shepherdess, Clorinda, who begins: "Ay mee, to who shall I my case complaine? / That may compassion my impatient griefe?"[15] Sidney's sighs, "Ay mee," and her questioning effort to find an audience for her complaint are echoed in Wroth's song 2:

> All night I weepe, all day I cry, Ay mee;
> I still doe wish though yett deny, Ay mee;
> I sigh, I mourne, I say that still
> I only ame the store for ill, Ay mee; . . .
> Whether (alass) then shall I goe Ay mee;
> When as dispaire all hopes outgoe Ay mee;
> Iff to the Forest, Cupid hyes,
> And my poore soule to his lawe ties Ay mee. (P14)

Sidney's opening sigh, "Ay mee," has become Wroth's insistent refrain. Instead of Mary Sidney's iambic pentameter lines and six-line stanza, Wroth invents an exploded ballad form. That is, she extends the ballad's four-line stanzas of tetrameter verse in lines 1, 2, and 4 by an additional foot, with her "Ay mee" refrain. If, at first, the refrain sounds a note of defeat, as the song goes on, the "I" both in the refrain and in the repeated "i" rhyme (cry, deny, hy, ly) becomes an assertion, an "Aye," and a declaration of the life of an "I." Wroth's challenge to the ballad form, disrupting it by the bold repetition of the refrain, asserts a new, unashamed voice, ready to retell the story of Petrarchism. Because of the more salient mediation of Mary Sidney's poem, the Petrarchan signature antitheses seem remote indeed. The sigh, "Ay mee," is the breath that takes us inside.

Mary Sidney's and Wroth's poems share the subject of the loss of a loved one. While Sidney's poem asks where she should "enfold" her "inward paine," Wroth's asks where she shall "goe." In Sidney's initially inner-directed approach, she asks, "To heavens?" and "To men?," rejecting both in favor of her "selfe." By the fourth stanza, she seems to have resolved her grief in inward resources. But the elegy's closing stanzas assume a more public role, celebrating the eternal glory of Astrophel, as "Joy of the world, and shepheards pride." Wroth's six-stanza song again echoes Clorinda's questions, asking if she should run "To the Court?" to relieve her distress. Like Clorinda, the speaker of Wroth's song rejects the outward resources her culture provides. But Wroth's briefer poem stops with its repose in "quiett rest." Neither the court nor the forest serve as refuge for this lover: "All places ar alike to love Ay mee." Addressing herself, the speaker empowers herself through the truth of her love: "Your true love all truth discovers." Wroth, then, does not provide a resolution of loss through apotheosizing the beloved, but celebrates an examination of a new subject, the female "I."

Wroth addresses the issue of female authorship in her thematics of writing. In sonnet 22, for example, she compares the requisite hiding of her verses, "the marke" she makes to express Cupid's power, with open sacrificial rites of Indians (P25). Just as the sun abuses with sunburn those Indians who worship it, so the speaker's worship of her beloved leads only to "hopes undunn." But the sestet suggests that the Indian's relationship to the sun may indeed be more rewarding than hers to her beloved:

> Beesids theyr sacrifies receav'ds in sight
>   Of theyr chose sainte: Mine hid as worthles rite;
>   Grant mee to see where I my offrings give,
> Then lett mee weare the marke of Cupids might
>   In hart as they in skin of Phoebus light
>   Nott ceasing offrings to love while I Live.

At least the Indians' sacrifice can be shown; hers must be "hid as worthles rite." Wroth's intricate puns on her name, "worth/wroth," and on her writing, "rite/write," encode the intimate entanglement of the activity of writing and the creation of female subjectivity. When the poem at its close turns inward to her "hart," it is not in despair but in determination that she will continue making her "marke," her "off-rings to love while I Live." However devalued her "rite" may be in a public forum, she attests to its "worth" in the sonnet. Wroth takes her metaphor of the Indians from Ben Jonson and Inigo Jones's *Masque of Blackness* (1605) in which she had appeared as Baryte, one of the Daughters of the Niger. In that Jacobean court masque, she had participated in one of those "pleasing pastimes" invented by men. Returning in this sonnet to rewrite the experience, she reclaims it as her own.

Part of Wroth's work in reclaiming poetic invention for women occurs in *Urania*, where she imagines communities of women who read, support, and generate each others' writing.[16] In the lyrics, Venus, Night, Time, Fortune, Folly, and Philomela speak with the voices of female authority from mythology, allegory, and philosphy. The song series following the corona in *Pamphilia to Amphilanthus* develops this female community. In song 2, Silvia and her nymphs hide in the woods, viewing Cupid's solipsistic play:

> All naked playing with his wings
>   Within a mirtle tree
> Which sight a soddaine laughter brings
>   His godhead soe to see;
> And fondly they beegan to jest,
>   With scoffing and delight,
> Nott knowing hee did breed unrest,
>   And that his will's his right. (P92)

Instead of a comic encounter, Cupid turns the incident into a violent assault on the nymphs when he shoots his "murdring dart." The poem explains such a turn through the punning assertion, "his will's his right." But Wroth replaces "powrfull Cupids name" in her next song with the powerful Ovidian name of Philomela, "Philomeale in this arbour / Makes now her loving harbour." By providing Philomela with a song, Wroth returns a voice to that violated heroine. Further, the female community of Silvia and her nymphs generates the creation of Philomela's song.

Similarly, Wroth revises the misogynist representation of Lady Fortune, for example, in sonnet 31. In the interior drama of that sonnet, Fortune offers warmth, comfort, and resolve to the speaker:

Till, rise, sayd she, Reward to thee doth send
 By mee the servants of true lovers, joy:
 Bannish all clowds of doubt, all feares destroy,
 And now on Fortune, and on Love depend. (P36)

The speaker withdraws into an interior realm where the once indifferent or hostile figure of Fortune becomes instead a friend. The peace Fortune brings is reiterated in the closing sonnet of *Pamphilia to Amphilanthus*. There, the speaker first acknowledges her muse in a farewell:

My muse now happy lay thyself to rest,
 Sleepe in the quiett of faithfull love,
 Write you no more, but lett thes phant'sies move
 Some other harts, wake not to new unrest. (P103)

In contrast to Sir Philip Sidney's chiding muse, who opens his sequence with her summons, "Fool . . . look in thy heart and write," Wroth's muse has been an assumed partner, not absent, but a tacit collaborator.

Wroth's community of women recalls Christine de Pisan's *Book of the City of Ladies*, where, to undo the damage misogynist texts have wrought, allegorical figures of Reason, Rectitude, and Justice appear to the author. These worthy women lead Christine de Pisan to rewrite history, mythology, and religion. In a similar way, the female population of Wroth's lyrics pays silent, but no less eloquent, tribute to the origins of female subjectivity in reading and writing: the twelfth-century letters of Heloise, the fables and lays of Marie de France, the allegories of Christine de Pisan, *The Book of Margery Kempe*, and the lyrics of Louise Labé and Gaspara Stampa. They, too, should be numbered in Wroth's company, in the invention of female poetic subjectivity.[17]

NOTES

1. All references to Wroth's poetry use Roberts's edition.
2. See also Masten's and Jones's discussions of this poem in their essays in this volume.
3. Giuseppe Mazzotta, "The *Canzoniere* and the Language of the Self," *Studies in Philology* 75, no. 3 (Summer 1978), 271–96; Anne Ferry, *The "Inward" Language* (Chicago: University of Chicago Press, 1983).
4. Thomas M. Greene, "The Poetics of Discovery," *The Yale Journal of Criticism* 2, no. 2 (Spring 1989), 129–43. See also Nancy Vickers, "Diana Described: Scattered Woman and Scattered Rhyme," *Critical Inquiry* 8, no. 2 (Winter 1981), 265–81.

5. For discussion of those sacred writings, see Margaret Patterson Hannay, ed., *Silent But for the Word: Tudor Women as Patrons, Translators, and Writers of Religious Works* (Kent, Ohio: The Kent State University Press, 1985), pp. 238–56.

6. From Drayton's *Poly-Olbion* (1613), quoted in Wendy Wall, "Disclosures in Print: The 'Violent Enlargement' of the Renaissance Voyeuristic Text," *Studies in English Literature* 29, no. 1 (Winter 1989), 40.

7. See Masten's analysis in this volume of Wroth's emphasis on privacy and withdrawal from circulation, in both her poems and her life; see also Lamb's discussion in this volume of Pamphilia's subjectivity as a reader.

8. Gervase Markham's list of women's duties from *The English Housewife* (1618) appears in Sara Heller Mendelson, *The Mental World of Stuart Women* (Amherst: University of Massachusetts Press, 1987), p. 8.

9. Joan Kelly, "Early Feminist Theory and the *Querelle des Femmes*, 1475–1640," in *Women, History and Theory* (Chicago: University of Chicago Press, 1984), p. 88.

10. Stephen Greenblatt, *Renaissance Self-Fashioning* (Chicago: University of Chicago Press, 1980), pp. 1–9.

11. On this issue, see Carol Thomas Neely, "Constructing the Subject: Feminist Practice and the New Renaissance Discourses," *English Literary Renaissance* 18 (1988), pp. 5–18.

12. Tilde Sankovitch, "Inventing the Authority of Origin: The Difficult Enterprise," in *Women in the Middle Ages and the Renaissance: Literary and Historical Perspectives*, ed. Mary Beth Rose (Syracuse: University of Syracuse Press, 1986), pp. 227–43.

13. See Masten's and Jones's discussions of Sonnet 42 in this volume. Naomi J. Miller, "Rewriting Lyric Fictions: The Role of the Lady in Lady Mary Wroth's *Pamphilia to Amphilanthus*," in *The Renaissance Englishwoman in Print: Counterbalancing the Canon*, ed. Anne M. Haselkorn and Betty S. Travitsky (Amherst: University of Massachusetts Press, 1990), pp. 295–310, differentiates the male and female "I" in comparing Wroth's poetry to that of her uncle, Philip Sidney, and her father, Robert Sidney.

14. Joel Fineman, *Shakespeare's Perjured Eye: The Invention of Poetic Subjectivity in the Sonnets* (Berkeley: University of California Press, 1986).

15. Gary F. Waller, ed. *The Triumph of Death and Other Unpublished and Uncollected Poems by Mary Sidney, Countess of Pembroke (1561–1621)* (Salzburg, 1977), pp. 176–79. On pages 53–60, Waller discusses the question of authorship.

16. See Naomi J. Miller, "'Not much to be marked': Narrative of the Woman's Part in Lady Mary Wroth's *Urania*," *Studies in English Literature* 29 (1989), 121–37.

17. I wish to thank the NEH for its support of two summer programs, Anne Middleton and Lee Patterson's 1988 seminar, "Late Medieval Lives," and Giuseppe Mazzotta's 1989 "Yale Petrarch Institute," during which I completed much of the research and writing of this essay. Thank you to the directors of these programs and to my fellow participants.

Theatricality and Female Identity
in Mary Wroth's *Urania*

Heather L. Weidemann

Critics of seventeenth-century women's writing are by now familiar with the details of the controversy which surrounded Mary Wroth's *The Countesse of Mountgomeries Urania* upon its publication in 1621. A number of prominent men at the court of James I voiced their objections to the work; the most outspoken of such critics, Edward Lord Denny, went so far as to address a venomous directive to Wroth. "Hermophradite in show, in deed a monster / As by thy words and works all men may conster, / Thy wrathfull spite conceived an Idell book / Broughte forth a foole which like the damme doth looke" wrote Denny to the woman he addressed as "Pamphilia," advising her to "leave idle books alone / For wiser and worthyer women have writte none."[1] Denny's charge of monstrous self-display captures the essence of a general reaction to Wroth's writing — a reaction which led male readers to view the *Urania*'s author as an unnatural sight, or, even more precisely, as a scandal. Besieged by this sort of criticism, Wroth was forced to withdraw the *Urania* from sale after only a short time in print.[2]

The Renaissance view of women writers as unseemly is by now a commonplace; recent scholars have noted that many directives in the period enjoined women to stay out of the public eye at all costs.[3] But it is not the fact of a general bias against female authors that I wish to discuss here, for by itself it seems to provide only a partial explanation for the furor which surrounded Lady Mary Wroth's brief publication venture. Wroth, after all, was not the first Englishwoman to publish a work under her own name; in addition, she was a member of the privileged Sidney family, a fact which might have been expected to afford some protection against criticism or censorship. The violent suppression of her *Urania*, however, seems to indicate that no kind of historical precedent, even that of famous literary ancestors like Sir Philip Sidney and the Countess of Pembroke, could give Wroth the appearance of propriety in the eyes of her outraged audience. To understand why, I would like to look beyond the larger climate of dis-ease in which Renaissance women wrote to the *Urania*'s particular vision of female identity and authorship. I will contend that the "scandal" of the *Urania* lay in the specific nature of its intersection with the politics of spectacle and self-representation, for Wroth's work introduced a new figure to the world of English letters: the figure of the theatrical woman.[4]

This figure performs several functions in the *Urania*: it evokes sympathy, induces admiration, and construes social experience as theatrical. Most importantly, it denotes an innovative (one might even say "novel") vision of female identity in particular, a vision which insists that a woman's innermost self is often in conflict with her outward appearance. When the female body is fetishized as an object, as in so much male-authored Renaissance literature, its meaning is supposedly only present on the surface, thereby foreclosing the possibility of a theatricalized or fictional self. In Wroth's writing, however, the female body functions in a different way: its visibility becomes signifier rather than signified, indicating a depth underneath the surface. Women like the *Urania*'s troubled queen Pamphilia are presented not so much as spectacles as revelatory subjects; their appearances often point to a subjective female identity which is hidden but nonetheless authentic. The enabling potential of this new identity directly contrasts with the classic misogynist equation of women and duplicity, reassigning theatrical femininity a positive value and entering it into discourse in the narrative. If Lord Denny's comments are any indication, it is the discursive "show" of this deliberately elusive female self which constitutes at least part of the *Urania*'s shock value. Wroth's configuration of dramatic subjectivity effectively proposes various forms of "coherent" feminine identity as acting — a scandalous proposition for conventional seventeenth-century readers.

Nowhere in *Urania* is the link between feminine identity and acting more evident than in the tale of Lindamira, an account which a narrative voice-over tells the reader is "more exactly related than a fixion"

(429) and which, as Josephine Roberts has shown, precisely parallels
the life of Lady Mary Wroth in its surrounding details.[5] Lindamira is
a faithful servant who is disgraced when a malicious rumor destroys
her reputation:

> . . . all [the queen's] favor was withdrawn as suddenly and directly, as if never
> had: Lindamira remaining like one in a gay Masque, the night pass'd, they are
> in their old clothes againe, and no appearance of what was; she was grieved to
> the heart because she truly lov'd her mistris, as her disgrace went further then
> only discontent for the losse, or the notice the world might take of it, which
> must like their reports be wiped away, or washed like linnen, which would bee
> as white again as ever. But this pierced her heart, and she was inly afflicted, at
> all times she nevertheless attended, never failing her duty, yet desirous to know
> the cause of her misfortune. (424)

Although the beleaguered Lindamira is compelled to act the conventional role of a cheerful lady-in-waiting for fear of further alienating
the queen she serves, the text asserts that her outward composure is
not to be mistaken for her inward state. Her grief is deeply felt and
contrasts with any specular appearance; it cannot be "wiped away, or
washed like linnen." This portrait of a seventeenth-century woman
vigorously opposes surface exterior to interior truth, inscribing the
notion of a "desirous" and ultimately autonomous inner self. "Remaining like one in a gay Masque," Lindamira is presented here as a two-
leveled text; hence, the narrative implies, she must perform to conceal
the fact of a potentially unruly female subjectivity or an emotional state
which might contradict her assigned social role. Wroth's allusion to
both herself and her personal misfortune thus depicts the story of her
life as a forced performance—and insists on the female subject's experience of social life as theatrical.

Given this portrait of the female courtier as an actress in a period
which officially denied women the freedom to act, we can perhaps begin to understand why the *Urania*'s vision of theatrical selfhood was
greeted with such a mixture of outrage and horror. For in constructing
her narrative Wroth not only dramatized her own autobiographical
self; she staged other characters as well. Some of these characters were
based in part on real-life acquaintances, evidently including Edward
Lord Denny—a fact which may provide another clue to the nature of
the controversy unleashed by *Urania*'s publication. By publishing a
work which referred to actual events at the court of James I, Wroth

asserted her right to generate, possess, and sell not only her own life story but also that of others.[6] Through its allusions to contemporary events, the *Urania* offers the spectacle of a woman attempting to cast herself both as an actress and a playwright, rehearsing and scripting provisional identities in direct opposition to both theatrical and anti-theatrical discourse. Not surprisingly, her audience reacted to this new form of female self-representation by censoring her work, in effect ordering her off both stage and page. In what follows, I will attempt to arrive at a more precise understanding of Wroth's historical dilemma by examining some of the prevailing constructions of theatricality and female identity in her day. I will then move to a consideration of several episodes in the *Urania* which are notably affected by those constructions, examining their implications for Wroth's vision of femininity as theater.

I

"Who shall measure the heat and violence of the poet's heart when caught and tangled in a woman's body?" writes Virginia Woolf in her famous speculation on the fate of a possible "Shakespeare's sister."[7] Woolf describes this hypothetical seventeenth-century woman as having "a taste for the theater" and a burning desire to act — a desire which exposes her to ridicule, abuse, and eventual ruin. In Jacobean England, as every drama student knows, women were not permitted to appear as actors in the public theaters; Shakespeare's sister, if she ever existed, would never have been given license to professionally represent anyone on stage, including herself. Theatrical self-display is often denounced as incompatible with proper feminine behavior in the discourse of the Jacobean theater; in Ben Jonson's *Volpone*, for example, Corvino decries Celia's appearance at a window precisely as an unseemly performance: "You smile, / Most graciously, and fan your favors forth, / To give your hot spectators satisfaction! . . . You were an actor with your hand-kerchief."[8] The impropriety of Celia's action lies in the fact of her acting: theatricality in a woman suggests that her identity has somehow become inauthentic or alienated, akin to that of a professional actor. Ironically, of course, the part of Celia would have been performed in

this era by an "inauthentic woman," a boy player whose presence technically enforced the prohibition against women on the professional stage.[9]
Women might properly be designated on stage by male representatives,
but the possibility of staging their own bodies remained closed to them.

If women could find no encouragement for dramatic self-representation
in the world of the public theaters, they fared little better in the private,
absolutist vision of the court masque.[10] In Jonson's *The Masque of Queens*,
Bel-Anna, Queen of the Ocean, played by James I's consort, Queen
Anne, is described solely as a reflection of her husband's masculine
virtue, "humbling all her worth / To him that gave it." James, the
principal observer of the masque, is urged to accept Anne's appearance
as a tribute to his sovereignty: "you . . . cannot but embrace / A spectacle so full of love and grace / Unto your court."[11] The queen is the
"spectacle" here as surely as the masque itself; her privileged visibility
is aestheticized and controlled through its display to the monarch's eye.
As the iconic depiction of Bel-Anna makes clear, Renaissance noblewomen appeared in Jacobean masques in a highly circumscribed manner: although they danced and wore spectacular costumes, they never
asserted themselves in speaking roles. Female characters did speak in
court masques, but on stage at Whitehall Banqueting House (as at the
Globe Theater) their parts would have been taken by boy players. Similarly, although the revels which were an integral part of the masque
drew in women participants, those courtly ladies who descended from
the audience to dance were never more than unproblematic objects
whose jewels and dresses were themselves part of the show.[12] The in-
junction against women's speech in masques effectively promoted the
myth of a coherent gender identity, identifying real women's bodies
(when they appeared on stage at all) as essentialized sites of spectacle
and submission.

The idea of woman as spectacle is not, of course, an innovation pe-
culiar to the masque genre; the work of Nancy Vickers, among others,
has recently reminded us that Renaissance rhetorical tradition often attempts to take control of a woman's body through a gesture of display.
As Vickers remarks, the body "as object or matter is . . . submitted to
a double power-relation inherent in the gesture itself: on the one hand,
the describer controls, possesses, and uses that matter to his own ends;
and, on the other, his reader or listener is extended the privilege or

pleasure of 'seeing.'" Literary forms like the lyric poem or the blazon "publish" the woman they describe by noting the particulars of her appearance, establishing her as an object to be gazed on and seen.[13] Working out of this well-established discursive tradition, the juxtaposition of verbal and visual forms in the Stuart masque doubly extends the pleasure of narrative "seeing" by displaying the muted bodies of real women on stage, relegating those bodies to object status under the gaze of the spectators.[14] Such emblematic gestures, of course, presuppose the objectified woman's silence: to paraphrase Vickers, the world of making words, of making texts, is not hers.

Given this historical and literary context, it seems somewhat remarkable at first to find a Renaissance woman actively attempting to cast herself as an actress or, even worse, a transcendent playwright/author. Setting the fact of *Urania*'s reception aside for the moment, however, the fact that Wroth could construct her particular vision of dramatic subjectivity at all suggests that she may have been able to draw on an existing, if alternative, discourse concerning theatricality and representation. Further inspection reveals that many of the apparently prescriptive constructions of identity in Renaissance texts betray an inability to elide the knowledge that appearance, even the appearance of a seemingly obedient young woman, encompasses the possibility of deception or concealment. Even Jonson's *The Masque of Beautie* finally admits this aspect of theatricality when one of its male characters worries aloud about the women on stage: "say the dames should, with their eyes / Upon the hearts here mean surprise / Were not the men like harmed?"[15] The female body ultimately cannot exhaust its signification even in the masque genre; despite the best efforts of dramatists like Jonson, its surface appearance can never be completely tautological. To the extent that Renaissance texts presuppose that social experience is theatrical, they necessarily open up that Pandora's box of questions: to what extent do women play roles — and by what means may their roles be controlled? It is this question, logically grounded within an alternate discourse — the discourse of "all the world's a stage" — which I would suggest Wroth attempts to "answer" through her efforts to re-envision the female self as a theatrical subject.

Several recent studies have reminded us of the importance of the theatrical metaphor for Renaissance literature; one such analysis, Stephen

Greenblatt's *Renaissance Self-Fashioning*, asserts that "the manuals of court behavior which became popular in the sixteenth century are essentially handbooks for actors, practical guides for a society whose members were always on stage."[16] Despite the inclusive tone of this statement (which I think, as will become clear, is essentially correct), most contemporary studies of theatricality in Renaissance culture have ignored or marginalized the possibility that performing and role-playing, the defining traits of male courtly identity, may in fact have been constitutive features of female courtly identity in some measure as well. Several pieces of historical evidence suggest that at least at the court of James I, some women may have been able (if not exactly encouraged) to engage with theatrical forms and stage representations. Jonson's preface to *The Masque of Queens*, for example, cannot avoid acknowledging what the masque text's representation of Bel-Anna, Queen of the Ocean, denies: that his show was actively shaped in part by a woman's desire. Despite the fact that the masque is intended to honor the king, it is, ironically, the queen's wish which appears to have determined its form: "her majesty (best knowing that a principal part of life in these spectacles lay in their variety) had commanded me to think on some dance or show that might precede hers and have the place of a foil or false masque." Similarly, in the preface to his first court entertainment, *The Masque of Blackness* (a work in which Lady Mary Wroth herself appeared), Jonson rather grudgingly notes that although he shaped the presentation of the queen and her ladies as the Daughters of the Niger, the original concept of having them appear in blackface was a product not of his own imagination but rather of "her majesty's will."[17] While Queen Anne's official role in masques was steadily delimited and diminished as her absolutist husband's reign wore on, it is worth noting that Jonson and other masque writers were at least initially required to reflect a woman's wishes in their texts.

Queen Anne's historical contribution to the genesis of the Jacobean masque suggests an active interest in theatricality on the part of a seventeenth-century woman; she is linked to further role-playing and performing, along with the Jacobean noblewomen who attended her, by the comments of that sharp-tongued observer of court life, Arbella Stuart:

> But out of this confusion of imbassages will you know how we spend our time
> on the Queenes side? Whilst I was at Winchester there weare certain childeplayes
> remembred by the fayre ladies. Viz. I pray my Lo. give me a Course in your park.
> Rise pig and go. One peny follow me.&c. and when came to Court they were
> as highly in request as ever cracking of nuts was. so I was by the m.rs. of the
> Revelles not onely compelled to play at I knew not what for till that day I hever
> heard of a play called fier. but even persuaded by the princely example I saw to
> play the childe againe. This exercise is most used from .10 of the clocke at night
> till .2 or .3 in the morning but the day I made one it beganne at twilight and
> ended at suppertime.[18]

In addition to noting the courtly obsession with games, led by Anne
as "mistress of the revels," Stuart also observes that Anne's ladies-in-
waiting apparently raided the dead Queen Elizabeth's wardrobe for
costumes for a masque on at least one occasion.[19] The vision of court
ladies pawing over and trying on Elizabeth's three thousand ruffled, be-
jeweled dresses is striking in and of itself: taken in tandem with descriptions of after-dinner charades as those ladies' chief pastime, it suggests
a consuming interest in role-playing on the part of Jacobean female
courtiers. More importantly for the study of Lady Mary Wroth, this
picture of Anne and her ladies makes it clear that performing was a requirement for membership in the queen's inner circle. As a member
of that circle almost from the moment of James's ascension, Wroth was
quite probably one of those ladies who drew Arbella Stuart's scorn
through a fondness for games such as "One penny follow me" and "rise
pig and go." In such a context, performing would obviously assume
crucial significance for Wroth's identity: skill and ability at games would
have been the available means to preserve her standing at court.

The notion of Wroth as a "lady at play" assumes even greater significance when considered in the light of courtesy-books, those courtly
behavior manuals which defined real life in terms of a performance.
Baldesar Castiglione's treatise *The Book of the Courtier* (*Il Libro del
Cortegiano*), translated into English in 1561 and reprinted several times
through the seventeenth century, has been well established as the "master
text" for the Renaissance view of courtly behavior as play; a fact often
undernoticed, however, is that Castiglione's rhetoric sets out a model
for female as well as male role-playing. In Thomas Hoby's influential
1561 translation, Castiglione's Lord Julian states that he will make a
"briefe rehersall" of the ideal courtly woman: she should "cultivate a

certain bashfulnesse, that may declare the noble shamefastenesse that is contrarie to headinesse . . . She ought also to frame her garments to this entent, and so to apparell her selfe, that she appeare not fonde and light." Julian sees this lady's theatricalized consciousness as salutary, assuming it will better enable her to please men; his opponent in debate, Lord Gasper, predictably "reherses" its less flattering side. Gasper claims that women's innate theatricality often leads to "doubtfull words" and "fained disdaines," painting a picture of hapless men ensnared by feminine wiles: "not satisfied with this only torment of jealosie, after the lover hath declared all his token of love and favorable service . . . [women] beginne to bethink themselves . . . and faining new suspitions that they are not beloved, they make a countenance that they will in any wise put him out of their favor."[20] Despite the ostensible contrast between their views of female role-playing, neither Julian nor Gasper suggests that it is probable, or even possible, that women will not act at all.

The most influential Renaissance courtesy-book, then, invokes performance in terms which suggest its inevitability for women; despite the fact that it does so as an attempt to construct a passive and conformist vision of female selfhood, the suggestion effectively provides a model for women's acting. Theatricality, it would seem, plays havoc with Gasper and Julian's intentions: calling for careful monitoring of a female courtier's appearance, *The Book of the Courtier* belatedly presumes that women can indeed alienate and conceal their identities if they so desire. It is this possibility of theatrical self-alienation, I would argue, that Lady Mary Wroth's *Urania* draws on as it repeatedly insists on the difference between a woman's implied true self and her self-representation. Not only Wroth's narrator but also several of her female characters appear to view existence as in some way theatrical: to take only a single example, we are introduced at one point to a woman called Alarina, who declares: "I love myself; my selfe now loveth me" (107). Alarina's declaration may appear simple at first, but it reveals a complex formulation of subjectivity: she draws a distinction between herself and her "self," assuming self-fracture or alienation as a condition of identity. Her comment is especially interesting because it refers to the cessation of her desire to become a wife; having passed up a conventional, coherent feminine role, she moves toward a condition which assumes that female selfhood has more than one face. If the *theatrum mundi* metaphor delineates the inescapable context within which such a protean vision of identity must be enacted, it also opens up a space for woman to do some of the acting, giving the *Urania*'s female characters the opportunity to explore (if not, finally, to authoritatively define) the kinds of roles a woman might actively play.

II

In the opening scenes of the *Urania*, Wroth signals her incipient concern with the problems of theatricality and female identity by placing a "masked" woman on center stage. The work's title character appears as a shepherdess who has recently learned that she is high-born; she has no clues, however, to the details of her identity. "Alas Urania," she laments, " . . . of any misfortune that can befall woman, is not this the most and greatest which thou art falne into? . . . Why was I not still continued in the beleefe I was, as I appeare, a Shepherdess, and Daughter to a Shepherd? My ambition then went no higher than this estate, now flies it to a knowledge; then was I contented, now perplexed" (1). Although the specifics of Urania's genealogy are eventually disclosed in the narrative, her plaintive query might serve as an epigraph for the work which bears her name. For what Urania posits in her opening lines is a gap between who she is and what she would "appeare" to be: in other words, a division which fractures the notion of feminine identity as wholeness. Urania's self-division obviously projects more than one face for female selfhood; the resulting plurality admits the possibility of an individual female subject — and one which actively "flies it to a knowledge." Speaking within the context of a theatrical culture, Wroth dramatizes a woman's self-awareness and, at the same time, challenges conventional paradigms of "coherent" feminine identity.

From the outset of the narrative, then, Wroth's model of female selfhood is unavoidably conditioned by its intersection with the politics of self-display. Moving from "thou" to "I," Urania's self-disclosure marks the engendering of a subjective consciousness; the narrative presents that incipient consciousness, which heightens Urania's awareness of herself as a spectacle, as both a troubling and crucial aspect of representing the female subject. A woman's appearance in the public eye is troubling, because visibility possibly denotes availability to the gaze of a beholder, yet it is also crucial because it affirms that something is there to be seen. One of Wroth's poems, affixed to the text of the *Urania* and possibly alluding to her real-life performance as a "lean-cheek'd Moor" in Ben Jonson's *The Masque of Blackness,* defines the conflicts involved in staging the female self:

Like to the Indians, scorched with the sunne,
  The sunne which they do as theyr God adore
  So ame I us'd by love, for ever more
  I worship him, less favors have I wunn.
Better are they who thus to blackness runn,
  And soe can only whiteness want deplore
  Than I who pale, and white ame with griefs store,
  Nor can have hope, butt to see hopes undunn;
Beesids theyr sacrifies receav'd in sight
  Of theyr chose sainte: Mine hid as worthless rite;
  Grant mee to see wher I my offrings give,
Then lett mee weare the marke of Cupid's might
  In hart as they in skin of Phoebus light
  Nott ceasing offrings to Love while I Live. (P25)

The speaker invokes a higher authority to recognize her sacrifice ("Grant mee to see wher I my offrings give"), implying that her pain is "worthles" if it is not "receav'd in sight." While her inner emotion must be visible if its existence is to be perceived by an audience, however, its display is also its potential undoing. As the speaker notes, the longer you stay out in the sun (or on the world's stage), the more you get burned: "So ame I us'd by love, for ever more / I worship him, less favors have I wunn." Faced with the competing claims of concealment and self-disclosure, the female body finally becomes a site traversed by spectacular contradictions: "lett me *weare* the mark of Cupid's might / *In hart* as they in skin." As a metaphor for presence (of the female subject or the woman writer), the body is a subject both in and of representation; if it is dependent on the perception of another for recognition, it is also ineluctably resistant to it.

This depiction of a theatrical woman thus paradoxically stages identity both as a provisional role and as an inward self that remains concealable.[21] Not surprisingly, the contradictory pressures imposed by such a vision of dramatic selfhood become a source of some anxiety

for the *Urania*'s female characters as the narrative progresses. The conflict inherent in Wroth's figure of the theatrical woman notably affects
Pamphilia, for example, as theatricality at once affirms and unsettles her
ability to retain complete command over her emotions. Time and time
again the unhappy queen, grieving over the faithlessness of her beloved
Amphilanthus, feigns happiness in the presence of an audience: "Pamphilia made some signe of Joye, but a Signe indeed it was for how
could joye come where such desperate sorrow did abound, yett the
Seeming gave great content to all the beholders" (I:fol.21). The difference between sign and substance allows Pamphilia to preserve her authority; yet she also laments such a difference as the primary cause of
her victimization: "I might sooner have seene, if not maskt with innocent belief, and abusd with truth" (396). Within the ontological gap
opened up by the split between Pamphilia's appearance and her innermost thoughts, Wroth locates the queen's individual subjectivity, asserting her detachment from a world only interested in outward "seeming." But Pamphilia's lingering desire to believe in the authenticity of
signs — a belief which forecloses the possibility of femininity as a form
of role-playing — also delimits her identity, effectively masking the signs
of her activity with paradigms of assigned and passive behavior.

The pressures imposed by Wroth's theatrical vision of female selfhood become most insistent in a lengthy discussion of the value of Pamphilia's constancy, perhaps the most notorious "critical crux" of the
Urania to date. When Urania suggests to Pamphilia that she might ease
her inner pain by disavowing its source (her passion for the wayward
prince Amphilanthus), the lovesick queen claims that standing by this
faithless man will in fact enable her to claim a constant self:

> To leave him for being false would show my love was not for his sake, but mine
> owne, that because he loved me, I therefore loved him, but when hee leaves I
> can do so to. O no deere Cousen I loved him for himselfe, and would have loved
> him had hee not loved mee, and will love though hee dispise me . . . Pamphilia
> must be of a new composition before she can let such thoughts fall into her con-
> stant breast, which is a Sanctuary of zealous affection, and so well hath love in-
> structed me, as I can never leave my master or his precepts, but still maintain a
> vertuous constancy. (400)

Pamphilia insists here that the play of difference between her faithful-
ness and Amphilanthus's inconstancy marks out a space for her assumption of a subject position.[22] If he is the unstable term in the opposition,

she is the stable one, and through this contrast she locates positive value—the power to engender a constant self-representation, independent of male control—within herself. However, Pamphilia's speech also suggests that this position entails subjection to another: "so well hath love instructed me, as I can never leave my master to his precepts." An autonomous female identity is perceptibly compromised here by the idea of love as a "master," for within the system of oppositions that Pamphilia uses to affirm her self only one term can be ascendant at one time. Given such a system, the objectification of the (male) master requires the oppression of the (female) subject, restabilizing the signs of conventional gender identity and ordering language and sexuality back in place. If dominance plays a critical role in representing selfhood here, then, for Pamphilia, choosing love means that she can never be both the simultaneous subject and object of desire. "Oh love," she sighs elsewhere in the narrative, "thou dost master me" (52). And this mastery makes her a prisoner of conventional representation, the very condition she was hoping to avoid.

Pamphilia's attempt to revise the role of the virtuously passive woman, then, comes surprisingly close to reinscribing it. Several of Wroth's critics have noted that Pamphilia's virtue constitutes her emotional "ruine"; less noted, however, is the surprising role which theatricality plays in constructing such an effect. When a group of court ladies decide to go sailing and invite Pamphilia to join them, the queen's first concern is to avoid the appearance of unseemliness: "Pamphilia went to the shore with them, but then considered her gravity was too much in the opinion of the world to enter into so slight an action, wherefore desired pardon." The ladies manage to convince her to "venture her constant self" with them; predictably, however, a storm comes up and all on board are shipwrecked. While the other women despair, Pamphilia frets that her behavior may be perceived as dissembling by a worldly audience: "why did I ever play so foolish a part? justly may I be condemned for this error, and blamed for so much lightness" (321). In an earlier episode, Pamphilia had appropriated theatrical forms in order to free some captive friends trapped in the House of Love, appearing as a vision of Constancy to unlock doors which were "not to be open to all, but to few possessed with that virtue" (39). Now, however, theatrical forms work against her, for in the course of exploring their new surroundings she and her friends become imprisoned in "a round building like a Theater." Like conventional fairy-tale heroines, we are told, the ladies must sit and wait for "the man most loving, and most beloved" to arrive and set them free.

It might correctly be objected that theatrical forms are not synonymous with conventionality, for the fact of the ladies' imprisonment in a theater does not necessarily signify their acquiescence to traditionally passive roles. Selarinus, lover of one of the imprisoned ladies, Philistella, in fact rails against the theater as an unsuitable place for a woman: "am I not a more proper Keeper for such excellencies? and is not Epirus a more convenient place for her to passe her time in, then a stone Theater? where should she play her part, but with her love? where live, but in his breast?" (353). Yet the tension between theatricality and passivity hinted at in the shipwrecked Pamphilia's reaction to the idea of an audience is at once more subtle and more complex. As the episode continues, Amphilanthus heroically shows up to free the trapped ladies; accompanying him, however, is his new mistress, Musalina, with whom he has become involved in Pamphilia's absence. The consequent irony of his designation as "the man most loving, and most beloved" is all too obvious, and Pamphilia's joy at his arrival turns to misery as she returns "to the seate, she had before sate in, not only as she did alone, but viewed by all to be so" (377). Amphilanthus's arrival effectively unmasks Pamphilia: his public infidelity provokes her to reveal her secret unhappiness, exposing her as an actress rather than as a constantly composed monarch. Pamphilia's resulting chagrin, moreover, effectively resubjects her to a theatrical imperative: if she wishes to preserve her dignity and authority in front of a courtly audience, she must do a better job of controlling her appearance. The presence of an audience, rather like the interjection of an all-seeing "master," dictates both Pamphilia's submission to the norm of performance and the self-divided consciousness which enforces that submission.

The *Urania* thus registers an intimate if disturbing connection between the terms of spectacle and those of women's subjection, a connection dramatized not only in the episode of the stone theater but in descriptions of other courtly performances. During one of their many reconciliations, Pamphilia and Amphilanthus take public vows of fidelity to one another. To celebrate this unofficial "marriage," Pamphilia's friend and erstwhile suitor the King of Tartaria stages a masque. Cupid, the traditional figure of Love, is forced to become "a Servant to honor, and a page to truth," while the allegorical figure of Honor is hailed by the maskers as "the Monarch true" (I:fol.7). If Honor's subjection of Cupid represents the triumph of virtue over passion, it also closely resembles that moment in the Jacobean masque when the real-life monarch banishes the professional actor from the stage. As an actor, Cupid is allied with passion or willfully choosing one's own role; Honor, as the sovereign, obviously plays a much more carefully delimited part. In light of the King of Tartaria's own courtship of Pamphilia, the symbolism of the masque seems obvious enough: Honor's banishment of Cupid would appear to foretell Pamphilia's coming attempt to banish passion (and Amphilanthus) from her life by marrying the more conventional Tartarian. But if this is true, women are the subjects of the masque in more ways than one, for the vanquished Cupid also represents the dashed hopes of a group of loving ladies who wish to keep their men at home. Allied with the professional actor playing Cupid, these women are effectively prevented from acting in their own interest and forced to resubmit to proper authority. Honor, the men's chosen "guide," reaffirms traditional gender hierarchy at the same time that he restores his monarchy, charging Cupid and, presumably, women, "never to meddle wher true Honor governs" (I:fol.8).

Indeed, in viewing the King of Tartaria's masque one has the impression that its true director is less the King himself than the larger cultural forces behind the scenes (call them the theater management) which endorse a conservative order of representation. Shortly after the masque, however, when this order seems to have effectively denied the power of female theatricality or at least the power of women to assert themselves on stage, the master's authority starts to look oddly vulnerable again. Pamphilia is visited by another friend, the sage Lady Mellissea, who presents her with "a very pretty show" designed "only to please the Queene." This masque features a young sailor, who is in love with a nymph who lives "in the segges, or grassy ouse." The sailor sings a song to this marshy nymph as "the Goddesse sole of love," concluding with a vow of submission: "Bow hart, and soule to her least frowne / And sensur'd thus ly downe." As a rejoinder to this display of affection, a scornful old shepherd sings a song decrying the deceptions and frauds of love: "Love butt a phantasie light, and vaine / Fluttering butt in poorest braine . . . Implore not heaven, nor deities / They know too well his forgeries." After the old man's instruction the sailor disavows love as his "commaunder" and joins in singing the last two lines of the shepherd's song: "Nor saints by imprications move / 'Tis butt the Idolatry of love" (I:fol.41). Significantly, the nymph joins in the last two lines also, explicitly rejecting both the governance of love and the sailor's highly idealized vision of her as a goddess. Pamphilia quickly gets the message, noting "if everyone should soe soon mend, love's Monarchy would have a quick end," and although Lady Mellissea disclaims any overt didacticism ("*you* are none of this madam"), her staging of the nymph's choice forms an instructive contrast with the spectacle of subjection proffered by the King of Tartaria's masque.

If the *Urania*'s "masque-like" moments can stage opposing possibilities for women, then perhaps subjection and theatrical forms are not irrevocably linked after all. Certainly the numerous textual attestations to Pamphilia's importance beyond her love for Amphilanthus provide examples of the way in which a theatrical formulation of female selfhood can produce self-affirmation; in the face of unhappiness, "she lost not her selfe, for her government continued just and brave, like that Lady she was, wherein she shewed her heart was not to be stir'd, though her private fortunes shooke round about her" (429). Display here confirms Pamphilia's autonomy, as do the numerous sonnets and monologues she produces—productions which, in a cultural context of absence and silence for women, provide dramatic evidence of a distinctively female voice. The fact that Pamphilia's productions are often concerned with the relationship between a subjective female self and a self-alienated, specular Self denotes an ongoing probing and potentially even a reversal of conventional notions of feminine wholeness. As she enacts the role of the constant woman, Pamphilia's theatricality calls attention to that role as a fiction; both identified with and distanced from her own representation, like an actress on the stage, she manages to locate a space to effectively rehearse her own concerns.

Such a willful rehearsal proposes identity, to say nothing of subjectivity, as constructed by and within discourse. Indeed, it could conceivably be argued that a dynamic relation is at work in the *Urania*, one in which the female subject is both shaped by a theatrical culture and actively reshapes that culture in the process of addressing and representing it.[23] The distinctive authorial persona which emerges as a result of this process effectively claims the right to direct and delimit her readers' interpretive activity—in other words, the right to her own authority. Although this right did not go historically unchallenged, as the checkered story of *Urania*'s reception indicates, it is significant that we have a final retort from Wroth addressed to her most notorious critic. Identifying herself as "Mistress Mary Wrothe," the author of the missive takes up and transforms Edward Denny's verse attack on her published work: "Hirmophradite in sense in Art a monster / As by your railing rimes the world may conster / Your spitefull words against a harmless booke / Shows that an ass much like the sire doth looke."[24] This stunning reversal of the terms of Denny's critique, complete even down to the substitution of metaphors of scandalous masculine "show" for those of feminine display, re-produces literary relations in a new way: it asserts the woman writer's equal right to control over representation and discourse. It is this new and authoritative vision of female authorship, I want to conclude, that Wroth synthesizes out of the age's available notions of theatricality and identity. For despite the obstacles and frustrations she encountered as a woman writing in the seventeenth century, Wroth's image of herself as a distinctive subject able to re-present images of men and women in effect "rewrites the Renaissance," denoting the way in which literary productions may offer very real, if limited, appropriations of power.[25]

NOTES

1. For further discussion of the controversy, see Roberts, *Poems*, pp. 31–36, and Roberts, "An Unpublished Literary Quarrel Concerning the Suppression of Mary Wroth's *Urania* (1621)," *Notes & Queries* 222 (1977), 532–35.
2. See Masten's essay in this volume for further discussion of the significance of this withdrawal from circulation.
3. Joan Kelly, "Early Feminist Theory and the *Querelle des Femmes*, 1475–1640" in *Women, History and Theory* (Chicago: University of Chicago Press, 1984) and Angeline Goreau, *The Whole Duty of a Woman: Female Writers in Seventeenth-Century England* (Garden City, N.Y.: Dial Press, 1984).
4. See Miller's essay in this volume for a comparison of Wroth's theatrical women and Shakespeare's female characters.

5. See Roberts, *Poems*, pp. 30–31.

6. My understanding of this authorial move is indebted to Catherine Gallagher's discussion of seventeenth-century female authorship in "Who Was That Masked Woman? The Prostitute and the Playwright in the Comedies of Aphra Behn," *Women's Studies* 15 (1988), 23–42.

7. Virginia Woolf, *A Room of One's Own* (New York: Harcourt, Brace, Jovanovich, 1957), p. 50. Miller has recently noted the relevance of Woolf's hypothetical account of a censured Renaissance woman writer for studies of Lady Mary Wroth in "'Not much to be marked': Narrative of the Woman's Part in Lady Mary Wroth's *Urania*," *Studies in English Literature* 29 (1989), 121–37.

8. Ben Jonson, *Volpone* (II.iii.7–9, 40) in *Complete Works*, ed. C. Herford and P. Simpson (Oxford: Clarendon Press, 1925–52). Cited in Katherine Eisaman Maus, "Horns of Dilemma: Jealousy, Gender, and Spectatorship in English Renaissance Drama," *English Literary History* 54 (Fall 1987), 561–83, which discusses the invective against feminine (and "effeminate") self-display in Renaissance theatrical texts and treatises.

9. Lisa Jardine discusses the uneasiness provoked not just by the idea of female theatricality but by the actual presence of boy players on stage in *Still Harping On Daughters: Women and Drama in the Age of Shakespeare* (Brighton: Harvester, 1983).

10. For a historical overview of women as performers in Jacobean and Caroline masques, see Suzanne Gossett, "Man-maid, begone! Women in the Masques," *English Literary Renaissance* 18 (Winter 1988), 96–113.

11. Ben Jonson, "The Masque of Queens," ll. 410–13, 474–76, in *Ben Jonson: The Complete Masques*, ed. Stephen Orgel (New Haven, Conn: Yale University Press, 1969).

12. Stephen Orgel notes this aspect of the audience's role in masques in *The Illusion of Power: Political Theater in the English Renaissance* (Berkeley: University of California Press, 1975), p. 30.

13. Nancy Vickers, "Diana Described: Scattered Woman and Scattered Rhyme," *Critical Inquiry* 8 (1981), 265–79. See also Patricia Parker's related discussion in the chapter "Rhetorics of Property: Exploration, Inventory, Blazon," in *Literary Fat Ladies: Rhetoric, Gender, Property* (London: Methuen, 1987).

14. Laura Mulvey, "Visual Pleasure and Narrative Cinema," *Screen* 16 (Autumn 1975), 6–18, comments on the silencing of women in film, another visual medium: "Woman then stands in patriarchal culture as signifier for the male other, bound by a symbolic order in which man can live out his phantasies and obsessions through linguistic command by imposing them on the silent image of woman still tied to her place as bearer of meaning, not maker of meaning." Mulvey's analysis is especially suggestive for the Jacobean masque in light of surviving designs by Inigo Jones which assign the king the only perfect seat in front of a perspective stage: the specular gaze at a masque is inevitably that of a sovereign male. Such a vantage point dovetails neatly with King James's ideas about absolutism as well as with his notorious misogyny: the personal becomes political as his queen and the other ladies reflect his authority back to him in a dazzling display. For Jones's stage designs, see Stephen Orgel and Roy Strong, eds., *Inigo Jones: The Theater of the Stuart Court* (Berkeley: University of California Press, 1973).

15. Orgel, ed., *Complete Masques*, p. 72.

16. Greenblatt, *Renaissance Self-Fashioning*, p. 162.

17. Ben Jonson, "The Masque of Queens," ll. 9–12, and "The Masque of Blackness," l. 18, in Orgel, ed., *Complete Masques*.

18. Arbella Stuart, Sloane Mss 4164 (British Museum), 182–83ff.

19. "The Queene intendeth to make a mask this Christmas, to which end my ladie of Suffolk and my ladie Walsingham have warrants to take of the late Queenes best apparell out of the Tower at theyre discretion." Arbella Stuart, Addison Mss 563 (British Museum), v. 22, f. 47.

20. Thomas Hoby, trans. *The Book of the Courtier* (London, 1928), p. 194, p. 254. Linda Woodbridge discusses Hoby's relation to formal Renaissance debates about women in *Women in the English Renaissance: Literature and the Nature of Womankind* (Urbana: University of Illinois Press, 1984), pp. 52–58.

21. For an alternative view, see Masten's discussion, in this volume, of Wroth's antitheatricality.

22. Maureen Quilligan has made this point in the context of Pamphilia's assumption of a recognizably Petrarchan subject position in "Lady Mary Wroth: Female Authority and the Family Romance," in *Unfolded Tales: Essays on Renaissance Romance*, ed. George M. Logan and Gordon Teskey (Ithaca, N.Y.: Cornell University Press, 1989), p. 273.

23. My language here closely echoes that of Louis A. Montrose in "The Elizabethan Subject and the Spenserian Text," in *Literary Theory / Renaissance Texts*, ed. Patricia Parker and David Quint (Baltimore: Johns Hopkins University Press, 1985), pp. 302–40.

24. Roberts, *Poems*, p. 34.

25. I'd like to thank Margaret Ferguson, Catherine Gallagher, and the Beatrice Bain Research Group at the University of California, Berkeley, for encouraging my initial research on Wroth; Mary Beth Rose and the staff of the Newberry Library for their assistance and hospitality; Judith Rosen for many helpful discussions of women and theatricality; and my family for the support which allowed me to complete this project.

Women Readers in Mary Wroth's *Urania*

Mary Ellen Lamb

Within its cultural context, Mary Wroth's *The Countesse of Mountgomeries Urania* is unusual for its sheer volume as well as for its genre. Running to almost 590,000 words in its published and unpublished portions, *Urania* is a massive work written when Englishwomen, unlike male writers of the sixteenth or early seventeenth centuries, produced few original fictions of substantial length. Wroth's choice to write a romance was also unique for an Englishwoman. For the most part, women wrote nonfiction: translations, diaries, occasional poems, books of domestic or maternal advice, letters, and defenses of women. While recent scholarship has ably demonstrated the impressive accomplishments of Renaissance women writers such as Mary Sidney, Queen Elizabeth, Elizabeth Cary, and Jane Anger, a comparison to the writings of Renaissance males reveals the extent to which Renaissance ideologies of gender limited the amount and kind (but not necessarily the quality) of writing possible for most women.[1] A few decades earlier, the censure possible even for a woman's translation of a romance was expressed in Margaret Tyler's defense of her translation of a book from Diego Ortunez de Calahorra's *The mirrour of princely deedes and knighthood* (1578) against some "il willers" who might enforce women "either not to write or to write of divinitie."[2]

In defending her translation from the position of a woman reader ("It is all one for a woman to pen a story, as for a man to address his story to a woman," A4v), Tyler anticipates one strategy through which Wroth authorized herself as a writer of an original romance. Wroth opened a space for her original work within a Renaissance ideology of gender by subverting one of its primary strategies: the cultural construct of the woman reader, a highly gendered sign which usually functioned to restrict women's writing. The categories of women readers which I discern in Wroth's romance range from the sexual woman reader, passive before dominating male desires, to the independent woman reader whose reading provides autonomy within a marital relationship, to the intellectual woman reader whose reading does not reflect her sexuality. These categories reveal Wroth's complex relationship to dominant versions of the woman reader already present within her culture. The very contradictory nature of these versions opens up a space for resistance. Like any subject, Wroth was neither entirely free from nor entirely controlled by the gender constructions of her culture. Wroth's romance capitalizes upon the contradictions within gender ideology to subvert, adapt, and push the edge of her culture's discourse to invest women's reading with the independent subjectivity necessary to produce writing. But even when subverted, this powerful cultural discourse necessarily still exerted a significant influence upon the kinds of reading and writing imagined possible for women in Wroth's romance.

READING AS A WOMAN

Gender differences implied in the phrase "reading as a woman" are not, or at least not primarily, natural or innate; they are produced by the exclusion of women's roles as readers in texts.[3] Thus, Wroth's construction of women readers in her romance was itself an act with political ramifications. In the Renaissance as in modern times, the concept of the woman reader poses complex ideological and textual issues, and Jonathan Culler's question, "What does it mean to read as a woman?" is as pertinent to the understanding of Renaissance women readers as of modern ones.[4] This exclusion of women as implied readers represents one powerful means by which women writers are excluded from active participation in the formation of ideologies within a culture. Various critics have explored the ways in which reading as a woman, or as a member of any marginalized group, constitutes a political act in any culture in which most books, written by and for heterosexual males, portray the male experience as universal.[5]

In any culture, a woman's reading of texts written to male readers and reflective of male experience is limited to a few options. She can submit to the text, identifying with male protagonists to read "against" herself; this submission alienates her from her own identity as a woman. She can confront the text by pointing to her own absences, to the strategies through which she is excluded as a reader. Ideally, she can somehow do both, simultaneously remaining "inside" as well as "outside" the text, precariously maintaining a split perspective. Whatever her choice, the problems posed by women's reading are only exacerbated by the writing which it inevitably informs. Essays by recent feminist critics such as Fetterly, Jacobus, De Lauretis, Schweikart, and Showalter construct reading as a political act of interpretation not only of a text but of a relationship with patriarchy.[6] This construction is equally applicable to the representations of women's reading in Wroth's *Urania*. Like the women readers constructed in feminist criticism, the women readers in Wroth's romance represent sites of ideological struggle. Even more than the women readers constructed in feminist criticism, however, Wroth's women readers provide a sense of the very real problems inherent in maintaining any acceptable balance between adaptation and subversion; for in any age, a writer's resistance to patriarchy is necessarily composed of those very discourses disseminated through that culture which has formed her as a subject.

READING AS A RENAISSANCE WOMAN

The problematics of Renaissance women's reading were rendered even more complicated than those of modern women by a long tradition representing women's reading as contaminated by a particularly virulent form of sensuality. According to St. Bonaventure, misreading began with Eve; restricting herself to the sensual superficiality of the external "book" of the first temptation, she neglected to read the interior book which would have released for her the inevitable meanings of her capitulation.[7] In the Renaissance, women readers of love poetry and romances were especially depicted as dangerously sensual. In his much reprinted *Instruction of a Christian Gentlewoman*, Juan Luis Vives warns husbands to restrict their wives' reading of chivalaric romance: "And verily they be but foolishe husbandes and madde, that suffer their wives to waxe more ungraciously subtyle by readinge of suche bokes."[8] In a work which defines women solely according to their chastity, this subtlety seems to connote a transgressive sexuality. With more sympathy, Boccaccio imagines for his *Decameron* an audience of gentlewomen readers afflicted with the pains of love, for which he advances his book as a partial remedy.[9] The association of this sexualization of women's reading especially with romances was evident in the reception of Sidney's *The Countess of Pembroke's Arcadia*. When women readers were imagined as reading this romance, their response was usually imagined as sexual. Wye Saltonstall, for instance, warns against permitting a woman to read "loves historyes" such as *Amadis de Gaule* and the *Arcadia*, for in them she "courts the shaddow of love till she know the substance."[10] Clearly, then, the sexualized woman reader was a common construction within gender ideology of early modern England.

A counter-discourse arose to represent women's reading of selected authors as signifying chastity. Richard Hyrde's introduction to Margaret Roper's translation of Erasmus's commentary on the Lord's Prayer presents women's reading of the appropriate books as a form of control over women's thoughts superior even to spinning:

> Redying and stydyeing of bokes so occupieth the mynde / that it can have no leyser to muse or delyte in other fantasies / whan in all handy werkes / that men saye be more mete for a woman / the body may be busy in one place / and the mynde walkying in another / while they syt sowing and spinnyiny with their fyngers / may caste and compasse many pevysshe fantasyes in theyr myndes.[11]

The chastity signified by women's reading of approved books remained precariously dependent upon a reading list limited primarily to church fathers and a few classical writers. Rather than revising notions concerning women's sexual nature, this counter-discourse merely repositioned women's reading as a restraint rather than an incitement to sexuality; it still represented women's reading according to their erotic desires.

Hyrde's representation of reading as a means of preventing women's "pevysshe fantasyes" exposes an underlying patriarchal project: to erase women's independent subjectivity.[12] In this way, the containment of women's reading performed a similar function as the containment of women's sexuality with which it was associated. At stake both in their reading and their sexuality is the status of women as subjects, able to think, to desire, to produce meanings in their minds and bodies sometimes at variance with patriarchal objectives. Both extremes of represent-ing women readers as lascivious or chaste formed divergent aspects of a single strategy: to limit the kinds of independent meanings imagined possible for women to produce in their reading as well as in their lives. The erotic meanings supposedly produced by women readers of ro-mances could be dismissed as frivolous or inappropriate: the serious meanings produced by chaste women readers of church fathers demon-strated, in theory, their absorption by patriarchy. By narrowing the space within contemporary discourse available for women to construct themselves as subjects, either representation of women readers — as lasci-vious or chaste — worked to prevent or to inhibit women's authorship.

READING AS THE COUNTESS OF MONTGOMERY

Wroth's title, *The Countesse of Mountgomeries Urania*, demonstrates the complexity of her manipulation of the woman reader as a cultural sign. On the one hand, the privileging of a woman reader in Wroth's title is consonant with the cultural stereotype of women as the primary readers of romance. By situating her romance outside male reception, Wroth's title works to disarm potential accusations of her assertion of inappropriate authority over male readers. On the other hand, by echo-ing Sir Philip Sidney's title, *The Countess of Pembroke's Arcadia*, Wroth's privileging of a particular woman reader elevates her authorship as analogous to her famous uncle's. Wroth was not just any woman writer; she was a Sidney, the inheritor of a powerful literary legacy. From this perspective, the woman reader named "the Countess of Montgomery" functioned as a rhetorical construct mirroring Sir Philip Sidney's literary power, which Wroth's title attempts to appropriate.

Even in its imitation of her uncle's title, however, Wroth's title repre-sents a radical textual act. Sidney's title attributed a role as a strong reader to the Countess of Pembroke, a role deriving in part from her physical presence while Sidney drafted out much of his work. Like Sid-ney's title, Wroth's invests a great degree of subjectivity in a woman reader. Wroth's representation of the Countess of Montgomery as a strong reader was probably accurate; for Susan de Vere Herbert was Wroth's neighbor while much of Wroth's romance was written, and so the proximity of their estates made it possible for her to read Wroth's manuscript drafts.[13] These representations of the Countesses of Pembroke and Montgomery as strong readers possessed important implications for women's authorship. Sir Philip Sidney's title describing his *Arcadia* as in some sense belonging to the Countess of Pembroke was no doubt one factor empowering the countess to prepare her brother's manuscript for publication. This literary act apparently worked to pave the way for her translations, some of which she published, as well as for her composition of some original poetry. In Wroth's case, the opportunity to imagine full subjectivity for a woman reader in her title apparently worked to authorize, not the Countess of Montgomery, but Wroth herself.

Wroth's title provides various possible and contradictory meanings for the woman reader: a marginalized reader of romance, a mirror of masculine authority, a subject in her own right. Similar inconsistencies appear and reappear in representations of women readers in Wroth's *Urania*. Rather than confusion or even conscious obfuscation, they reveal the extent to which the construct of the woman reader in Wroth's romance remained a site of a struggle never wholly resolved. By opening a space for women's subjectivity within the written discourse of the period, the representations of women readers in Wroth's romance finally enabled forms of women's authorship which, however, necessarily replicated rather than resolved the ideological struggle waged through the construct of the woman reader.

REREADING ROMANCE

Wroth's choice of genre inevitably made her work vulnerable to the Renaissance sexualization of women's reading, and especially the reading of romances. Rather than opposing this sexualization by presenting her work (and her authorial self) as chaste and pious, Wroth responded by writing a romance which was not only flagrantly sexual in itself but which even implicated her own personal history in its sexuality. As Gary Waller has demonstrated earlier in this volume, the overarching narrative concerning the sometimes adulterous love of Pamphilia for Amphilanthus includes numerous correspondences implying its allusion to a probable real-life sexual involvement between Wroth and her cousin William Herbert, third Earl of Pembroke, by whom she apparently had two illegitimate children. Soon after the publication of the folio portion, an angry response from Edward Denny, Baron of Waltham, witnesses her inclusion of scandalous episodes from the personal lives of contemporaries as well.[14]

Rather than diffusing this cultural paranoia surrounding the sexuality imagined for women's reading, *Urania* embodies some of its worst fantasies. Wroth's romance justifies the sexual preoccupation of romance by dignifying the erotic impulse itself. This romance defends sexuality, especially women's sexuality, by creating constancy even to an unfaithful lover as a heroic trait.[15] The most prominent of the array of constant heroines unswervingly true to their erring lovers is Pamphilia herself, despite the inconstancies of her lover Amphilanthus as he obsessively acts out the meaning of his name, "lover of two." Except for the rebellion of the independent Allarina and a few others, most sympathetic women characters conform to the self-representation of the lovely Philistella as "made, maintaind by love, and in love shaped, & squared only to his rule" (277). In Wroth's romance, love confers nobility and even a form of spirituality: "Love who is the Lord of all brave royall minds, hath like the heavens beheld my lowly breast, and in it taken lodging, gracing it with humbling his great Godhead, to embrace a true, and yeelding heart . . . love dwels in me, hee hath made me his hoste" (277). This representation of constancy, even sexual constancy to an adulterous lover, as a heroic trait, is a strategy justifying the composition of *Urania* itself, whose main plot is transparently displayed as reflecting the continuing love of Wroth for her own "Amphilanthus."

READER RECEPTION

The heroism of women's sexual constancy dignifies several scenes of reading in *Urania*; the sexuality implicated in the reading of Dalinea, the daughter of the King of Achaia, is rendered even more piquant by its association with wealth. The combination proves overwhelming to Parselius, a friend of Dalinea's brother but a stranger to her, as he finds her reading to her gentlewomen. The erotic arousal this scene elicits in Parselius moves him to forswear his (previously) beloved Urania. The immediacy and the strength of Parselius's reaction suggest the extent to which the eroticism associated with women's reading made of the woman reader herself an erotic object. The eroticism of this scene is dignified, however, by its association with wealth, for Dalinea's book represents one of several signifiers of conspicuous affluence in this vision of elegant domesticity: "Her Ladies who attended her, were a little distant from her in a faire compasse Window, where also stood a Chaire, wherein it seemed she had been sitting, till the newes came of his arrivall. In that Chaire lay a Booke, the Ladies were all at worke; so as it shewed, she read while they wrought" (103).

Dalinea's book distinguishes her from her less privileged ladies, who sew while she reads to them. Like the oddly specific detail of the "faire compasse Window" and the harmonious presence of the attending ladies themselves, Dalinea's reading reveals her aristocratic taste. Her graceful use of affluence is demonstrated through her literacy, an achievement more common among aristocratic Renaissance women than those of the lower classes. The canopy or "State" under which Dalinea seats Parselius while he conducts his precipitate wooing confirms the text's focus upon signifiers of wealth: "Then she brought him under the State, where two Chaires being set, they passed away some time, discoursing of adventures" (103).

In a sense, Parselius's strikingly discursive form of wooing represents a continuation of Dalinea's reading; for Parselius woos her through his skill in narrating the exploits of her brother and himself: his "discourse had made his way, by taking first her eares prisoners" (103). Already a lover of reading, Dalinea proves highly receptive to Parselius's text, as well; and she immediately falls in love. This apparent connection between a woman's reading and her receptivity to romantic advances is dignified by subsequent events. Dalinea maintains heroic constancy in her marriage to the initially faithless Parselius. Parselius deserts Dalinea when his once-loved Urania reproves him in a dream. Her love unwavering, Dalinea dresses in black and appears with their child in the court where he resides. In the meantime, however, Parselius has been cleansed of his love for Urania by the purifying sea at St. Maura, and he claims Dalinea joyfully, never to desert her again in the space of the book.

In justifying Dalinea's erotic impulse through her constancy, the text also justifies the sexuality associated with women's reading within that culture.

PAMPHILIA REREADS ROMANCE

Pamphilia's scene of reading specifically adapts the culture's sexualization of women's reading of romances through renaming women's sexuality as constancy. Preoccupied with her love for Amphilanthus, Pamphilia retires to a "delicate thicke wood" (264) to read a book whose subject is explicitly revealed as love, the central topic of romances. In fact, its plot is strikingly similar to Pamphilia's own story shortly to be narrated in Wroth's *Urania*. A woman in love reading a book about love: a scene like this had elicited grave warnings from writers such as Vives concerned with the consequences of allowing women to "waxe more ungraciously subtle." Rather than denying the sexual content of Pamphilia's book, Wroth's romance affirms the heroism of faithful women by using that sexuality to criticize unconstant men: "The subject was Love, and the story she then was reading, the affection of a Lady to a brave Gentleman, who equally loved, but being a man, it was necessary for him to exceede a woman in all things, so much as inconstansie was found fit for him to excell her in, hee left her for a new" (264).[16] Without apology, Pamphilia's book presents love as a significant topic, worthy of attention in its own right. The bitter irony of this passage represents a revaluation of the amorous content of romance, including Wroth's romance, by shifting the focus from the romantic thoughts of the woman reader to the inconstancy of male lovers. Far from frivolous, Pamphilia's book was soon to prove an accurate record of cultural codes painfully lived out in the lives of Pamphilia and other characters. The transparent topicality linking Pamphilia to Wroth herself suggests that Wroth's romance was similarly to reflect the inequitable codes of love then (dis)organizing lives in seventeenth-century England. Thus, rather than denying its presence, the romance justifies the erotic content of Pamphilia's book — and, by implication, Wroth's as well — by demonstrating its accuracy.

The erotic content of Pamphilia's book is also justified by Pamphilia's loyalty to love, which causes her to throw her book away:

> Poor love saide the Queene, how doth all stories, and every writer use thee at their pleasure, apparrelling thee according to their various fancies? canst thou suffer thy selfe to be thus put in cloathes, nay ragges instead of vertuous habits? punish such Traytors, and cherrish mee thy loyall subject who will not so much as keepe thy injuries neere me; then threw she away the booke and walked up and downe, her hand on her heart. (264)

The relationship of this passage to cultural stereotypes of women who read romances in a state of sexual arousal is complex. In one sense, Pamphilia embodies this stereotype. As she walks "up and downe, her hand on heart," this woman reader is undeniably a woman preoccupied by love. Rather than denying women's erotic impulse, Wroth's romance has again created of women's love a source of heroism. Far from seeming foolish in her error, her protest against love's detractors dignifies her love through her loyalty.

This scene presents another form of revaluation of the woman reader of romance. Accusers and apologists alike represented women readers as passive vehicles of a text's message. Accusers assumed sexual arousal for women readers of inappropriate texts; defenders assumed that appropriate texts would inculcate chastity. Pamphilia, however, acts out her active disagreement with her book by throwing it away. Her resistance to her text creates for her the independent subjectivity denied by contemporary constructions of the woman reader. Even though subsequent events show her faith in love to be misplaced, she has been granted the freedom to be wrong.

INDEPENDENT READINGS

A counter-discourse emerges within *Urania* representing women readers as uninterested in love; but this alternative to the sexualized woman reader proves unstable.[17] An unnamed Sad Lady provides an example of a woman character whose act of reading indicates her freedom from, rather than her entanglement in, sexual desire. Scorning Cupid, she walks alone in the woods carrying her bow and her book: "(I carried) with mee a booke in my pockett to recreate my spiritts with when I pleased, for no thing could I thinke on butt how to please my self best, and a bowe with Arrows which I threw att my back, for my defence" (II:fol.59v). Like her bow and arrow which conventionally evoked resonances of Diana, goddess of chastity, the Sad Lady's book signifies her independence from men. Her book demonstrates her self-sufficiency, her ability to "recreate" her "spiritts" when she pleased without the aid of a male companion. The independent subjectivity suggested by her self-sufficiency results in authorship, for she proceeds to write a poem expressing her contempt for Cupid. Yet this counter-discourse is contaminated by its opposite; for her disinclination to love becomes itself a trait eliciting love. Blown away by the wind, her poem dispraising Cupid is read by the valiant knight Andromarcko, who immediately loves its author. After she spurns his advances, he embarks on a search for his father. The melancholy of the Sad Lady proceeds from her belated realization of her love for this man she may never meet again.

This instability of the book as signifying either receptivity or defiance of love perhaps reveals a need expressed within the text to have it both ways: to retain the subjectivity independent from men ascribed to a self-sufficient woman but within a relationship with a man; to enjoy the pleasures of marriage without a sense of engulfment of the separate self. This balance between the needs for separation and relatedness pervades another of Pamphilia's scenes of reading, in which she receives the marriage proposal of the King of Tartaria. Still in love with the recently married Amphilanthus, she initially refuses his proposal, claiming to prefer the companionship of books: "Yett is my sad, and soe determined to be sad lyfe, as makes mee farr undeserving of such a fortune, a booke, and solitarines beeing the onely companions I desire in thes my unfortunate dayes" (II:fol.21v).

Far from denying Pamphilia the independence signified by her reading, the King of Tartaria proposes to incorporate it within their marriage. In maintaining her rights as a reader, he affirms her rights to a subjectivity separate from his even in marriage:

> Love your booke, butt love mee soe farr as that I may hold itt to you that while you peruse that, I may Joye in beeholding you, and som times gaine a looke from you if butt to chide mee for soe carelessly parforming my office, when love will

by chance make my hand shake, purposely to obtaine a sweet looke, for surely you can nott be soe cruell, as that love will not with all sweetnes shine in thos cleerest lights; bee solitarie, yett favour mee soe much as that I may butt attend you, when you waulke in deserts, and woods, I will serve you as a guard. (II.fol.21v)

In asserting Pamphilia's independent subjectivity, the King of Tartaria denies his own, to represent himself as utterly absorbed in his adoration of Pamphilia. She perceives his proposal as an expression of submission inappropriate to a ruler: "Noe my lord you are borne to rule, and god forbid I should assume any such power over you" (II:fol.21v). Soon changing her mind, Pamphilia agrees to marry him. Because of her love for the faithless Amphilanthus, however, she remains in conflict, reaching her decision "against her owne minde, yett nott constrain'd" (II:fol.22).[18]

The independent subjectivity allowed Pamphilia by her husband appears to be shaped by the anxieties of her culture concerning the sexual nature of the woman reader, for Pamphilia employs her independent subjectivity not only in reading, but in her continued relationship with Amphilanthus during her marriage with the King of Tartaria. The exact extent of the physicality of this relationship is not clear. Soon after Pamphilia's marriage, Amphilanthus "with deep groanes stoped her mouth with kisses" (II:fol.25); yet concerning her love for Amphilanthus, Pamphilia agrees with her confidante Leucenia that "Love is happy, by ten times more hapy when injoyde with Chastitie" (II:fol.50v). The emotional independence granted by the King of Tartaria to Pamphilia as a reader is consistent with his tolerance of her friendship with Amphilanthus, whom he invites to his court. As in other episodes, Wroth's romance invests Pamphilia's love for Amphilanthus with dignity rather than scandal; all three live contentedly together, Amphilanthus with Pamphilia "in the court of his true and loyall friend the Great Cham, who lived butt in ther sights" (II:fol.55).

READING SCIENCE

The Countesse of Mountgomeries Urania pushes the representation of the woman reader as defined by erotic impulses (her own or others') toward a representation of the woman reader as defined by intellectual achievement and perhaps even by worldly power. The version of woman reader presented by Sophia, the rightful heir of lands usurped by her evil uncle the Sophie, at first resembles that of Dalinea. Like Dalinea's book, Sophia's books manifest her wealth, as she conducts the courtly stranger Rosindy to her gallery and library, "the most sumptious in the world for a woeman to have and the rarest, since non butt the rarest of bookes were permitted to bee ther" (I:fol.61v). Rosindy is delighted when Sophia expresses her trust in him by giving him a key to the study. Their immediate camaraderie, together with the key admitting Rosindy to Sophia's private space, would seem to presage romantic involvement. But unlike Parselius, Rosindy remains constant to his previous beloved. The passage moves from a depiction of Sophia as a graceful embodiment of wealth to a figure of learning in her own right. Unlike Pamphilia's book about love, Sophia's books contain factual information or knowledge in the "siences," a word then used to refer to "knowledge acquired by study" or "a recognized department of learning" (*OED* IX, 221).

> [Sophia's books were] all chosen ones, and as choisely chosen, and as truly used, and imployed by the owner, she beeing exactly, and perfectly learned in all siences, and learning well bestowed on her who honored learning for the truth of learnings sake, perfect knowledg. (I:fol.61v)

Various discourses, implicit in the name Sophia itself, worked to empower Wroth's romance to move beyond the woman reader as predominantly an erotic figure. The name Sophia contained meanings both of worldly power and of wisdom. Most clearly, "Sophia" was the feminine form of "Sophy," the contemporary title of the Persian ruler, which in fact the Sophia of Wroth's romance was by right. In addition, the name "Sophia" itself was the Greek word for wisdom, and in the previous century the variant form "sophy" had been used to mean "wisdom" or "one or other of the various sciences" (*OED* X, 437). The currency of these conflated meanings of "Sophia" becomes evident a few pages later in the *Urania* when a learned shepherdess Clorina was judged worthy of the name, primarily for her skill in natural sciences:

> And often for her skill in all arts, and siences, as well as of the letters, as other the cheifest knowledges in the cheifest of Natures works well called Sophia, a name most proper for her since itt portendeth wisdome, and exquisitt understanding in all things both in Nature, and for the highest deserned, ore with presumption to bee knowne in the heavens, or in the seas, or in any sort of hearbs, and in the proper uses of them. (II:fol.4)

The text's endowment of Clorina with these scientific knowledges, including her knowledge of herbs, provides insight into a cultural discourse enabling its representation of Sophia as an intellectual reader of factual knowledges rather than as a sexualized reader of romance. This discourse affected, and was affected by, Clorina's probable real-life referent, Mary Sidney, Countess of Pembroke.[19] According to John Aubrey, the countess's "genius lay as much towards chimistrie as poetrie," and she permitted Adrian Gilbert, half-brother to the family friend Sir Walter Raleigh, to keep a laboratory at her estate. Chemistry, not yet dissociated from alchemistry, was closely allied to medicine; for the philosopher's stone was able not only to turn any element to gold but to heal any ailment, as well. There is some evidence for the countess's interest in medicinal aspects of chemistry in Aubrey's further statement that she attempted to attract to Wilton a Salisbury chemist, "who did great cures by his art" before he died impoverished in his search for the philosopher's stone.[20] An attribution around 1620 of a medical recipe composed of roses, oranges, lemons, and cinnamon to a Countess of Pembroke probably represents a contribution to this written knowledge of healing herbs by Mary Sidney or by a successor.[21] This recipe is similar in kind to a medical recipe attributed to Adrian Gilbert also including roses, cinnamon, and other herbal ingredients, but with the addition of the more difficult-to-obtain ebony and unicorn's horn.[22]

The Countess of Pembroke was unusual for her time in providing patronage to male chemists/alchemists; her patronage, or attempted patronage, of male (al)chemists implies her identification of these knowledges as appropriate for male authorities. But her knowledge, and the knowledge of "Clorina," in the uses of herbs formed a natural extension of a skill rendered acceptable for Renaissance gentlewomen by contemporary cultural practice. At that time, various aristocratic women assumed the burden of elementary medical care for families on their estates. Margaret Hoby's diary, for example, records her care for a woman in childbirth.[23] Guidance in this capacity was apparently provided primarily by books; for Hoby's supervision of the dressing of a "poore mans Legg" apparently prompts her reading of an "arball" or "herbal," perhaps William Turner's *New Herball*.[24] Similarly, one of three books included in a contemporary portrait of Margaret Clifford, Countess of Cumberland, was a manuscript of medical remedies.[25] The

fairly extensive library represented in a portrait of her daughter Anne
Clifford includes John Gerard's *Herball* (1957).

Thus, the learning of Sophia and Clorina in "siences" would seem to
offer a substantial advance from the more common depictions of women
readers according to their lack or excess of sexual interest. But the figure
of the woman reader of science, particularly of herbal science, casts disturbing shadows. Wroth's romance was written during the height of
the witch craze between 1580 to 1650.[26] Like the self-representations
of Renaissance women readers of herbals, Wroth's representation of
women readers of science signified an acquiescence to male authority
implicating their author in a cultural demonization of a primarily female oral tradition. The reading of herbals not only demonstrated the
medical knowledge of aristocratic women and their care for those in
their charge; the reading of herbals also functioned to distinguish them
from other women practitioners who depended upon an oral tradition
rather than on books written by male authorities. This oral tradition,
practiced for centuries primarily by women, provided one central underlying reason for the burning of women as witches; for the ability of
women to heal posed a barrier to the ongoing masculinization of the
medical profession. As early as 1511 the English parliament outlawed
the practice of medicine to "common artificers as smythes, weavers, and
women" for "they partly use sorcerye and witchcrafte."[27] Vulnerable
to identification as witches, non-authorized practitioners placed themselves in danger of death by burning. As William Perkins argued, a sick
person who receives aid even from a good witch is cured by the devil
rather than by the Lord; even or perhaps especially the "blessing Witch"
must suffer the death penalty.[28] Thus, a woman who drew instead from
a body of written knowledge compiled by male authors protected herself from charges of witchcraft by validating the masculine authorities
then laying claim to the medical profession.

The reading of herbals or of science provides a particularly sharp
example of the way in which the reading of books implied entry into
a primarily masculine domain. The reading of other kinds of books was

also capable of fostering a sense of alienation of women from other women and from themselves. If Walter Ong is correct in his discernment of irremediable changes in consciousness created by literacy, this entry into literacy may well have also represented a departure, a separation from an oral society composed not only of many middle-class women but of numerous aristocratic women as well, including Wroth's own illiterate mother.[29] Moreover, to a much greater extent than in the twentieth century, most books were written by males to an implied male readership. Those relatively few books, primarily romances, which inscribed a female audience often eroticized the act of reading by addressing "gentlewomen readers" inscribed as preoccupied by matters of the heart rather than of the mind.

Thus, literacy represented not only an intellectual achievement. Willingly or not, consciously or not, whether they resisted or acquiesced in destructive gender assumptions underlying the written word, women readers participated in some way in a masculine discourse. An understanding of this pressure towards self-alienation implicit in women's reading enables appreciation for the sheer brilliance of Wroth's manipulation of cultural constructions of the woman reader to provide some degree of dignity to women's reading. Within this cultural context, however, the very act of reading, whether by Wroth's characters, herself, or her literate women contemporaries, implicitly validated a masculine discourse based in part upon the erasure of women's subjectivity. The terms of Sophia's choice were set by her larger culture. The words a woman read, and the words a woman wrote, were inevitably corrupted by the discourses of her culture. Yet only through such participation in a masculine discourse could ideologies be molded. The alternative was silence.

NOTES

1. Recent scholarship is documented ably in Elizabeth Hageman's two bibliographies, "Recent Studies in Women Writers of Tudor England," *English Literary Renaissance* 14 (1984), 409–25, and "Recent Studies in Women Writers of the English Seventeenth Century," *English Literary Renaissance*, 18 (1988), 138–67.
2. Margaret Tyler, trans., "M.T. to the Reader," in Diego Ortunez de Calahorra's *The Mirrour of princely deedes and knighthood* (London, 1578), A4v.

3. Some gender differences in readers are documented by Elizabeth Flynn, "Gender and Reading," in *Gender and Reading: Essays on Readers, Texts, and Contexts*, ed. Flynn and Patrocinio P. Schweickart (Baltimore: Johns Hopkins University Press, 1987), pp. 267–88. Judith Kegan Gardiner, "On Female Identity and Writing by Women," in *Writing and Sexual Difference*, ed. Elizabeth Abel (Chicago: Chicago University Press, 1982), pp. 177–92, grounds gendered differences in readers' relationships with texts in psychoanalytic theory, particularly Nancy Chodorow.

4. Jonathan Culler, "Reading as a Woman," in *On Deconstruction: Theory and Criticism after Structuralism* (Ithaca: Cornell University Press, 1982), pp. 43–64. For an extension of Culler's discussion into the writings of the Sidney family women, see Gary Waller, "The Countess of Pembroke and Gendered Reading," in *The Renaissance Englishwoman in Print: Counterbalancing the Canon*, ed. Anne M. Haselkorn and Betty S. Travitsky (Amherst: University of Massachusetts Press, 1990), pp. 327–45.

5. See, among others, Gary Waller, "Struggling into Discourse,: The Emergence of Renaissance Women's Writing," in *Silent But for the Word: Tudor Women as Patrons, Translators, and Writers of Religious Works*, ed. Margaret Patterson Hannay (Kent, Ohio: The Kent State University Press, 1985), pp. 238–56, and Elaine Showalter, "The Other Bostonians: Gender and Literary Study," *Yale Journal of Criticism* 1 (1988), 179–87. John Guillory, "Canonical and Non-Canonical: A Critique of the Current Debate," *English Literary History* 54 (1987), 483–527, discusses the politicization of literacy especially well.

6. Judith Fetterly, *The Resisting Reader: A Feminist Approach to American Literature* (Bloomington: Indiana University Press, 1978); Mary Jacobus, "Is There a Woman in This Text?", in *Reading Woman: Essays in Feminist Criticism* (New York: Columbia University Press, 1986), pp. 83–110; Teresa De Lauretis, "The Technology of Gender," *Technologies of Gender: Essays on Theory, Film, and Fiction* (Bloomington: Indiana University Press, 1987), pp. 1–30; Schweickart, "Reading Ourselves: Toward a Feminist Theory of Reading," in *Gender and Reading*, pp. 31–62.

7. Susan Noakes, "On the Superficiality of Women," in *The Comparative Perspective on Literature: Approaches to Theory and Practice*, ed. Clayton Koelb and Susan Noakes (Ithaca: Cornell University Press, 1988), p. 347.

8. Juan Luis Vives, *Instruction of a Christian Gentlewoman* (London, 1557), D3.

9. Giovanni Boccaccio, *The Decameron* (London, 1620), A4. The sexualization of women's reading, together with writing, receives further attention in the introduction to my book, *Gender and Authorship in the Sidney Circle* (Madison, Wisconsin: University of Wisconsin Press, 1990). For the association of women's silence with chastity, see especially the fine article by Margaret Ferguson, "A Room Not Their Own: Renaissance Women as Readers and Writers," in *The Comparative Perspective on Literature*, ed. Koelb and Noakes, pp. 93–116.

10. Wye Saltonstall, *Picturae Loquentes. Or Pictures Drawne forth in Characters with a Poeme of a Maide* (London, 1631), E6v. Moralists' fears concerning sexual effect of romances on women readers is also discussed in Tina Krontiris, "Breaking Barriers of Genre and Gender: Margaret Tyler's Translation of *The Mirrour of Knighthood*," *English Literary Renaissance* 18 (1988), 19–39.

11. Richard Hyrde, ded. Desiderius Erasmus's *Devout Treatise upon the Pater Noster*, trans. Margaret Roper (London, 1526), A4r.

12. My use of this much-fraught term to emphasize the subject as a locus of meaning has been influenced by Catherine Belsey, *The Subject of Tragedy: Identity and Difference in Renaissance Drama* (London: Methuen, 1985); its secondary meaning which also represents the subject as contained within a culture, discussed well by Montrose, "The Elizabethan Subject and the Spenserian Text," is also pertinent.

13. Roberts, *Poems*, p. 27.

14. Roberts, *Poems*, pp. 31–32.

15. Pamphilia's striking constancy is noted in most criticism on Wroth; see especially Elaine Beilin, "Heroic Virtue: Mary Wroth's *Urania* and *Pamphilia to Amphilanthus*," ch. 8 in *Redeeming Eve: Women Writers in the Renaissance* (Princeton: Princeton University Press, 1987). Carolyn Ruth Swift, in "Feminine Identity in Lady Mary Wroth's Romance *Urania*," *English Literary Renaissance* 14 (1984), 391, represents Urania's argument to Pamphilia against constancy as a dissenting voice, but the text describes Urania as arguing "against her owne minde" to save Pamphilia's life.

16. This passage is noted in Beilin, "Heroic Virtue," p. 220, Swift, "Feminine Identity," p. 336, and Nona Fienberg in her essay in this volume.

17. On the radical instability of discourses, see Michel Foucault, *The History of Sexuality, Volume I: An Introduction* (New York: Vintage, 1980), pp. 100–102.

18. See Roberts's discussion of this passage, earlier in this volume.

19. Clues connecting Clorina to the Countess of Pembroke are even stronger in an expansion of this episode in Wroth's play *Loves Victorie*; in the play, however, the countess figure is depicted as in love rather than independent. See Roberts, "The Huntington Manuscript of Lady Mary Wroth's *Loves Victorie*," *Huntington Library Quarterly* 46 (1983), 166–68.

20. John Aubrey, *Brief Lives*, ed. Oliver Lawson Dick (Harmondsworth: Secher & Warburg, 1950), p. 139; *The Natural History of Wiltshire*, ed. John Britton (London: J. B. Nichols for the Wiltshire Topographical Society, 1847), pp. 89–90).

21. Sloane MS 1988, f. 138.

22. Ashmolean MS 1499, f. 209b.

23. Margaret Hoby, *Diary*, ed. Dorothy M. Meads (London: Routledge, 1930), p. 63.

24. Hoby, *Diary*, p. 72, 250n.

25. George C. Williamson, *Lady Anne Clifford, Countess of Dorset, Pembroke & Montgomery, 1590–1676*, 2nd ed. (East Ardsley: S. R. Publishers, 1922), p. 339.

26. Brian Easlea, *Witch Hunting, Magic and the New Philosophy: An Introduction to Debates of the Scientific Revolution, 1450–1750* (Sussex: Harvester, 1980), p. 11.

27. Cited by Easlea, p. 39.

28. William Perkins, *Discourse of the Damned Art of Witchcraft* (London, 1608), pp. 174–76, 256.

29. Walter Ong, *Orality and Literacy: The Technologizing of the Word* (New York: Methuen, 1982); David Cressy, *Literacy and the Social Order: Reading and Writing in Tudor and Stuart England* (Cambridge: Cambridge University Press, 1980), pp. 20–25.

Annotated Bibliography

PRIMARY WORKS

Published Editions

POETRY

Pamphilia to Amphilanthus. Ed. Gary Waller. Salzburg: Universität Salzburg, 1977. Reprints the 1621 edition, with additional poems from the Folger ms.

The Poems of Lady Mary Wroth. Ed. Josephine A. Roberts. Baton Rouge: Louisiana State University Press, 1983. The invaluable standard edition.

DRAMA

"Love's Victorie." Ed. C.H.J. Maxwell. M.A. thesis, Stanford University, 1933. An edition of the incomplete Huntington manuscript.

Lady Mary Wroth's Love's Victory. Ed. Michael G. Brennan. London: The Roxburghe Club, 1988. An edition of the Penshurst manuscript.

PROSE ROMANCE

The Countesse of Mountgomeries Urania. London, 1621. Also includes *Pamphilia to Amphilanthus.*

The Countess of Montgomery's Urania. Ed. Josephine A. Roberts. English Renaissance Text Society, forthcoming.

Manuscripts

The Secound Part of the Countess of Montgomerys Urania. Newberry Library Case MS fY 1565. W 95.

Sonnets and Songs. Folger Ms v.a.104

SECONDARY WORKS

Baker, Ernest A. *The History of the English Novel.* New York: Barnes and Noble, 1936. Dismisses *Urania* as a prolix imitation of Sidney's *Arcadia.*

Beilin, Elaine. "'The Onely Perfect Vertue': Constancy in Mary Wroth's *Pamphilia to Amphilanthus.*" *Spenser Studies* 2 (1981), 229–45. On Pamphilia as an emblem of female constancy.

————. *Redeeming Eve: Women Writers in the Renaissance.* Princeton: Princeton University Press, 1987. Ch. 8, "Heroic Virtue: Mary Wroth's *Urania* and *Pamphilia to Amphilanthus*," discusses Wroth's representation of constancy as heroic virtue.

Bond, W.H. "The Reputation and Influence of Sir Philip Sidney." Ph.D. diss., Harvard University, 1935. Includes Wroth as an imitator of Sidney.

Brennan, Michael. *Literary Patronage in the English Renaissance: The Pembroke Family.* London: Routledge, 1988. References, mainly biographical, to Wroth's relations with Pembroke.

Brydges, Sir Egerton. *Restituta, or Titles, Extracts, and Characters of Old Books in English Literature Revived.* London: T. Bensley, 1815. Vol. 2 prints some extracts from *Urania,* with comments.

Collins, Arthur, ed. *Letters and Memorials of State.* London: T. Osborne, 1746. Inaccurate but still invaluable transcription of the Sidney correspondence.

Croft, Peter, ed. *The Poems of Robert Sidney.* Oxford: Clarendon, 1984. See esp. Appendix C, pp. 342–46: "Echoes of Roberts's Sequence in His Daughter Mary Wroth's Verse."

Duncan-Jones, Katherine. Review of Roberts, *Poems. Review of English Studies,* n.s.36 (1985), 565–66.

Fleay, H.G. *A Biographical Chronicle of the English Drama.* London: Frederic Gard Fleay, 1891. Refers to Jonson's connection with Wroth: asserts she is the Celia of Jonson's poems.

Galli, Antonio. *Rime di Antimo Galli all'Illustrissima Signora Elizabetta Talbot-Grey.* London, 1609. Stanza 70 describes Wroth in *The Masque of Beauty.*

Gartenberg, Patricia, and Nina Thames Whittmore. "A Checklist of English Women in Print, 1475–1640." *Bulletin of Bibliography* 34 (1977), 2. Calls attention to Wroth's female viewpoint in *Urania.*

Gebauer, Andreas. *Von Macht und Mäzenatentum: Laben und Werk William Herberts, des dritten Earls von Pembroke.* Heidelberg: Carl Winter, 1987. A biography of Pembroke, with many references to Wroth.

Greg, W.W. *Pastoral Poetry and Pastoral Drama.* New York: Russell and Russell, 1959. Brief remarks on *Love's Victory.*

Greer, Germaine, Susan Hastings, Jeslyn Medoff, and Melinda Sansone, eds. *Kissing the Rod: An Anthology of Seventeenth-Century Women's Verse.* New York: The Noonday Press, 1988. Prints eight sonnets from Roberts, with a brief introduction, pp. 61–67.

Hackett, Helen. "'Yet Tell me some such Fiction': Lady Mary Wroth's *Urania* and the 'Femininity' of Romance." In *Interventions: Women, Texts, and Histories, 1575–1760,* ed. Diane Furkiss and Clare Brant. London: Routledge, forthcoming.

Hall, Kim. "Acknowledging Things of Darkness: Race, Gender, and Power in Early Modern England." Ph.D. diss., University of Pennsylvania, 1990. Ch. 4, "The Daughters of Eve and the Children of Ham: Race and the English Woman Writer," looks at types of blackness in Urania.

Hannay, Margaret Patterson. "Lady Mary Wroth." In *Women of the Renaissance and Reformation,* ed. Katharina M. Wilson. Athens: University of Georgia Press, 1984. A selection of poems with an introduction, pp. 548–65.

————. "Lady Wroth." In *An Encyclopedia of British Women Writers,* ed. Paul and June Schleuter, p. 491. New York: Garland Press, 1986.

————. "Lady Mary Wroth." In *British Women Writers: A Critical Reference Guide*, ed. Janet Todd, pp. 740–43. New York: Continuum, 1989.

————. *Philip's Phoenix: Mary Sidney, Countess of Pembroke*. London: Oxford University Press, 1989. Biography of Wroth's aunt: contains a number of references to Wroth.

Hay, Millicent V. *The Life of Robert Sidney*. Washington: The Folger Shakespeare Library, 1984. A study, largely biographical, of Wroth's father.

Historical Manuscripts Commission: De L'Isle and Dudley. London 1925–66. An invaluable source for the lives of the Sidney family.

Jones, Ann Rosalind. *The Currency of Eros: Women's Love Lyric in Europe, 1540–1620*. Bloomington: Indiana University Press, 1990. Ch. 4, "Feminine Pastoral as Heroic Martyrdom," compares Wroth's sonnets and Gaspara Stampa's.

Jonson, Ben. *Discoveries 1641: Conversations with William Drummond of Hawthornden*. New York: Barnes and Noble, 1966. Refers to Wroth's poetry and her unhappy marriage to a "jealous husband."

Jusserand, J.J. *The English Novel in the Time of Shakespeare*. 1908; rpt. New York, AMS Press, 1965. Dismisses *Urania* as an inferior imitation of Sidney's *Arcadia*.

Kennedy, Gwynne. "Feminine Subjectivity in the English Renaissance: The Writings of Elizabeth Cary, Lady Falkland, and Lady Mary Wroth." Ph.D. diss., University of Pennsylvania, 1989.

Kohler, Charlotte. "The Elizabethan Woman of Letters: The Extent of her Literary Activities." Ph.D. diss., University of Virginia, 1936. Identifies Wroth's importance in historical rather than literary terms.

Lamb, Mary Ellen. *Gender and Authorship in the Sidney Circle*. University of Wisconsin Press, 1990. Ch 4: "The Heroics of Constancy in Mary Wroth's *Countess of Montgomery's Urania*.

Lee, Sir Sidney. "Lady Mary Wroth." *Dictionary of National Biography*, vol. 53, pp. 161–62. London: Smit, Elder, 1900. Brief biographical account.

MacArthur, Janet. "'A Sydney, Though Unnamed': Lady Mary Wroth and Her Poetical Progenitors." *English Studies in Canada* 15 (1989), 12–20. Relations with family's other (and the wider tradition of male Petrarchan) poets.

MacCarthy, Bridget G. *Women Writers: Their Contribution to the English Novel, 1621–1744*. Cork: Cork University Press, 1946. Suggests Urania united "realistic" and "romantic" genres.

McClure, Norman E., ed. *The Letters of John Chamberlain*, 2 vols. Philadelphia: American Philosophical Society, 1939. Occasional references to Wroth.

McLaren [Witten-Hannah], Margaret. "Lady Mary Wroth's *Urania*: The Work and the Tradition." Ph.D. diss., University of Auckland, 1978. A pioneering study that, while widely cited, has unfortunately never been published. Especially valuable on the publishing and printing of the *Urania*.

————. "'An Unknown Continent': Lady Mary Wroth's Forgotten Pastoral Drama, 'Loves Victorie.'" In *The Renaissance Englishwoman in Print: Counterbalancing the Canon*. Ed. Anne M. Haselkorn and Betty S. Travitsky, pp. 276–94. Amherst: University of Massachusetts Press, 1990. Although restricted to the shorter version of *Love's Victory*, has some valuable comments on the contradictory erotic discourses in the work.

Miller, Naomi J. "'Not much to be marked': Narrative of the Woman's Part in Lady

Mary Wroth's *Urania*." *Studies in English Literature* 29 (1989), 121–37. Examines Wroth's treatment of female friendship in *Urania* with reference to literary and cultural conceptions of gender roles in the early modern period.

———. "Rewriting Lyric Fictions: The Role of the Lady in Lady Mary Wroth's *Pamphilia to Amphilanthus*." In *The Renaissance Englishwoman in Print*, ed. Haselkorn and Travitsky, pp. 295–310. Discusses gender and voice in Wroth's sequence, in comparison to the sequences of Philip and Robert Sidney.

———. "Strange Labyrinth: Pattern as Process in Sir Philip Sidney's *Arcadia* and Lady Mary Wroth's *Urania*." Ph.D. diss., Harvard University, 1987. Compares Sidney's and Wroth's representations of community through attention to the interrelated claims of gender, genre, culture within their texts.

O'Connor, John J. "James Hay and the Countess of Montgomery's *Urania*," *Notes & Queries* 200 (1955), 150–52. Provides historical context for the withdrawal of the *Urania* from sale after its 1621 publication.

Pam, D.O. *Protestant Gentlemen: The Wroths of Durants Arbour, Enfield, and Loughton, Essex*. Enfield: Edmonton Hundred Historical Society, n.s.25 (1973). An account of the Wroth family.

Parry, Graham. "Lady Mary Wroth's *Urania*." *Proceedings of the Leeds Philosophical and Literary Society, Literary and Historical Section* 16 (1975), 51–70. Defines *Urania* as a product of the courtly-chivalric ethos prevalent in Renaissance England.

Paulisson, May Nelson. "Forgotten Love Sonnets of the Court of King James: The Sonnets of Lady Mary Wroth." *Publications of the Missouri Philological Association* 3 (1985), 24–31. Summary of the following item.

———. *The Love Sonnets of Lady Mary Wroth: A Critical Introduction*. Salzburg: Universität Salzburg, 1982. Examines classical, courtly, and metaphysical strains in Wroth's poetry.

Pigeon, Renée. "Prose Fiction Adaptions of Sir Philip Sidney's *Arcadia*." Ph.D. diss., University of California, 1988.

Quilligan, Maureen. "The Constant Subject: Instability and Female Authority in Wroth's *Urania* Poems." In *Soliciting Interpretation: Literary Theory and Seventeenth-Century Poetry*, ed. Elizabeth D. Harvey and Katherine Eisaman Maus, pp. 307–35. Chicago: University of Chicago Press, 1990.

———. "Lady Mary Wroth: Female Authority and the Family Romance." In *Unfolded Tales: Essays on Renaissance Romance*, ed. George M. Logan and Gordon Teskey, pp. 257–80. Ithaca, N.Y.: Cornell University Press, 1989. Analyzes the cultural struggles over gender in *Urania*; includes a valuable reading of the Sidney family portrait (c. 1596).

Roberts, Josephine A. "The Biographical Problem of *Pamphilia to Amphilanthus*." *Tulsa Studies in Women's Literature* 1 (1982), 43–53. Indicates relevance of the link between Wroth and William Herbert to Wroth's sequence, but concludes that Wroth limited the degree of personal reference in her poems.

———. "The Huntington Manuscript of Lady Mary Wroth's Play, *Loves Victorie*." *Huntington Library Quarterly* 46 (1983) 156–74. Identifies personal allusions to Wroth's family and draws connections with other pastoral plays.

———. "Labyrinths of Desire: Lady Mary Wroth's Reconstruction of Romance." *Sidney Newsletter* 10, no. 1 (1990), 70. *Urania*'s critique of traditional forms and gender stereotypes.

————. "Lady Mary Wroth's Sonnets: A Labyrinth of the Mind." *Journal of Women's Studies in Literature* 1 (1979), 319–29. Examines subjugation, frustration, and loss of self in the poems.

————. "Lady Mary Wroth's *Urania*: A Response to Jacobean Censorship." *Proceedings of the Renaissance English Text Society* 3 (1987), 21–26. Account of the protests against the *Urania*.

————. "Radigund Revisited: Perspectives on Women Rulers in Lady Mary Wroth's *Urania*." In *The Renaissance Englishwoman in Print*, ed. Haselkorn and Travitsky, 187–207. Discusses Wroth's ambivalent views of female rule, in relation to *The Faerie Queene*.

————. "An Unpublished Literary Quarrel Concerning the Suppression of Mary Wroth's *Urania* (1621)." *Notes & Queries* 222 (1977), 532–35. Discusses social context of the controversy.

Roberts, Josephine A., and James F. Gaines. "Amatory Landscapes in Lady Mary Wroth's *Urania* and Mlle. de Scudery's *Clelie*." In *Love, Sexuality, and Marriage in Early Modern Europe*, ed. James Grantham Turner. Cambridge: Cambridge University Press, 1991.

Rowton, Frederick, ed. *The Female Poets of Great Britain*. London: Longman, 1848. Briefly discusses two of Wroth's songs, from *Pamphilia to Amphilanthus* and from the *Urania*.

Salzman, Paul. "Contemporary References in Mary Wroth's *Urania*." *Review of English Studies* 29 (1978), 178–81. Provides historical context for the suppression of the *Urania*.

————. "*Urania* and the Tyranny of Love." In *English Prose Fiction, 1558–1700*, pp. 138–44. Oxford: Clarendon, 1985. Addresses the significance of contemporary details in Wroth's romance.

Shapiro, Michael. "Lady Mary Wroth Describes a 'Boy Actress.'" *Medieval and Renaissance Drama in England* 4 (1989), 187–94. Discusses boys as actors playing the roles of women.

Shaver, Anne. "Outspoken Women in Book I of Lady Mary Wroth's *Urania*." *Sidney Newsletter* 10, no. 1 (1990), 89. Argues that Wroth's heroines assert themselves relatively successfully in spheres other than sexual choice.

————. "A Woman of Romance." *Modern Language Studies* (forthcoming). An account of gender politics in *Urania*.

Swift, Carolyn Ruth. "Feminine Identity in Lady Mary Wroth's Romance *Urania*." *English Literary Renaissance* 14 (1984), 328–46. Argues that Wroth reveals in her romance the loss of identity that women experience in a society that victimizes them.

————. "Feminine Self-Definition in Lady Mary Wroth's *Loves Victorie* (c.1621)," *English Literary Renaissance* 19 (1989), 171–88.

Travitsky, Betty, ed. *The Paradise of Women: Writings by Englishwomen of the Renaissance*. Westport, Conn.: Greenwood Press, 1981. Prints brief selections from *Urania* and the poetry.

Valiant, Sharon "Sidney's Sister, Pembroke's Mother . . . and Aphra Behn's Great-Grandmother?" Paper, American Society for Eighteenth-Century Studies conference in New Orleans, 1989. Argues for Wroth's daughter Catherine Lovell as Behn's mother.

Wall, Wendy. "The Shapes of Desire: Politics, Publication, and Renaissance Texts." Ph.D. diss., University of Pennsylvania, 1989. Ch. 6, "Dancing in a Net: Renaissance Women and Print," pp. 281–333, discusses Wroth.

Waller, Gary. *English Poetry of the Sixteenth Century.* London: Longman, 1986. Ch. 8, "Reopening the Canon," comments on Wroth's belated Petrarchanism and her attitudes to the Jacobean court.

———. "Five Poems on a Seventeenth-Century Romance." In *Other Flights, Always.* Braunton, Eng.: Merlin Books, 1991. Poetic recreation of aspects of Wroth's relation with Pembroke.

———. "Mother/Son, Father/Daughter, Brother/Sister, Cousins: The Sidney Family Romance." *Modern Philology,* 1991. Psychoanalytical/cultural reading, focusing on recent work on Wroth and Pembroke.

———. "Representing Alternatives: Rereading the Sidney Women Today." *Sidney Newsletter* 10, no. 1 (1990), 72–73. On Wroth's adventures breaching ideological norms in the early modern period.

———. "The Sidney Family Romance: Gender Construction in Early Modern England." A study of the literary, cultural, and psychoanalytic patterns in the Wroth/Pembroke relationship. In preparation.

———. "Struggling into Discourse: The Emergence of Renaissance Women's Writing." In *Silent but for the Word: Tudor Women as Patrons, Translators, and Writers of Religious Works,* ed. Margaret Patterson Hannay, pp. 238–56. Kent, Ohio: The Kent State University Press, 1985. Focuses on the exclusion of women, including Wroth, from masculinist discourse.

Waller, William Chapman. "An Extinct County Family: Wroth of Loughton Hall." *Transactions of the Essex Archaeological Society,* n.s.7 (1903), 156–80. On the Wroth family.

Wright, Louis B. "The Purposeful Reading of our Colonial Ancestors." *English Literary History* 4 (1937), 110. Notes that *Urania* enjoyed a considerable vogue in Virginia and New England.

Yeager, Sandra. "'She who still constant lov'd': *Pamphilia to Amphilanthus* as Lady Wroth's Indictment of Male Codes of Love." *Sidney Newsletter* 10, no. 1 (1990), 88–89. Argues that Wroth affirms mutual love and wedded sexuality.

Zurcher, Amelia. "'Dauncing in a Net': Representation in Lady Mary Wroth's *Urania.*" M.Phil. diss., Oxford University, 1989.

Contributors

Nona Fienberg is associate professor of English at Keene State College. She is the author of *Elizabeth, her Poets, and the Creation of the Courtly Manner*. Her articles on Medieval and Renaissance topics have appeared in such journals as *Modern Philology, Studies in English Literature*, and *Shakespeare Quarterly*. Her current project is a study of early modern women.

Margaret P. Hannay is professor of English literature at Siena College. She is the author of *Philip's Phoenix: Mary Sidney Countess of Pembroke* (1990) and editor of *Silent but for the Word: Tudor Women as Patrons, Translators and Writers of Religious Works* (1985). She has published articles on the Sidney women, and she is currently editing, with Noel J. Kinnamon, the collected works of Mary Sidney, Countess of Pembroke for the Oxford English Texts Series.

Ann Rosalind Jones is professor of comparative literature at Smith College. She is the author of *The Currency of Eros: Women's Love Lyric in Europe, 1540–1620* (1990) and has published widely on feminist issues and Renaissance literature, especially on women poets, the Sidneys, and tragic heroines. She is a consultant to Verso Books' Questions on Feminism series, for which she has edited a translation of Catherine Clement.

Mary Ellen Lamb is associate professor of English at Southern Illinois University at Carbondale. She is the author of *Gender and Authorship in the Sidney Circle* (1990). She has also published on Shakespeare and the Countess of Pembroke in such journals as *English Literary Renaissance, Shakespeare Survey*, and *Shakespeare Quarterly*.

Barbara K. Lewalski is William R. Kenan Professor of English literature and of history and literature at Harvard University. Her scholarship and teaching center on English literature of the early modern period. Her extensive publications in this area include *Paradise Lost and the Rhetoric of Literary Forms*, which won the James Holly Hanford Award of the Milton Society of America, and *Protestant Poetics and the Seventeenth-Century Religious Lyric* (Princeton, 1979), which won the James Russell Lowell Prize of the Modern Language Association. She has recently published articles on Aemilia Lanyer and Lucy, Countess of Bedford, and is now completing a book entitled *Writing Women in the Jacobean Era: Social Roles and Literary Images.* She is also at work on a critical biography of Milton.

Jeff Masten teaches in the Department of English at Harvard University. His current project is a study of collaboration, authorship, and sexuality in Renaissance drama.

Naomi J. Miller is assistant professor of English literature and women's studies at the University of Arizona. Her publications include several articles on Wroth. She is currently at work on a book-length study of Wroth's works in their literary and cultural contexts.

Josephine A. Roberts is William A. Read Professor of English at Louisiana State University. She has written books on Sidney's *Arcadia* (1978) and Shakespeare's *Richard II* (1988) and is the editor of *The Poems of Lady Mary Wroth* (1983). Her articles on Renaissance topics have appeared in such journals as *English Literary Renaissance, Tulsa Studies in Women's Literature, Journal of Women's Studies in Literature, Comparative Literature,* and *Huntington Library Quarterly.* She is editing Wroth's *Urania* for the English Renaissance Text Society.

Gary Waller is Professor of Literary and Cultural Studies in the Department of English at Carnegie Mellon University, where he was for six years head of department. He is the author of some fifteen books, mainly on Renaissance literature and culture, including *The Strong Necessity of Time* (1976), *Mary Sidney Countess of Pembroke* (1979), *Sir Philip Sidney and Renaissance Culture* (1984), *English Poetry in the Sixteenth Century* (1986), *Reading Texts* (1987), and editions of the poetry of the Countess of Pembroke and Lady Mary Wroth. Forthcoming books include a study of Spenser for Macmillan and a study of gender construction in the seventeenth century, *The Sidney Family Romance.* His essays and articles range across Renaissance literature, contemporary fiction and poetry, theory and curricular studies. His second collection of poetry, *Other Flights, Always,* has just been published by Merlin Books. In 1987 he was a Guggenheim Fellow.

Heather Weidemann is a doctoral student in the Department of English, University of California, at Berkeley. She is writing a dissertation on dramatic metaphors and authorial self-representation in seventeenth-century literature.

Index

Reading Mary Wroth
was designed by Dariel Mayer,
composed by Lithocraft, Inc.,
and printed by McNaughton & Gunn, Inc.
The book is set in Bembo
and printed on 50-lb Glatfelter Natural.